FLYING DRUNK

A Northwest Airlines Flight, Three Drunk Pilots, and One Man's Fight for Redemption

Joseph Balzer

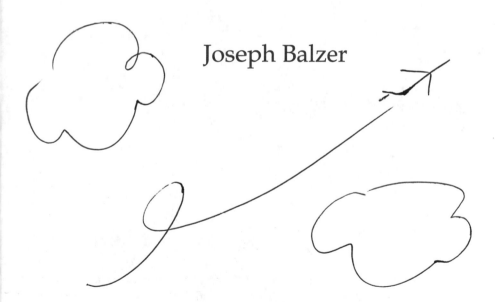

SB 865-360-9472

Savas Beatie
California

June 27, 2015

Printed in the United States of America.

Cataloging-in-Publication Data is available from the Library of Congress.

ISBN 978-1-61121-164-1

05 04 03 02 01   5 4 3 2 1
First Paperback Printing, First edition

SB
Published by
Savas Beatie LLC
989 Governor Drive, Suite 102
El Dorado Hills, CA 95762
Phone: 916-941-6896
sales@savasbeatie.com
www.savasbeatie.com

Savas Beatie titles are available at special discounts for bulk purchases in the United States by corporations, institutions, and other organizations. For more details, please contact Special Sales, P.O. Box 4527, El Dorado Hills, CA 95762, or you may e-mail us at sales@savasbeatie.com, or visit our website at www.savasbeatie.com for additional information.

All photos courtesy of the author unless otherwise stated.

To the alcoholics who still suffer, and the brave souls who are willing to reach out and help them. To my first "sponsor," the late Buddy Stockard, and the late Dr. Audie Davis, the recovering pilot's humble hero, whose dedication to the cause of alcoholic pilots has put thousands of us back into the air, sober.

Joe Balzer, a proud pilot with American Airlines.

Contents

Contents (continued)

A photo gallery follows page 130

Foreword

by Dr. Audie Davis

D r. Audie Davis managed the Aeromedical Certification Division (ACD) of the Federal Aviation Administration for more than thirty years. The ACD serves as the focal point for deciding whether pilots are medically fit to fly, according to regulatory mandates.

These are seldom easy or simple decisions. But enlightened and progressive leadership of the FAA's medical office established a policy under which pilots who developed what appeared to be career-ending medical conditions could become certified under a procedure known as "Special Issuance." Pilots who had experienced heart attacks, bypass surgery, cancer or other grave conditions, including alcoholism, were considered on a case-by-case basis to determine whether they could be returned to flying without compromising passenger safety.

This was the arena in which Dr. Davis and Joe Balzer first crossed paths. One early morning in March 1990, Dr. Davis received a call regarding Balzer and two other "impaired" crew members on a compromised flight from Fargo to Minneapolis. That was the first time he heard Joe's name—but it was not to be the last. In 1994 Dr. Davis heard Joe speak at a National H.I.M.S. conference. H.I.M.S., which stands for Human Intervention Motivational Study, began in 1972 as an experimental program to help recovering alcoholic pilots get healthy and return to work.

*   *   *

When I first heard Joe Balzer speak he was a pilot without a license to fly; he was also a man with a broken heart. His talk described the radical changes he had brought about in his life, made possible by applying the 12-Step principles of recovery. His words touched everyone in the audience.

Joe's life demonstrates to all of us how to bravely get up when you've been knocked down by alcoholism. He was able to surrender, yet persevere, and overcome the detrimental consequences of his tumultuous past.

Drawing on his prescribed Daily Spiritual Reprieve, Joe had to constantly meet the challenge to stay focused and move forward, in spite of the continual rejection he—a convicted felon—experienced while trying to find meaningful work. Key to his motivation was the desire to share his tribulations with humility and grace, as he reached out to help other people who suffer from alcoholism.

Joe's amazing story shows how he was able to find hope in the midst of despair. It is a tale of gratitude, courage, passion, humility, acceptance, and especially perseverance in the face of seemingly insurmountable obstacles.

It is a powerful story of victory and hope for us all.

Prologue

The first week of March 1990 was one I will never forget. But not for the reasons I had hoped.

The sacrifices I had made for the previous twelve years had just begun to pay off. I was a newlywed, married to a lovely woman with whom I wanted to spend the rest of my life. We had just spent a wonderful vacation with friends, skiing in the magnificent high country of Colorado.

I left for work with optimism and hope for our future, knowing that I was about to finish probation as a "new hire" pilot with Northwest Airlines. My evaluations from previous Captains had all been excellent, which meant I was passing my probationary period with flying colors.

My wife Deborah and I were looking forward to my full pilot status and a healthy raise, finally putting behind us the low first-year pay an airline pilot receives. We were so close to buying our dream house on a lake in Nashville, Tennessee, that we were giddy with excitement. Everything was going our way. We had nothing to fear—or at least, that's what we thought.

And then my world crashed down around me on the morning of March 8, 1990.

* * *

Outside it was a cold, wet morning in Fargo, North Dakota—but not as cold as inside the cockpit, due to the working relationship between the Captain and the other two pilots of our jet. That morning I was the Flight Engineer on a Northwest Airlines Boeing 727. As the plane entered the dark runway for takeoff, then raced down the runway, accelerating to attain takeoff speed, my insides were ripping apart in turmoil. I watched as the First Officer pushed the three engine throttles forward. The air inside the engines was being compressed under tremendous pressure—as were the thoughts overwhelming my brain. Fear bounced between my ears; the situation was rapidly spiraling out of control.

With the engines developing thousands of pounds of thrust, the aircraft rapidly approached the speed necessary to develop sufficient lift on the wings to become airborne. The shaking of the airframe paralleled the shaking inside me. I was aching to scream "Stop!" and return to the gate, but I could not form the words. I'm convinced no one there would have listened to me, anyway; nonetheless, had I known what was waiting for us later, I would have done things differently.

Something that rarely happens in a modern commercial airliner was taking place. The crew coordination, communication and teamwork so important for the safe outcome of a flight had been completely compromised days earlier by the poor leadership of the overbearing Captain. This officer, rude to the point of being downright mean, had nothing but criticism to offer anyone. The icy air hanging between all of us comprised a dangerous element in the cockpit.

The gear handle was raised and the landing gear rumbled into the wheel wells. The airspeed increased dramatically as the drag from the main gear was eliminated from the slipstream. As the airplane climbed higher into the dark morning sky, I contemplated the unfolding situation. Earlier, my repeated requests and desperate attempts to prevent this flight from ever taking place had failed miserably. Now everything I had ever worked for was at stake. My short airline career—a career that I had made so many personal sacrifices to attain—might end with this flight.

The reason: I was sitting in the cockpit of a commercial jet unsure whether there was alcohol running through my veins. I had done everything I could do to get this airplane properly pre-flighted and ready for takeoff—but I had failed to preflight myself. My life-long struggle with alcohol had resumed, and this time I had carried it into the cockpit with me, compromising my own personal value system. And I was not alone. At the time, I could not remember exactly how much I, along with the Captain and First Officer, had drunk the night before—but it had been considerable. Now shame, embarrassment, even anger washed through me, followed by a feeling of total, absolute defeat. Thank God we had not been discovered—yet.

So there I sat, part of a dysfunctional crew, working under a "leader" who was himself out of control. I was trapped in a situation I did not understand, and my decision to take this mess into the air had been one of the worst of my life. Just a few days before, my wife and I had experienced deep joy and happiness as we looked forward to a bright future together. Now, on this dark March morning, I was a pilot on a flight unlike that made by any three pilots I had ever heard of: we were at the controls of a commercial airliner with innocent passengers on board, and we were intoxicated.

We were flying drunk; and Federal officers had already been alerted. Everything that could go wrong was about to.

Acknowledgments

There are so many people to thank.

My wife and children were the underwriters of this effort. My kids asked, "Mom, what is wrong with Dad?" during the time I wrote about being in prison. Deborah is a special woman. As a newlywed, her life as she knew it fell apart, yet she found it in herself to support me, stand by my side, and endure many years of pure, emotional Hell and doing without. She is an angel, and I am fortunate to love her and have her as my wife.

For three years I lugged around my manuscript and wrote in hotel rooms, libraries, parks, airplanes, and the dungeon. The dungeon is where Deborah sent me. It is also (now) sacred ground. I was banned from the house due to the cacophony of papers I continually left strewn all over our living room. It was my idea to get two giant card tables and put them together against the wall. That straw did it, and the camel was toast. I finally moved into the workshop-basement office, where it is cold in the winter and warm in the summer—but it was all mine. It is here that I experienced the pain, loss, and suffering all over again. I also felt deep joy, elation, and gratefulness, realizing over and over how blessed I am in my life. I reached a place of forgiveness and understanding, and only wish for others to do the same.

My family beyond Deborah and the kids is incredible. My mother wrote me a letter or sent me a card every day I was in prison. My father, in spite of impossible odds, continued to encourage me to pursue my dreams, as he always has. My sister Barbara has been my mentor and friend in recovery, and helped guide me back along some of the treacherous roads I had traveled. My sister Brenda and her husband Dick have also been great supporters, and were there for us when the chips were way down. My brother Jim and his wife Annie remain encouragers, and help to keep me focused on what is important in life.

Buddy Stockard was my first sponsor, therapist, and now good friend. He found me at the lowest point in my life, taught me how to live sober, and accept life on life's terms. He is the best example of what good sobriety can do. Buddy has served countless others with his wisdom, giving away with love what he knows to be true.

I have the deepest gratitude and appreciation for all the fine people who took time out of their lives and drove several hundred miles to visit me in prison on Saturdays. The Boshiers of Nashville—a true aviation family— were my staunchest supporters. Geoff, Carole, Hailey, Jeff, Robin, Antony, Tracy, Kurt, Tony, Tish, Mac, Abby, John, and all my family members who traveled such great distances to warm my heart in the shadows of the pen, your kind gestures will never be forgotten.

Thanks are also due to Don F. and Al C., my great pilot friends from Eastern Airlines who are sober and wonderful men. They encouraged me to get out and tell my story. I hope they approve of the final result.

My friend and mentor Captain Skip Swift and his wife Mary have been exceptional supporters of my spirit, and have provided me with unlimited counseling and gentle, patient guidance through the lowest valleys a man could walk through. He took me fishing when I had nothing else but pain and rejection to look forward to. Skip has been telling me for years to write this book, and he will receive the first signed copy. I think so much of him that I named my son after him.

Dr. Audie Davis has dedicated his life to helping pilots recover from alcoholism and drug addiction. As Chief Aero surgeon for the Federal Aviation Administration for more than thirty years, he helped save countless pilots' lives, and then aided them to return to the cockpit healthy and sober. Davis is a leader in the field of recovery, and his encouragement, support, and kind words written in the Foreword of this book motivate me to reach out to others who still suffer.

Thanks also to Chris Morton, my new friend in East Tennessee. I didn't know how to do much with a word processor, and Chris got me started. Daniel Burnham in Dallas printed the first part of the book and helped me believe in the story I was trying to tell. Dr. James Milam, author of *Under the Influence*, directed me to my first editor, Cliff Carle. I owe Cliff a great deal of thanks. We edited this book five different times, and each time he brought out more from me than I ever knew I had. He was great to work with.

Someone once told me that finding a good publisher is like running around outside hoping to be struck by lightning. I was struck by Theodore P. "Ted" Savas, of Savas Beatie LLC. He read my manuscript, called me on the phone and exclaimed, "Joe, what a story!" The passion in his voice was everything I hoped it would be. A mentor of mine, Francine Ward, author of *Esteemable Acts*, told me, "Joe, you need to go with the person who is passionate about your story." She was right. The Savas Beatie team is passionate, tireless, friendly, and hardworking. Ted assigned Captain Rob Ayer, a professor at the US Coast Guard Academy as my editor. Rob helped developmentally edit the manuscript and worked closely with me on the final edits. He really made the book flow smoothly and quickly. Marketing director Sarah Keeney, together with marketing assistants Veronica Kane and Tammy Hall are setting up a great campaign. I am thankful for all the help and hard work that Sarah, Veronica, and Tammy are doing for me.

I would also like to thank Oasis Audio for producing an audio version of *Flying Drunk*. Val Laolagi, web designer and artist, has done a great job on my website, which is located at www.flyingdrunk.com. I hope this site will point people in a positive direction to change their lives.

My friend, mentor, drum judge, and fellow Cavalier Gary Moore is the author of the simply outstanding book *Playing with the Enemy*. Gary encouraged me to pursue a great publisher—his own, Savas Beatie—and offers endless advice and encouragement for my success whenever I need it.

Captain Cecil Ewell, Captain Mike Smith, Captain J. C. Doerr, and the late Mr. Bob Baker are great men who offered me hope with American Airlines—the greatest and most supportive airline in the world. Thank you also to the thousands of baggage handlers, aircraft cleaners, gate agents, flight attendants, mechanics, pilots, schedulers, and airport workers who have over the years encouraged me to tell this story. Your inspiration and kind words mean more than you can ever know.

Family and friends are really all that matter in this life. God has blessed me with a family I love, a profession I love, and the best friends in the world. I pray that you will enjoy this book, and share it with someone you love with the greatest hope, that they too can make a change in their lives.

SPLOOIE!

Joe Balzer

A Note on Sources

Most of this book has been written from my own personal recollections. I also relied upon letters, discussions with friends and family, fellow pilots, flight attendants, and many others who have helped me so much along the way. Much of it is confirmed in writing. A few of these sources refreshed my memory; most of them served to confirm it.

The section describing my five-day nightmare flying assignment, including our encounters with the FAA, our arrests, and the trial and convictions is based upon my experiences and memory, the complete trial transcript, conversations with many others (pilots, attorneys, flight attendants, gate attendants, witnesses, FAA personnel, etc.), letters and communications received (before and after the trial) from others, and dozens of articles (published in hard copy and on the Internet) from a wide variety of sources, including *The Seattle Times*, *Newsweek*, *New York Times*, and many other publications. You can easily find these yourself on the Internet.

Some people don't want my story told—one man in particular. He recently sent me (through my publisher) a threatening email. After lying about me, my life, and my current job standing with American Airlines, he concluded with this: *"If his book is truthful then there should be no difficulties. If it is not, then there will be consequences."* Once you read this book, it will become obvious who sent me this. He is still trying to bully others. Sadly, some things never change.

To the best of my ability, I have not embellished, enhanced, or otherwise exaggerated any of my experiences. I don't need to—because it is all true, and now part of the record of aviation history.

Chapter 1

Early Life

I can remember things that happened to me at a very early age. As unlikely as it sounds, I remember my first birthday party; I can even recall some of the people who were there. But not all of my early memories are happy ones.

Our house was very small, about a thousand square feet, located in a blue-collar neighborhood in Dayton, Ohio. It was a rough little place—actually, the roughest place I would ever live as a child. When I was only two years old someone smashed me in the face with a brick. My face swelled up, and our family doctor had to make a house call to examine it and treat the damage.

Several months later, my dad brought home a new tricycle for me. I can still see him pulling it out of the trunk of the car. It was the first "new" thing I ever remember receiving; most of my stuff was handed down from my older brother and sister. Even the brown "family" teddy bear was a hand-me-down. When too many hugs and punches and the passage of time wore it down, my mother would sew it back together, then press it back into our little arms. That bear was so old that much of his fur had rubbed off, but his baldness didn't make him any less wonderful in my heart and mind.

My new tricycle was something special. No kid in my neighborhood had ever seen anything quite like it. It was painted black and white and had police markings on it. This amazing tricycle even had a windshield like a police motorcycle, and a siren to boot. But I only enjoyed my new trike for a few days before someone decided he didn't like the windshield and smashed it with another brick, right in front of me. I wasn't yet three, but my heart broke. I never did get a new windshield, and that trike was never the same. I don't remember who smashed up my little dream toy, and I don't recall whether anyone was ever held accountable.

But I remember to this day the deep impression this incident made upon me: nobody cared about my feelings.

Sputnik

Our town was buzzing with excitement. Heck, the entire world was stunned: the Russians had launched Sputnik. It was 1957, and I remember standing outside, with what seemed like the entire neighborhood, looking into the chilly October night sky in an effort to spot the first satellite ever launched into space. People were overcome with awe and amazement as the tiny Sputnik streaked across the starry heavens. I don't remember whether I actually saw what everyone was so excited about, but I know my father didn't want us to miss the opportunity. Everyone wanted the chance to be a part of this historic moment.

What I do remember with perfect clarity is that this was the beginning of my fascination with things that fly. It all just seemed so incredible to me. A rocket in space? That was pure science fiction in the 1950s. After that, my eyes were often looking up.

Although everyone was in awe of this major scientific breakthrough, there was also a lingering undercurrent of fear. I remember the adults talking about it: something about Russia, and how those Russians were some downright scary people. My young mind couldn't quite sort it out, of course, but Sputnik seemed to be good and bad at the same time.

On the Move

My family moved away from that neighborhood before I started school, into the first new house we ever lived in. It was in Beavercreek, Ohio, which in 1958 was a small town outside Dayton next to Wright Patterson Air Force Base. For a young boy, moving into this new house was like moving to paradise. Fields and woods, abundant with running creeks and ponds, surrounded the small house. Wild apple, mulberry, and cherry trees dotted the landscape. One of my favorite memories is of making my way up into the branches of those trees, finding a comfortable place to sit, and eating the sweet fruit.

With Wright Patterson just a stone's throw away, aircraft frequently flew over our house. Every time one passed overhead I would stand and watch until it passed from view. My brother and I played with gliders and model airplanes in the large fields, listening as sonic booms shook the ground when Air Force jets broke the sound barrier. We often climbed to the top of a hill at the end of our neighborhood to watch aircraft take off and land. The Air Force was always coming up with something new, and we were often the first ones to see it. We looked forward all winter long to the incredible summer air shows at Wright Pat. When I discovered that pilots let young kids go inside the airplanes and sit in the cockpits at the controls, no one could keep me away.

One sunny day an aircraft flew overhead while I was outside playing. Its wings seemed to move forward and backward during its maneuvers. What an awesome sight for a little kid who had never seen anything like that before! I ran into the house and described to my dad what I'd seen. The airplane's wings started from a delta-wing, swept-back configuration, then moved forward into a more-conventional, straight-wing configuration in midair. He listened carefully to what I said, then took me by the hand to our neighbor's house. Colonel Lunsford was an Air Force pilot, and my dad must have known that he could tell us about the airplane I had seen. The Colonel seemed impressed by my powers of observation and articulation. It was an F-111, he explained, a new type of aircraft the Air Force was developing. These and other similar experiences increased my dream of being a pilot when I grew up.

Sadly, our good friend Colonel Lunsford ended up missing in action during the Vietnam War.

My First "Flight"

In first grade, I formed a club called the "Flying Tigers." We ran around the playground at recess time with our arms out as if they were the wings of imaginary P-40s. The P-40 aircraft of the real Flying Tigers had tiger teeth painted on their noses—and I loved that. We shot down every German and Japanese "plane" in sight, flapping our arms, screaming like banshees, and running as fast as our legs would carry us. Ground combat also tickled our young fancies. When we got home from school, we put small branches from trees into the mesh web of our World War II Army helmets so we could hide from one another in the woods.

It was flying, however, that consumed my thoughts. In order to "fly" my own airplane, I made an aircraft instrument panel out of wood. It had a yoke just like a real airplane, and my mother let me hang my contraption over the front seat of her big, brown 1949 DeSoto. It was an airplane inside a tank. This was pure, imaginary paradise for this five-year-old boy. My mom let me "fly" all the way to the grocery store and back. She also took my friends and me to the Army-Navy surplus store to buy patches for our little army outfits. Back in the 1950s, there weren't many little boys I knew who didn't have an army outfit on which my mom had sewn some nifty patches.

We were the coolest little kids on the planet.

The Parade

I saw my first parade in a small Ohio town called Yellow Springs. The impression the music made on me changed my life forever. I especially remember the sound of the drums as they beat the rhythms, or street beats, that moved the bands forward. My dad purchased a phonograph record for the family that featured the style of marching music played in the parade. I wore that record out while yearning to learn how to play the drums. Quaker Oats boxes and anything else I could find fell victim to my pounding. My dad had an old wooden drum he had played in the 1930s in a Boy Scout band, but the broken head never got fixed so I could play it. Looking back, I wish I had asked my dad to get that drum fixed for me. But maybe I was just used to certain things not getting fixed, like my police tricycle windshield.

On the Road

My dad served in the Navy during WWII and in the Korean War. After his discharge, he went to work in a warehouse driving a forklift so he could go to business school at night and earn his college degree. He did this steadily for eight years, from the 1950s to the early 1960s. We didn't see our dad very much because he was working hard to better himself and provide for his family. My father was always a very industrious man, with a great sense of humor. People liked him right away when they met him, which really helped him in his sales career. He took a job with DAP Incorporated and sold caulking and putty all around the Midwest.

The road was hard on my dad. Back then, salesmen drove everywhere they went, and he spent long hours behind the wheel traveling from state to state to open and service new accounts. He was an exemplary salesman and a great role model.

I know my dad loved us very much. He would always try to get all of his work done so he could be home by mid-afternoon every Friday. I couldn't wait until my dad got home. He was always whistling a happy tune when he walked through the door.

And then things began to change. I remember listening once when my Dad tried to explain to my Mom about how hard it was being on the road all the time. The loneliness at night was killing him, and being away from his family for long stretches of time was tearing away at his soul.

My dad's behavior slowly began to change; he began to drink. He had always enjoyed a drink now and then, but drinking was quickly becoming a routine. He set out to drink for the same reasons other people did, but something was happening to my Dad over time, and he did not realize it: the alcohol was making him very sick.

In retrospect, I now know that my father had a genetic predisposition for the disease of alcoholism. As with any alcoholic, as the years passed his drinking increased. Slowly and painfully, our little family changed into something very scary.

Loss of Control

We were driving home from my grandparents' house in Cincinnati, Ohio. Dad and his brothers had been drinking all day at Grandma's house. At the time, I thought it was normal behavior for most families in the 1950s. After all, the men had grown up hard and fast, had seen a lot of war, and drinking was a part of the postwar culture, right?

The problem with Dad, though, was that he didn't stop drinking. He would get so drunk his speech slurred and he could not walk without staggering. This isn't such a problem when you are about to fall into bed, but when you insist on driving home on a dark, rainy night, it's a frightening problem. At times such as this Mom would beg Dad not to drive, but he never listened. I remember how she would sob, which of course would make us three kids start crying; if Mom was upset and afraid, we should be too, right? But Mom just wasn't healthy enough at the time to not get in the car with her kids when her husband was drunk. As the spouse of an alcoholic, her co-dependency kept her frozen and unable to do the right thing.

There are elevated bridges all over Cincinnati. Passing over the Cincinnati viaduct in the middle of the night, during a heavy rainstorm, with your drunken father behind the wheel, swerving all over the road, was enough to scare the hell out of anyone—even small children who did not fully appreciate the ramifications of what was happening. As the car swerved back and forth we nearly went off the side of the bridge. *I was scared to death, crying in the back seat, a helpless little child with no power to change anything.*

I think that, in order to survive these terrifying experiences with Dad, we all shut down emotionally. How would these episodes of confusing terror affect me in difficult situations in the future?

Chapter 2

Adolescent Years

W hen my dad was promoted to national sales manager in 1967, we moved away from my childhood outdoor paradise in southern Ohio. Moving was a real culture shock for me. The kids in Chicago were very different.

The main thing I remember was that it was okay to fistfight in school. Kids who ratted on other kids were looked down upon, and bullies got away with murder on the playground. Several kids made fun of me because I carried a briefcase to school and wore a brown corduroy hat. I loved corduroy and still do, but those kids at my new school hated that hat and wanted to fight me for it my first day in school!

The kids had been learning Spanish in school, but I was totally lost because we moved in February and the school year was nearly over. It was a tough time for all of the Balzer kids. My sister stayed back in Beavercreek so she could graduate with her high school class. That was a great move. She never stuck around much, and married at age nineteen soon after moving to Chicago.

Almost Heaven

I remember getting up one Saturday morning in 1967 to go out to the local airport in Lombard, Illinois. This was a magical place with several hangars and lots of airplanes. Sometimes, kids got lucky. My friend John told me about a fellow who was taking him up in his helicopter. I figured if I hung around up there long enough, I might find somebody willing to take me up for an airplane ride, especially if I offered to help wash his plane.

As I rode my bike down the block toward the airport, I could hear the sounds of roaring bulldozer engines and tearing metal, followed by loud bangs. I pedaled closer and spotted clouds of dust and piles of twisted metal where the hangars had been.

The airport was being shut down! I just could not believe it. Later, I learned that the airport property had been sold to developers who wanted to build condominiums. As a twelve-year-old kid, I had remained totally unaware of the local battle that had raged over this valuable piece of real estate. So I was devastated—it all happened so fast, and I had no advance warning. Now the airport was gone, piled up and twisted—and along with it my hope of getting an airplane ride and learning more about flying, at least for the time being.

Music as My Salvation

I was very small for my age. I loved sports and played everything, but by the time high school rolled around I wasn't good enough to compete with so many kids in such a large school. I couldn't hit a baseball to save my life.

But I still loved beating pots and pans. To my delight, I discovered a small but very talented drum and twirling corps called the Velvet Viking Cadets. The group practiced in the parking lot of a shopping center right up the street from our house in Lombard. It was a precision unit, and I loved to watch it practice. One night I mustered up the courage to ask the director if I could join.

She looked me over carefully. "Do you think you can cut it?"

I had no prior experience, not even with the basic snare drum, but I stuck out my chin and confidently replied, "Yes, I can!"

When she agreed to give me a chance, I was bound and determined I would not let her down; I practiced hard every day. When I was 17 years old I won the individual snare drum solo championship at Notre Dame University. Our unit won several national championships. The city council threw a big party for us, and I got to ride in a parade through town in the back of an early-model Corvette convertible.

Drum corps was the best thing that ever happened to me. It was great for my self-esteem, and for the first time I really felt part of something special.

Plus, it was such a great group of kids; everyone worked so hard. Many of those "kids" remain my close friends to this day.

After high school I joined the all-male Cavaliers Drum and Bugle Corps out of Chicago. What an incredible experience that was, traveling throughout the country and competing with other corps from across the United States. During my years with the outfit I marched with a driven and incredibly talented drum line.

The discipline, dedication, teamwork, and commitment to excellence I learned in these two fine drum corps would serve me well in the coming years.

The Beginning of Drinking

I have a confession to make. The first time I got staggering drunk I was three years old.

My mother had left me with my great grandfather, and we were sitting in front of his house on a beautiful summer day. He handed me his "long neck" brown beer bottle to hold. I don't remember whether he expected me to drink, or told me to, but when he went into the house to get something I helped myself to his beer. At that age, just a few gulps was all it took.

When my mom discovered her little boy flat-out drunk and unable to stand, she exploded. That was the last time I ever saw my great-grandpa. I don't know whether my mom banished him, or whether he just passed away. He was 94 years old—and he loved his beer.

High School Teetotaler

Thankfully, there was never any occasion for me to drink in high school. My friends who were athletes did all the drinking, while I hung out with the musicians. We musicians did other things besides drinking, such as play music and practice, practice, practice. The jocks, as a general rule, loved to drink beer—or at least pretended they loved it. I figured that out during my senior year when I went to a few parties and found that nearly everyone but me was totally loaded. I just didn't have any interest in drinking at that time in my life. Besides, my dad was doing it at home.

I enjoyed the sober time I spent with my girlfriend, and marching and learning new rhythms in drum corps. I also had a great job at the local drugstore, which kept me busy three nights a week and on the weekends. I often rode my bike the twelve miles one-way to my girlfriend's house. How could you drink and do that?

Back then, drinking didn't make any sense to me. We even had a beautiful wet bar I helped my father build in our basement, but I never found a need or a reason to use it—at least, throughout high school.

College: A Different Story

The first time I truly went away from home was when I left for college. For some reason, I got it in my head that it was time to begin drinking, like everyone else. I was away from my girlfriend and really didn't know how to fit in with the college party scene, so I starting cracking beers alone in my room. At first, I didn't really like it, but a habit set in. I began with two quarts of beer every Friday night. My drinking never interfered with my studies, and I rarely drank on weekdays, although the school I attended—Northern Illinois University—was known for big parties that started every Thursday afternoon and ended late Sunday night.

Heavy drinking was the norm on campus. We students in the dormitories got together to host our own "keg" parties. We'd start with one keg of beer and go through as many as the liquor store would sell us or we could afford. All the freshmen were under the legal drinking age, but as long as you pitched in for the keg and invited some cute girls, you were welcome. And you could drink until someone had to carry you home.

Blackout #1

My first alcoholic blackout occurred at one of these dorm parties. The residents of a particular dorm, located across the campus, invited our entire university marching band to party one night. Four hundred members strong, the Husky Band was not to be outdone. We set out to prove that we could out-drink and out-party anyone on campus. Moreover, there were lots of upperclassmen in the marching band who could teach us the art of imbibing.

I set out to drink like everyone else at the party, but at some point I lost control and could not remember what I was doing. By that time there wasn't anyone left at the party I knew. I do remember being staggering drunk and trying to walk home in a freezing blizzard. The effect of the alcohol hit me rapidly, and continued to get worse even though I had stopped drinking. Within minutes my hands and feet were numb, my face was frozen, and I found myself staring a four-lane highway in the face. The wide concrete barrier stood between me and the dormitory I lived in. It was slick, covered with a thin layer of snow, and the college kids driving on it were moving way too fast for the existing conditions.

The drivers might have seen me on the highway if I had been walking or standing upright, but by this time it was impossible for me to stand. No matter how hard I tried, my legs just would not cooperate. So, determined to make it home, I decided the only way to cross the highway was to roll myself across. Literally . . . *roll my way across.*

For a while the idea seemed like a good one. But then I spotted the headlights of an oncoming car. My heart leaped into my mouth when I discovered I was unable to stand up and get out of the way. I began to roll with a new sense of urgency, knowing that in a few seconds, if I did not get out of the way, I would be smashed into human "road kill" in the middle of a four-lane highway. The car roared by so close to me that the tires threw slush from the road into my face.

Panic-stricken, I continued rolling my way across. Along the way I vomited until there was nothing left in my stomach; then the dry heaves started. I was so dizzy I could barely think. Exhausted and confused, I stopped to get my bearings. I made out the lights of my dormitory, and finally got back to my room. The only thing that saved my life that night was sheer luck in avoiding a car, and the heavy band uniform overcoat we wore during the winter days. Without the latter, I very easily could have fallen asleep and frozen to death.

For some warped reason, I really thought everyone drank like this—all the way to blackout, that is. Frankly, I was uncomfortable around people, and drinking made me relax and feel like a part of the crowd. I believed that without the alcohol I would feel very alone at school and would not fit in socially.

To this day I don't know why, but my drinking did not have a negative effect on my college work. I did quite well and graduated with my B.S. degree in the summer of 1977.

I did not have a car until my senior year, and I don't remember driving under the influence of alcohol. Still, there must have been times when I had no business driving, yet did so anyway. I definitely did not understand that drinking to blackout was a strong indicator for early stage-one alcoholism. It would be many years before I was able to put that information to good use. Until then, I was a train wreck looking for a place to happen.

Chapter 3

Dreaming of Flying

During my senior year in college, our university marching band flew on a United Airlines DC-10. We flew from Chicago to Los Angeles to support the football team in a game against Long Beach State and to play at the Los Angeles Coliseum during a Rams game.

It was my first flight in a jet aircraft. I will never forget the feeling I had when the pilots pushed the throttles forward for take-off. The entire plane shook, and something deep inside me woke up. I had been busy all these years, but flying had never been too far from my mind. Now, those engines re-ignited the passion I had experienced as a child when I watched Sputnik soar overhead or the latest incarnation of an F-111 zoom past. My zest for airplanes returned.

I knew that in the "old days" of aviation, passengers could go up and talk to the pilots during flight. Building up some courage, I asked one of the flight attendants if I could approach the cockpit to look inside and speak to the pilots. "Sure," she answered with a smile. "But you'll have to wait until we're on the ground in L.A. They stopped letting people up into the cockpit a few years ago."

I thanked her and stared out the window all the way from Chicago to California. I couldn't wait to talk to the pilots. Once we landed, I unbuckled as quickly as possible and scooted my way to the front of the plane. The nice flight attendant told the pilots someone was coming up there to see them. I still remember the moment I entered the cockpit, my eyes soaking in the flight instruments, gauges, and circuit breakers. The complexity staggered me. I had instant respect for anyone who could do this complicated job.

"What do I have to do to get a job like this?" I asked the Captain, sitting in the left-hand seat.

He smiled and answered, "Just finish up your degree, learn to fly, and get as much 'heavy' multi-engine time (pilot talk for experience) as you can." The idea of becoming a pilot for a major airline suddenly struck me as an attainable goal.

Once we returned to Illinois, I made straight for the university library. I was working there as a "book stacker" and remembered seeing a book called "Careers in America." I looked up "airline pilot." What I found blew me away: great wages, plenty of time off, a cool lifestyle, lots of travel, and all those female flight attendants. Wow! I wanted that fancy uniform and the respect that went with it!

The next day I went to see the Dean of the university. I told her I wanted to change my major from Music to Elementary Education. She was surprised, because she knew I had dabbled at several programs, but then worked hard to get into the music department. However, I knew it would take me another three years to finish a music degree, and I didn't want to wait that long. I wanted to graduate and find a job, so I could learn to fly.

"So now you are going to be a teacher? Joe, I know you'll make a really good one."

"Yes," I answered without missing a beat. "I am going to be a teacher while I learn to fly, and then I am going to become an airline pilot."

The look on her face told me she didn't doubt me for a moment.

Chapter 4

Joe the Teacher

After I finished my degree in the summer of 1977 I moved to Fort Lauderdale, Florida, a great place to learn to fly and build time. Once there, I enrolled in an evening private pilot ground school. My job as a schoolteacher gave me my afternoons free to pursue my goal. I flew small, single-engine planes as much as possible.

Northern Illinois University had provided an excellent Elementary Education program. We education majors had at least three internships before graduation. The last one, during my senior year, was for a full six months.

During my first assignment as a student intern, I was assigned to a teacher who had decided that one little boy could never learn math. The boy had a really rough home life and, predictably, was already struggling by the second grade. But I took "Ronnie" out into the hallway, put numbers on the floor, and within minutes had him jumping on them like a happy frog. Two weeks later he was keeping up with the other children in their math lessons. Reaching out to him really felt good.

In fact, teaching in the public schools was one of the most rewarding experiences of my life. There is nothing quite like helping children learn and sparking their interest in new things. I can still see those children and the excitement on their faces when we did special lessons that tickled their fancy. I still have the art pictures the kids drew for me one fall of a large tree growing just outside the second-story window of the schoolhouse. Each and every one of them was remarkable!

Getting Paid to Teach—Well, Sort Of!

My last full-time teaching job was in Deerfield Beach, Florida. All the kids were remedial students who had tested well below their grade levels in mathematics. At the beginning of the year most of the students in my seventh-grade class were working at the third- or fourth-grade level. But hard work, tremendous motivation, and some tough love pushed these kids to their true potential. I have to give it to them, because they worked hard, and by the end of the year nearly all were performing at grade level. I can still picture those kids, too. And the other teachers were very impressed with the results.

But I also had to eat, pay for a place to live, and save some money. Our function as teachers was critically important, but we were all paid so little money to teach at this school that it was hard to stay. It broke my heart to see talented people leaving the education system because they just didn't make enough to support themselves.

During my last year of public school teaching I volunteered to teach a group of children who had been removed from their regular classrooms due to discipline problems. I poured my heart and soul into those kids, and I am proud to say that they respected, and even loved, me for it. They made good progress. Even though those kids were the "rejects" from the regular classroom, they performed well for me because they knew I cared about them, demanded excellence, and would tolerate nothing less. The day we parted for the last time was an emotional one for all of us, and I still think about it.

Chapter 5

Liftoff

Although I loved my day job, every free moment was consumed with flying. I began taking actual flying lessons in an airplane in May of 1978; I augmented this by reading every aviation book I could get my hands on. To help supplement my meager teaching income, I parked cars at night at a busy nightclub in Fort Lauderdale. Each night's extra money helped pay for a flight lesson the next day. I was very aggressive with my plan to learn to fly, because my research in aviation magazines and professional aviation organizations all indicated the airlines would be short of pilots in the early 1980s, and I wanted to be part of the hiring boom. In fact, I wanted to be right in front of the pack, so my seniority number would be a good one.

Great expense, dedication, and sacrifice went into my commitment to succeed; I went after a piloting career like a starving lion. Although I witnessed many young pilots give up their dreams, nothing was going to stop me.

Who is Sober?

I am certain today that my first three flight instructors were alcoholics. One of them even called himself an alcoholic, although he had no intention of quitting drinking. My favorite instructor was a guy named Paul. I don't know what happened to him, but the last I heard he was deep into the later stages of alcoholism, and today is more than likely dead.

Being around an alcoholic such as Paul stirred a deep pain inside me. I felt compassion toward him and wanted to help; but, like most people who are involved in an alcoholic's life, I just didn't know what to do.

A Sad Story of a Hero

I took my first flight lessons from the man who was teaching the ground school through the board of education. He was a very good ground school instructor, so I figured he was a good flight instructor as well. Looking back today, he probably *was* a good flight instructor—but he just moved along too slowly for me. My first lesson in the airplane involved starting the engine and taxiing around the airport for forty minutes. People were shocked when I told them this. They'd never heard of a flight instructor taxiing around the airport with a student that long. The goal is to get students into the air as soon as you can; they will have plenty of time to practice taxiing the airplane as they learn how to fly it.

This instructor—Frank was his name—was also teaching another student, who happened to be a young boy in the seventh grade. The youngster's name was Mark Johnson, and he was an exceptionally bright kid. (So bright that he later graduated eighth in his class from the United States Naval Academy.) Mark's father, Herb, always accompanied him to the airport, and I became a friend of the family, a friendship that we still share to this day.

During our conversations I learned that Herb had been a WWII pilot and an honest-to-goodness war hero. He had flown the Corsair fighter for the Navy in the South Pacific. His men and superior officers all admired him. The part about Herb that I did not understand was why he was not the one teaching his son how to fly.

After knowing them for several weeks, the Johnson family invited me to their house for dinner. I decided to ask Herb why he was not teaching Mark to fly. He mumbled something about his license that I did not fully understand, but I got the feeling the subject was taboo. I was not supposed to be asking questions about Herb and his flying career.

As I learned the hard way, a certain secrecy follows the disease of alcoholism. It is an inescapable fact. After Herb passed away, his lovely wife sat quietly at the dinner table one night and explained to me that Herb had been forced to quit flying in the 1960s. During the war Herb and his buddies, like so many in the military—especially pilots—had drunk heavily and relied on alcohol to calm their nerves from the incredible pressures. Nonetheless, he had gone on to become a pilot with a major airline. But a woman observed him drinking heavily in a bar and turned him in because she believed he had consumed too many drinks to be flying an airplane the next day. In those days, any pilots having a problem with alcohol were forced to resign or were fired, and that is exactly what had happened to Herb.

At the time, I had only a very shallow understanding of what this man must have endured during the last twenty-five years of his life—without his wings of freedom. He carried the mail in his south Florida town until he retired many years later— and then he died of emphysema, from another addiction he had picked up during the Second World War. Yet Herb was a man of wisdom, and he and his wife raised an outstanding young man whom I am proud to call my friend today.

Secrecy

Partly as a result of the way pilots were treated by their companies, as well as the FAA's policy concerning alcohol at the time, most pilots agreed to "take care" of their buddies if they showed up to fly drunk, hung over, or under the influence of alcohol to any degree. In those days, your fellow pilots and flight attendants simply piled you into the cockpit to get you home. That saved your job and your butt to fly another day.

This practice continued for years. It had to: it was the only way pilots could save themselves from getting into big trouble with their companies or the FAA. Prior to 1972, if you were diagnosed with alcoholism you lost your pilot's license for life—no exceptions. It was a sad state of affairs, considering that most pilots came from the military, where they had never had any trouble finding alcohol; in fact, the military gave pilots beer rations.

After learning about Herb's dilemma, I could understand the underlying sadness that was always present in his demeanor. After all, he had sobered up and quit drinking—but he would never be allowed to fly again for the rest of his life.

That's an incredibly tough nut to swallow for anyone who really loves to fly airplanes. For those who do not fly it is very difficult to even begin to understand what Herb and others like him experienced. Flying gives them a feeling similar to what some people feel about fishing: once you are into fishing, it's all over. Some people just don't get hooked, and that's okay; but they really can't understand what they're missing.

I was very careful about my drinking and flying, and drew no parallels between my imbibing and Herb's, which had gotten him into so much trouble. Of course, I didn't know what any of the signs of early-stage alcoholism were, either. One day I found myself wondering if my ignorance and lack of education about alcoholism was going to lead to tragedy in my own life. Was I headed down the same path Herb had taken? In the end I decided that nothing like that could ever happen to *me.*

Sadly, how wrong I was.

Pursuing My Goal—and Paying the Price

While in the midst of learning how to fly, an acquaintance of mine gave me a poster that said, "Happy are those who have big dreams and are willing to pay the price to make them come true." That was me all over—I was dedicated and focused on my goal of becoming a pilot with a major airline.

Over the course of three years, I worked two or three jobs at a time and spent every penny I had in the pursuit of my flight ratings. Thousands of dollars later, I had every rating I would need to make myself very competitive with other young pilots who were going to be applying to the airlines.

The first thing I earned was my private pilot rating, which allowed me to fly passengers around south Florida, the Keys, and the Bahamas. I would walk up and down the beach in Fort Lauderdale with a sign that read "Fly to the Bahamas for Twenty Dollars." This got the college crowd's attention, and I flew many people to Bimini. They shared the expenses with me, and I made sure they had a wonderful time as I gave them a mini-tour in the lovely skies above the islands. It was beautiful, and they loved it; so did I.

My experience flying tourists pushed me over the 200-hour flight time requirement to test for a commercial pilot license. As part of this I pursued the qualification that would allow me to fly into the clouds without any visual reference to the ground—the coveted instrument flight rating. With that securely under my belt, I obtained my flight instructor rating, so I could teach other people how to fly. I could actually make a little money flying, rather than spending all of my money building up my flight experience. Then I added my multi-engine rating.

Soon followed my Airline Transport Pilot Rating. This rating, known as the A.T.P., is something many of the large airlines really look for in an applicant. It is an advanced instrument rating taken in a complex aircraft.

"Complex" means the aircraft has more advanced systems, such as retractable landing gear, fixed-pitch propellers, more powerful engines, and so forth. Pilots must also demonstrate that they can execute an instrument approach in an emergency situation with an engine failure. There is also a minimum flight experience requirement of 1,500 hours total flight time which, at the time I did mine, was verified in a personal interview with a Federal Safety Inspector. Having this rating shows the airlines you are serious about becoming a professional pilot.

All of this learning and accomplishment required tremendous sacrifice of time and energy. I knew before I began pursuing my goal of becoming an airline pilot that it was not going to be an easy endeavor. I saw several young people fail. Many quit after receiving their private pilot licenses, telling me they just could not figure out a way to build time. Some people would get all the way to their ATP, then quit after a few months of looking for a job. Not me. I knew I was going to succeed, and there was no way I was going to quit. I didn't listen to the naysayers who told me it was too hard, or too expensive, or too time-consuming, or that I would never have a chance to fly for a major airline. Others were welcome to believe in those limitations on their own lives, but I was determined and driven, and I pursued every opportunity as if it were my last.

Chapter 6

Delta is Ready When You Are

I left teaching in 1979 to go to work full time for Delta Airlines in the cabin service department. My dad wondered what the heck I was doing. After all, I had a college degree and a professional job, yet I was leaving to go clean airplanes in the middle of the night for Delta Airlines.

However, I thought this was a great idea, and tried to explain it to him. "I know some guys who worked for Delta on the ramp in Fort Lauderdale," I began, "and after they got 1,500 hours of flight time and their college degree, they were hired from within the company as pilots."

He wasn't convinced. "Wouldn't you be better off just flying planes and getting your experience so you could apply to all of the airlines?" he asked. It was a reasonable question. My problem was that by now I was fixated on Delta. I knew people who worked there who enjoyed their jobs.

So, in spite of good ol' Dad's advice, I went ahead and took the night job with Delta. I worked a midnight shift cleaning airplanes. The job involved dumping the lavatories into a "lav truck," cleaning and restocking the galleys, and cleaning the cabins. In those days, smoking was permitted in the cabins, and there were ashtrays that needed to be emptied. I walked, bobbed, bent, and kneeled all the way down the aisles, wiping out all of the ashtrays, picking up butts, and doing whatever was necessary to make that cabin spotless.

I remember how excited I was, early on, the first time I saw an announcement on the job vacancy board posted by the supervisors' office that Delta was getting ready to hire some Second Officers or Flight Engineers. This was around 1980. I met all the minimum requirements, and, knowing guys who had done it a few years earlier, I could not wait to go up and interview for a pilot's job. I applied by letter and in person.

But it didn't happen. They told us they were not going to put any employees in the classes. And that's how it went, from then on; they pretty much strung us along. Although I had no idea at the time, I would end up waiting *six long years* to get that pilot interview with Delta. Unbeknownst to me, something had changed within the Delta "family" philosophy, and they hadn't hired a pilot from within the company since those fellows from Fort Lauderdale six years earlier. But it was hard to know whether there had been a policy change, or just other factors intruding: the PATCO strike happened in 1981, and most airlines stopped hiring and actually furloughed pilots; plus Delta went through some big leadership changes.

But I was not the only one hanging around in hopes of getting hired from within the company to be a pilot for Delta. At least twenty-five of us interviewed with Delta in September of 1985. We were told by the head of personnel that—finally!—a class having twenty-five slots was going to be filled from within the company. We all interviewed, and we all felt we had done well. I even went in to visit the new chief pilot, and he told me, "I'll see you in class on Friday." After six years of waiting, sacrifice, and dedication to this company, it was difficult to contain my excitement.

And then I got the call. Someone on the other end of the phone informed me, three days before the class was going to start, that my hopes had been in vain. "We're sorry, but we can't offer you any encouragement!"

"What!?" I replied. Maybe I should have screamed into the phone, but I was too blown away and numb to do so. I was shaking when I hung up. After six years of being an exemplary employee, with full qualifications, they had turned me down flat.

Try as I might, no one would answer or return my calls. I had already moved out of my little apartment in Fort Lauderdale and had everything packed and ready for a move to Atlanta to begin my training. The news crushed my spirit and broke my heart.

It did not take long before several of the other employee applicants phoned me to share their own stories of disappointment. Delta had turned down every one of us; not a single person was going to be hired from within the company. Delta never gave any of us an explanation why. We were all great candidates and good employees, but some unknown executive decided to turn all of us down.

Two of the other guys I had met during the interview process told me they were going to leave the company. Who could blame them? My own carpet of dreams had been pulled out from under me, too. I wrote a resignation letter and slid it under the door of my supervisor's office. I was done with Delta.

Chapter 7

Paying My Dues

I had a friend, Steve—also a young pilot building time—who worked for a small company called Island Suppliers, which flew freight and passengers to the Caribbean islands in DC-3s, Curtis C-46s, and Convairs. Every Saturday they carried passengers to the Bahamas. One day, about a year after I went to work cleaning planes for Delta, Steve suggested that if I helped Island Suppliers load their airplane in the morning, the Captain might let me go on the trip as the flight attendant. So I did. When that flight's passengers got off the airplane in the islands, the Captain invited me to fly back with him in the right seat of the airplane. That turned out to be one of the most exciting days of my life: I was a flight attendant on the way over, and a pilot on the way back! They even ordered a pilot uniform for me. I felt like I was on my way to the big leagues!

Since I was flying the DC-3 while still working for Delta, I would get off my graveyard cleaning shift on Saturday at 6:00 a.m., then cross the airport property at Fort Lauderdale International to help load the DC-3. But I was thankful for the opportunity to fly these "old classic" airplanes with some old classic pilots.

And I was so proud of my little white shirt with the gold epaulets—even though before long it was stained with oil from flying the DC-3. The shift supervisor at Delta let me hang my "clean" pilot shirt behind the door in his office. Some of my co-workers at my cleaning job went happily nuts the day I showed up with my pilot uniform shirt.

However, I was surprised to discover the reactions of many other workers I had thought were my friends. They were distinctly unfriendly:

jealous and envious about my very hard-won "good fortune." I found it profoundly sad that people would feel that way toward a fellow employee who was just following a dream and trying to improve his lot in life. But the lesson stuck hard: many people, despite their "friendship," don't really want to see you get ahead and succeed.

Learning from the Legends

The fellows who taught me to fly those old airplanes had mostly begun as World War II pilots, and it was a real honor to fly with and learn from them. They never sweated the small stuff when you made a mistake, but they made darn sure that if you did something that might get yourself killed someday, you wouldn't be apt to do it again anytime soon. This feedback came in the form of a very tactful though sharp butt-chewing, followed by some humor so you wouldn't be totally demoralized.

Back then, pilots really knew how to have fun, and they were fun to be around. Those were some beautiful days in my life. There is nothing quite like flying an aircraft with very large reciprocating "round" engines. Pilots have a love for the music they make as they hum through the skies. The sound of the DC-3's engines could be heard from miles away as the planes flew back from their runs to the islands. It was sweet music to my ears. (Recently, my son ran outside yelling, "What is that sound, Dad?" It was a DC-3 flying over at low level—a rare sight in this day and age. The sound of those radial engines still moves a young boy's heart.)

Most of the young pilots like me dreamed of getting a chance to fly one of those great airplanes someday, and were willing to do just about anything to have that opportunity. For us that might mean loading cargo into every airplane the company had flying that week, in the middle of those hot, muggy Fort Lauderdale midsummer afternoons. We often loaded several thousand pounds of freight with only a two- or three-man team. Then the co-pilot—whoever's turn it was for that flight—would get cleaned up and join the Captain in the cockpit.

Many other young men, also hoping to build some time in DC-3s, showed up interested in learning how to fly these airplanes. But when they found out how hard we worked to get them loaded, they had a way of disappearing and not coming back.

We often took a third pilot along for those long—ten hours or more—days of hard flying to the out-islands, so each pilot could get some welcome rest along the way. We were younger then, and falling asleep on a load of freight in the back of a DC-3 or a Curtis C-46 on the way to our destination was almost as comfortable as being on a warm mattress.

Those of our pilot friends who were not afraid of hard work all had the chance to fly one of these airplanes at some point. Nothing, and I mean *nothing*, sounds like a C-46 when you sit in the cockpit and slowly bring the throttles up to maximum takeoff power. The engines are right there next to your head, as close as on any aircraft I have ever flown, and the vibration and sounds coming from the engines and the props whirling around really rattle your brain. You have to be a pilot to fully appreciate how great it is! Any pilot worth his wings would love to do this at least once in his lifetime.

Island Adventures

I remember one flight in particular. We were flying back to Fort Lauderdale from the Turks and Caicos Islands in a Curtis C-46 through some really heavy rain and dark, ugly clouds. The windows in the cockpit of this old bird come down to around your knees, so the visibility is great when you're looking out. This is a good thing when the airplane and the window seals are new, but when the airplane is old and worn and has been flying the islands and sitting in the sun for years, the window seals tend to dry up and crumble away. Ours had done so some years back.

On this day the result was a thorough soaking of the cockpit, including our radios. There are at least two kinds of radios in most airplanes: those used for navigation and those used for communication. They both failed. So I flew by what pilots call the "whiskey compass," a small magnetic compass that in most old airplanes is mounted on the glare shield in front of the pilots. A compass card floats on the liquid inside the glass. By today's standards it's a very crude instrument.

But it's superb so long as you know how to use it. I got plenty of practice that day because we were solidly in the clouds, and thus operating under Instrument Flight Rules (IFR), so we simply took up a heading which we hoped would eventually take us to the Florida mainland.

I think even old, crusty Captain Gene may have been a little nervous that day, because he smoked every single cigar he had, which was three packs of ten each. I will never forget the sight when we finally broke out of the clouds and turbulence and saw the late afternoon sun thirty degrees above the horizon to the west, and the mainland of the Florida coast shimmering in the distance. We both smiled. We were more relieved than we let on.

Another thing about the DC-3: it loved to drink oil. We carried the precious liquid, in large cans, with us onboard the airplane, and when we landed at some out-island after flying for a few hours, we climbed up on the wing and added oil to the engines. You could always tell which pilots flew radial-engine airplanes because they always had plenty of oil stains on their white shirts.

The hard work, oil stains, and long hours were well worth the beauty of the night sky in the Caribbean out-islands. Many of the islands to which we flew supplies had little in the way of development, so there was little if any electrical lighting and sky illumination. I have been blessed in my life to be in some remote areas, but nothing compares to the starlit sky of the 1980s in these small out-islands of the Sargasso Sea. On a clear night the heavens looked as if they contained a billion stars—and I felt as if I were among them, for the first time in my life. There is nothing like it anywhere. The clarity and brilliance is so lovely you can not help but think you are working in the presence of God.

At some of the stations in the out-islands we were met by little boys who showed up to unload the airplane and earn a dollar for doing so. At least they were being paid real money. I, however, was working for free—as so many young pilots have always done in order to gain the experience they needed to get better jobs.

I guess you could have called us "grocery boys," because, for the most part, that's what we were delivering. My pilot friends and I would stand in the airplane and yell out to the unloading boss, "Okay, we have a twenty-pound box of frozen steaks, Neill!" If it was something that was supposed to go to this particular island, he would yell back: "Let it come!" If not, his answer was just as simple: "Let it stay."

Trouble in the Air

One afternoon my radial-engine flying buddies and I were loading a C-46 full of freight. It seemed like a lot more than usual, but the boss wanted it loaded. We shrugged and, reluctantly, kept packing. You didn't ever want to complain about anything to the boss (owner) or you would find yourself out of a flying job with the snap of a finger. I say "job" even though none of us was ever paid for what we were doing. We were willing to load and fly for free because we hoped the experience would get us a job with one of the major airlines . . . someday.

This particular day started out like every other day. After starting the engines we taxied the aircraft out to the runway. We ran our checklists to make sure everything was ready for takeoff, then applied takeoff power. As the fuel poured into the engines they came to life with a mounting roar. Normally, the aircraft accelerates evenly down the runway. On this day, however, something was different. The aircraft accelerated very slowly. I considered aborting the takeoff, but it was not my decision because I was not the Captain. I looked anxiously at the engine instruments: manifold pressure, okay; R.P.M., okay; oil pressure, okay. All of the indications were normal, but this airplane was acting too much like a ground-loving machine for me to feel comfortable.

I had flown this runway hundreds of times, and knew full well a railroad track and a highway were waiting for us at the end. Were we going to stay on the ground, impact the railroad tracks, and disintegrate into a fireball, spewing flames and our bodies along Federal Highway? The thought crossed my mind as my eyes scanned the gauges. By this time we were running out of runway fast, and we only had one option: we had to get this airplane into the air before we turned into a couple of crash statistics.

We were almost at the end of the runway when the nose of the airplane eased off the ground. I gasped quietly, then held my breath as we flew in "ground effect" for several hundred yards. Ground effect is an aerodynamic condition in which an aircraft does not have enough airspeed to fly unless it stays close to the ground. And by close, I mean no more than one-half of its own wingspan above the earth, which is not very far. An aircraft in this slow condition will stall and crash if it flies above its ground effect distance.

Our plane was clearly not ready to fly when we pulled her off the ground. I raised the landing gear to get rid of some aerodynamic drag, and the aircraft flew better, but only slightly. At this point we were buying feet and inches, trying to clear the approach lights at the end of the runway and whatever unknown obstacles lay ahead of our flight path. Time and events passed in slow motion. I hawked the throttles and instruments to ensure we were getting everything we could out of the engines. It was the first time in my life when the outcome of a flight was in serious question; but, as I quickly discovered, my training kicked in and I didn't really have time to think much about it.

The Captain, whose turn it was to fly this leg, was doing a delicate balancing act, staying in "ground effect" to keep us from impacting mother earth, while subtly handling the controls in a way that would allow us to gain precious additional airspeed.

I remember looking out my window as we barely cleared Federal Highway at the end of the runway. I could see a lady in a convertible with a baby in a car seat. She must have wet her pants as this big, loud, lumbering C-46 cleared her car by less than ten feet. I know I would have.

The tower controller knew something was wrong before we even left the runway. "Are you going to be all right?" He asked this question over and over.

"Sure," I thought to myself, "as long as we don't hit the ground with all this gas and freight on board." If we did, there would be a big beach barbeque right in the middle of Fort Lauderdale, and the Captain and I would be the first guests to arrive.

By the time we reached the shoreline, just over a mile or so from the end of the runway, we were maybe thirty feet in the air, holding on to what little airspeed we had while sacrificing what airspeed we could for some precious altitude to clear the palm trees by the coast. We had every bit of power coming out of those engines we could muster without over-temping them, which would have caused one or both to overheat, guaranteeing a short swim offshore.

After clearing the coconut tree obstacles by mere inches, we flew low again, just twenty feet off the tops of the waves. Ground effect is the same whether over water or land, so we returned to it intentionally in order to pick up some airspeed, so as to be able to climb later, somewhere down range. We were eastbound, with nothing between us and Bimini, one of the first islands in the Bahamas chain, just east and south of Fort Lauderdale.

"That son of a bitch!" the Captain finally exclaimed. "I'll never let him do this to me again!"

I knew there wasn't anything I could do to change the situation or make the future operation any safer for me or the other pilots. A young pilot trying to build his flight experience always faced the dilemma of having enough air time for the next "better" job. Even a small company with a "light twin" might require the pilot in command to have 1,000 hours of flight experience in a twin-engine airplane. Where were you going to get that experience? I was just a young kid trying to build some flying time, and so was very replaceable with plenty of young fellows standing in line to fly one of these for the invaluable experience—even if it meant loading airplanes on a hot ramp, or risking my life on an overloaded plane.

But at that moment I was terrified enough to quit—providing I survived. As we flew over Bimini, just four hundred feet above the ground, I decided I would no longer offer my services free to Island Suppliers. After all, I might still be killed, or at least involved in some bad accident. Either outcome certainly would prevent me from getting a job with a major airline!

But, as it happened, we landed safely in Bimini. There we discovered that the center of gravity of the plane had shifted due to the heavy cargo moving. The C-46 was a magnificent airplane; but over-challenging it by overloading was the leading factor in its crashes. It killed many innocent pilots, and I just figured it was time for me to move on with my aviation career. This was going to be my last trip with the company.

Finally . . . Money to Fly

At this point I had a stroke of good fortune. I ran into someone on the field looking for a pilot to fly an Aztec—a small, light, six-seater, twin-engine airplane—to an out-island as a part-time pilot. The employer was a multimillionaire who owned his own island in the Bahamas. Part of my job was to smuggle in suitcases full of bathing suits for his wife to sell at the boutique at the resort hotel they owned. Sometimes they called me up just to fly in bottles of wine for elaborate dinners they hosted at the hotel. It was a magnificent place on a pretty little out-island where the rich people liked to go to get away from it all. The job even came with pay—a whopping $10.00 per hour!

The first time I spent the night there on a "layover" was New Year's Eve 1981. I was getting paid to fly across some tropical islands, and having the time of my life doing it. I was in young pilot heaven.

Sadly, the Captain who had taught me how to fly the DC-3 and C-46 was killed making an approach to one of the out-islands at night in a light airplane. Landings at night at that particular island were prohibited. He and his girlfriend were both killed when their airplane hit an obstacle on approach. Those islands are really dark at night, and it was not the first nor the last time a very experienced pilot and his passenger lost their lives trying to defeat that darkness.

Moving up to Jets

It was time for me to really try to make myself more competitive with the other applicants to the airlines, and jet time was the answer to that challenge. In Fort Lauderdale the best place to learn how to fly jets was with the great Harvey Hop and his company called Hop-a-Jet, Incorporated. Harvey Hop was a very demanding but very generous man. Many a young pilot who could not stand up to Harvey's yelling would walk away from his constant stream of confrontations and demands. I looked at it differently. I *wanted* a demanding instructor, so as far as I was concerned it was a tremendous opportunity. Harvey, a retired naval commander and professional pilot, had flown at Pearl Harbor during the Japanese attack and was almost shot down by friendly fire. He offered guys like me the chance to come out to the hangar and learn the ropes of the jet charter business.

The training wasn't all flying. A big chunk of time was spent doing Jeppesen revisions, or alterations to the charts pilots use to navigate aircraft in clouds and execute instrument approaches. New revisions came out every two weeks, and that meant that procedures changed with them. These revisions consumed hours of tedious work. The other pilots who were on the payroll paid close attention to whomever had a good attitude (i.e., was willing to sit down for long stretches of time and do the work), and the good attitude was awarded by a flight in the Lear jet whenever Hop-a-Jet had a charter.

We also spent our days swabbing the deck, which meant mopping the entire floor of his large aircraft hangar until it sparkled. We cleaned the restrooms in the hangar, emptied the toilet on the airplane after it came in from a charter—anything it took, no matter how hard, boring, or disgusting. I did these things because I knew the precious jet time and experience I would acquire under Harvey's mentoring would be invaluable in obtaining a job as a pilot. Jet time is something very difficult to attain as a civilian. A very small percentage of airline pilots in those days came out of the civilian ranks, so a young, non-military flier had to do something special to distinguish himself from all the other candidates.

Harvey liked to hold what he called "skull sessions." He would have you come into his office and would drill you on aircraft systems while teaching you about the Learjet. One afternoon, after the conclusion of one of our sessions, he told me, "If you stick around, I will turn you into one hell of a jet pilot." That suited me just fine.

Harvey mentored more than three hundred young pilots like me. The pilots who wanted to make it to a major airline usually did. But they had to stick it out to get there. Some airlines sought out Harvey's pilots because he had such a high reputation as an instructor. He had the most hours of any Learjet pilot flying, and I am proud to say I was flying with him when he logged his 17,000th hour in the Learjet on Christmas Eve 1984.

Thanks to Harvey's help, I was hired by a small commuter airline in late 1985. The company flew Cessna 402s and Bandits all over the Caribbean from West Palm Beach, Fort Lauderdale, and Miami. It was fun work, except we didn't have any radar on our airplanes, which really made it a challenge to fly over water at night. Thunderstorms tend to develop rapidly in the moist, tropical environment. The company was run well, but, as with most commuter airlines, it tended to push the pilots too hard, and pilot fatigue was a significant factor in the operation.

The commuter job was a stepping stone for me. My sights were set on a major airline—any major airline. I knew I was ready and I knew I was qualified, so I put in my application with Eastern Airlines within days of leaving my job at Delta in 1985.

And then came the phone call and interview that changed my life.

Chapter 8

Eastern: "The Pilot's Airline"

Shortly after my resignation from Delta in 1985, its fiercest competitor, Eastern Airlines in Miami, Florida, hired me as a pilot. The terrific thing was that Eastern offered me a *real* airline job with *real* airline people—as a Second Officer (flight engineer) on the Boeing 727. This was a once-in-a-lifetime break for me at a time when I was still trying to get over the rejection from the whole Delta experience. Eastern was a great company with a marvelous route structure and history. I made some new friends right away, and enjoyed many aspects of the airline culture at Eastern.

Unfortunately, the company had some issues with deregulation, issues that many of the other major airlines also would face in the coming years. However, Eastern had to face these issues much sooner than the other airlines. The result was that Eastern Airlines was sold out from under the employees in the middle of the night—which, as you can imagine, did not sit well with anyone working for the airline.

The new owner's name was Frank Lorenzo.

We've Been "Franked"

Watching Eastern Airlines get dismantled by Frank Lorenzo was a very painful experience. Nothing quite like it had ever happened in aviation history. This tremendous company had made so many contributions over its long and glorious past, but that didn't matter much when the corporate raiders came calling. Many fine people went down with this ship. I flew for Eastern Airlines for three years, and over the course of that time I saw people lose their careers—and their lives evaporated. I saw families lose their income streams—and fall apart. Single mothers who had worked as flight attendants or gate agents for twenty or more years lost their jobs and their pensions. Dreams died hard; the employees' morale went straight down the tubes. We were surrounded by sadness.

One of the sad, cold realities was that Eastern Airlines Captains would never be hired by any of the other air carriers. It was common practice in those days for airlines to not hire Captains from other airlines. Many of an airline's Captains would not want to go anyway, because at another company they would be forced to start at the bottom of the seniority list. Our pilots had put heart and soul into Eastern—and Lorenzo saw to it that their efforts ended tragically.

I did not realize it at the time, but all this upheaval had a tremendous impact on the way I dealt with the changes in my life. My drinking, which had been light and completely under control, began to pick up. This was especially true on layovers, during which we pilots licked our wounds and shared our sad stories of what our lives would be like without Eastern. Starting over at the bottom of another carrier's seniority list, with the lower pay scale, was not an option for most of the employees. Many found work in other fields.

Many of the younger pilots saw the handwriting on the wall early, and left the company in droves—especially when it became obvious that Lorenzo's ultimate plan was to liquidate the company. As one of my pilot friends put it to me, "Joe, we've been Franked."

A Man Who Helped Change My Life

I was flying one of my trips with Eastern during this difficult period when I met Captain Al. Al always managed to maintain peace of mind, even in the midst of the corporate crisis. On the second day of our trip together, I asked him what the triangle and circle were on his gold tie tack.

"I'm a recovering alcoholic," he explained, without missing a beat. "We can talk about it more over dinner if you like." That night he told me his powerful story and gave me a good education about what alcoholism is—and what it is not.

After I shared with him that my dad was an alcoholic, he strongly encouraged me to attend twelve-step meetings for adults who had a parent "who is an alcoholic," he continued. "It might help you a great deal." I agreed it was a good idea and told him I would attend.

Of course, I never went. There was always some excuse: I was tired, the meetings were too far away, and I really did not need to go. Everyone who has had a dependency problem knows these and a hundred other excuses. Honestly, the meetings did have some inner appeal to me, but the main stumbling block (at least, so I convinced myself) was the forty-five minute drive to Miami to attend. (Today, I will drive or walk an hour just to sit through a twelve-step meeting, and don't think twice about it.)

Looking back, I know now the real reason for avoiding the meetings was my fear of facing the pain in my life that had begun in my childhood. A father who was not sober much of the time was not a father who was able to meet the needs of his children. I know today that the loneliness and abandonment I felt were because of my dad's alcoholism and absence from our home, which prevented him from being there for me. He was gone as a result of his traveling; but he was also gone because of his drinking, so even when he was there, he was somewhere else. And not only was he *somewhere* else, but he was *someone* else. I felt alone, abandoned, and unguided. That's discouraging, to say the least. The simple truth is that children who do not have parental security find it harder to make sense out of the world. The pain, neediness, and disappointment I felt were the direct results of the lack of a consistent and positive role model in my dad. There was no buffer between me and the rest of the world, so I had to become my own protector. My family situation was unsafe and out of control, and I sensed this even as a young child. "I have to survive on my own" whispered that little voice inside my head. But this is a scary, angry, and insecure place for anyone, especially a child, to be. Fear and self-protection rose to the forefront of my life, and it resulted in my decision to take up my own self-sabotaging behaviors. My dad's abandonment of his family obligations contributed to my development of independent survival skills, which are common among children who grow up with a parent addicted to drugs or alcohol. The pain of not having a sober dad was too much to bear. The pain kept me locked in denial. My way out turned out to be . . . alcohol. But, as far as I was concerned, it was dad who had the problem with alcohol, not me.

Captain Al also told me to read *It Will Never Happen to Me,* a book by Claudia Black. He told me it would help explain a lot, and he was right. After reading it, I realized two things: that my father was definitely an alcoholic, and that he was going to die if he did not get help.

Several weeks later, Al and I decided to do a telephone intervention on my dad. It was an extremely emotional experience for my father and me, and he promised me he would never drink again. He was crying heavily when he said this to me. Somehow—God only knows how—my father quit drinking that day. By this time he was deep in the throes of later-stage alcoholism, but he was able to quit drinking because he was ready to surrender. That was more than twenty years ago. Today, my father has become the man God intended for him to be. He is sober and available to others. My father has not had a drink since he promised me he would never touch alcohol again.

Reading Black's book also gave me the courage to confront my little sister about her drinking. One day I took her to a beautiful park in Fort Lauderdale and tried to convince her that she might be an alcoholic. The book had a test on the last page with about twenty questions. If a person answered five or more out of twenty questions in the affirmative, he or she probably had a drinking problem. My sister answered five of the questions "yes," so I knew she had a problem. A few months later, my sister did a very courageous thing: she entered a treatment center for alcoholism, and ever since has been a shining example of what recovery looks like.

Of course, I wasn't being honest with myself; I had answered only two of the questions "yes." What I did not realize was that by directing the attention toward others, I was subconsciously shifting attention away from myself. My sister's success was even more amazing when you consider what was about to happen to me.

Return of the Blackouts

There was a ten-year period in my life during which I did not drink to excess or have any blackouts. This was from about the age of 22 until around my second year as a pilot for Eastern Airlines (1987). It wasn't until I had quit drinking for several years and then reflected back on some of my layovers as an Eastern pilot that I came to the realization that there had been several times when I drank to "blackout" on a layover the night before a trip.

I recall one particular episode in Aruba, an island in the Caribbean. The entire crew except the Captain drank into the early morning hours. The drinks were strong—that I recall with crystal clarity. I don't recall going back to my room or where I was in between. The last thing I remember was living it up in a casino with the other pilot and the flight attendants.

The next morning the only person who showed up to fly the airplane was the Captain. He hadn't gone out with us the night before, so he had no idea that his entire crew was in bad shape. In fact, we were all still in bed, fast asleep. The Captain hired a cab driver to send two cabs to the hotel and to go to our individual rooms, get us up out of bed, and drive us to the airport so we could work the outbound flight to Miami—and we did. The people who bought the tickets and depended upon us for their lives had no idea.

We repeated this pattern many other times in large cities such as New York and Boston. It was not uncommon for me to forget where I had spent the night, or how I got from the restaurant or bar back to the hotel.

Dad Goes for a Ride

In 1988 another hair-raising incident occurred in West Palm Beach, Florida. I was flying the Airbus with a very senior Captain and First Officer. The FO, named John, was an ex-Marine, and he really put pressure on the other young pilots to drink with him on layovers. In fact, if you didn't go out drinking with him you might end up getting the "silent treatment" from him while flying along in the cockpit, which was not a pleasant situation to deal with. Communication is, after all, essential in a cockpit. If the silent treatment was not on John's agenda, then taunting usually was. "Are you a pussy?" he demanded. "Are you afraid to drink with me?" On that particular 1988 night in Palm Beach, we all had so much to drink that I have no idea how I got from the bar back to the hotel.

However, before I blacked out the Captain had offered to take my dad along with us in the cockpit on the jump seat the next day on the flight to New York City. I called my dad and told him drive up to Palm Beach. Dad had a wonderful time up there, especially when we were flying over Manhattan on that clear morning. The view was spectacular, and his mind was racing with all his memories of being a young sailor during WWII and the great times he enjoyed visiting New York City.

Unbeknownst to Dad, all of us were hung over, and some of us were still under the influence of alcohol. As far as I was concerned, Dad had no way of knowing how much we had had to drink the night before. But I always wondered whether he sensed that we were not all that we should have been. He never said anything; but I still wonder.

That was my last blackout on a night before a trip early the next morning. But it was not my last alcohol-induced blackout. That one was coming—and it would transpire in the presence of some of my best friends in the whole world.

L.A. Blackout

Airline employees tend to have friends scattered about the country. One of my best friends is Chris, who lives in Mission Viejo, California. I have known Chris and his wife Kim individually for more than two decades. When he learned I was going to have a layover in Los Angeles, Chris invited me to come down to a Christmas party he was throwing at his house for several people from his company. I hitched a ride south from LAX with one of the first-class passengers.

In the car everything was great for a few minutes, until the passenger's wife pulled out a joint and began smoking as we rolled down the expressway. Now *that* scared the crap out of me! I was getting ready to have a pilot interview with Northwest Airlines in a few weeks, and I knew they were going to give me a drug test. My concern was that some of that smoke inside the car would get into my lungs.

"Excuse me," I said, turning to the husband. "I realize that you folks are being kind enough to give me a ride to my friend's house, but I can't have any of that smoke in my system, because it can cause me to lose my job and end my career."

The husband understood immediately. "Honey, please put out the joint." I breathed a sigh of relief; that had been easier than I expected. But I was wrong: the wife shot her husband a sharp glance, glared at me, and spat, "Hell no!"

They argued about it for about a couple of minutes, until I finally interjected, "Hey, don't worry about it, could you please just pull over at the next exit? I can take a cab to my friend's house from here."

The husband was embarrassed and very apologetic as I stepped out of the smoke-filled car to hail a cab. I felt sorry for him.

I arrived late at Chris' party, so I still had my airline uniform on, and his guests could see that I was a pilot with Eastern Airlines. I went upstairs to change my clothes and came down to join the party. I remember drinking lots of rum that night, and the blackout I experienced was so complete that I remembered nothing after that at all.

The Morning After

The next morning I staggered awake with a mile-sized hangover. Where was I? When I got my bearings, I tried to recall the night before, to no avail. My friends were already downstairs having breakfast and coffee by the time I stumbled down to wish them good morning.

The look on their faces is hard to describe. It was a blend of anger, sadness, confusion, and violation—the look many alcoholics are used to getting when they continually hurt the people they love.

"I don't remember anything about last night, but I must have done something terrible, based on the way you are looking at me."

"Joe," began Chris, fumbling for the right words. "We watched you do some weird things last night, I mean, totally out-of-character things I have never seen you do before." He paused before adding, "Things I can't even believe."

I could feel the blood rising into my face. It felt as if a fist had been slammed into my gut. "I am so, so sorry, really. What did I do?"

Both Chris and his wife shook their heads and refused to tell me what had happened. They were both in shock.

"For some reason I don't understand, I can't drink like other people." I hesitated to find the right words. "I am drinking more and more, and having blackouts, and I don't remember anything about the night before. It's getting very scary," I continued, "and I know I need to quit drinking before some innocent person gets hurt or before I end up getting into a lot of trouble."

And then I began to cry.

"I am so sorry for what happened at your party. Please accept my apology." I don't think I could have felt more embarrassed, humiliated and ashamed of myself. Why couldn't I just drink normally, like other people? I vowed to myself I would never drink again.

The fellowship of twelve-step programs was available to me, but I didn't put to good use any of their invaluable wisdom. Some combination of embarrassment, shame, and pride kept me from going to any meetings at all. Instead, I just stopped drinking cold turkey, and relied on my own willpower to stay away from alcohol.

But, as I would later learn, willpower alone would not save me.

Chapter 9

Northwest Airlines:
I'm Flying a Bowling Shoe!

F or several months there was no alcohol in my house: no beer, no wine, no hard liquor—nothing. I began to feel so confident that I interviewed with Northwest Airlines in early 1989. The interview went great, and the company offered me a job as a pilot and flight engineer. I was on cloud nine! My dream, after so many long hard years of work, was about to come true.

When I left for training, my sober father gave me a beautiful "praying hands" medallion with the serenity prayer written on the back to carry with me in my flight bag on all my flights. "Joe, whatever you do," he cautioned, "don't go out drinking with any of the flight crews in your first year at Northwest Airlines. Keep your nose clean and stay out of trouble."

His words rang in my ears long after they were spoken. Did my dad sense something had been wrong that morning he rode with three Eastern Airlines pilots to New York? I don't know, but one thing is certain: his words of caution were the best advice he ever gave me. Unfortunately, I didn't have a program of twelve steps or any special wisdom attached to that medallion, so the power of the program of recovery rested solely in my hands. I was trying to quit drinking on my own without any support, but with all the determination I could muster.

Having mentioned my dad's gift to me of the serenity prayer medallion, this is a good time to clarify my belief system. I have always believed in God, and come from a family of believers. While regular church or Sunday

School attendance was not part of my upbringing, my parents were people of faith who taught me lessons about God. I am grateful for these early experiences, because people who come from alcoholic childhoods often do not trust adults and other people in general, so they are not going to trust God, either. They are angry at their earthly father, so they are angry at their heavenly father, too, and usually feel a great distance from God; they won't let people in, so it is hard to let God in. As a young adult in my early twenties I attended church, where I met a man who opened me to God's possibilities, and I drew closer to God. So several years before the incident in Fargo, I was already attending a church: I was a man of faith, a seeker of God.

The Girl Next Door

After I had been hired by NWA and was in training, I lived in an older section of Minneapolis. A good friend of mine used this place as a crash pad, and another lived with me full time and ran a car repair shop out of the garage. It was during this busy and important crossroads in my life that I met the girl next door. I could tell right away that Mary had some serious issues with alcohol. Her brothers and her father drank heavily every day and were alcoholics. "Nobody in Minneapolis has anything to do in the winter," she explained, "so they drink and then drink some more." Of course, there actually is a lot to do in Minneapolis during the winter months, but when you are in denial it makes a great excuse to get hammered daily.

Mary was drinking, too. In fact, she was blacking out every Friday and Saturday night. When I found out, I did my best to explain to her that I had quit drinking because I was having blackouts and they scared the heck out of me. My prayer was that my message would influence Mary in positive way.

Looking back, it is obvious that even though I could recognize alcoholism in other people, I didn't have much insight to share because I didn't have a consistent, foundational recovery program of my own. Sure, I could communicate my own deep feeling of helplessness that I had been experiencing for most of my life, but I could do little else. Alcohol had stolen my inner humanity from me, and now it was doing the same to Mary. She was a sweet girl, but she was sick and needed help.

Just like me. The only difference was that I was in a desperate search inside myself to find a way to stop drinking permanently, to recover my dignity, to recover my lost soul. I had gone about three months without a drink, and I was feeling good about myself again. And that was a great feeling.

The Illusion of Stability

I wanted to fly for Northwest for one simple reason: it appeared to have the strongest balance sheet of any airline flying. It was difficult emotionally to leave all of my friends at Eastern, but Northwest offered a stable career opportunity as a pilot, even though I would have to start all over again on the seniority list. In all honesty, it really bugged me that I was voluntarily giving up three years of seniority at Eastern, but there wasn't anything I could do about it if I wanted to fly with Northwest. The other undesirable aspect of leaving one airline to go with another is the low pay and probationary status every pilot experiences for one year as a new hire.

I left Eastern Airlines with the hope that my new wife Deborah and I would have some stability in our lives as airline employees. That's right. I got married. I haven't told you that part yet. Backing up: we met in the fall of 1987, on a layover in Canada. Eastern had several different crews staying at the same hotel in Toronto. Deborah was down in the lounge with some crewmembers when I walked in with my flight crew to watch the World Series and relax. My future wife was sitting at a table with another woman talking and laughing when I first set eyes upon her. I walked over and we began chatting, and after a short time discovered she was with Eastern and based in Miami. She was pleasant, friendly, and pretty. I would be lying if I said I wasn't looking forward to seeing her again.

Deborah had never seen anything like the behavior my dad exhibited when he drank. Her parents didn't drink, ever. Years later, she admitted that sometimes when I drank my behavior scared her. I did things on our honeymoon that frightened her, she later revealed, but I don't remember them because I was in a "blackout." (This was before my L.A. blackout, and the ensuing period of self-imposed cold turkey.) Like most people in this situation, Deborah didn't recognize alcoholism for what it was.

Since the outlook at Eastern was bleak, we both decided to leave the company. When I joined Northwest in March of 1989, it was financially sound. It had all of its airplanes and untold millions in other assets, and its debt-to-equity ratio was impressive.

However, while I was in "new hire" training to become a pilot and flight engineer for Northwest, a local news channel announced that an investment group was buying the company. I was unsure what this would mean, and I quickly found out no one else was sure, either. Most of the employees I spoke with had mixed feeling about acquisition. Few were happy about the way Northwest had treated its employees in the past, and everyone hoped the new ownership would at least give them more respect. But the employees were also concerned that the new owners would change the structure of the company and begin selling off the assets that for so many years had helped the company retain a strong balance sheet. All I could do was hang on for the ride—again.

At the same time, a merger-turned-ugly between Northwest Airlines and Republic Airlines was underway, and my classmates and I were thrust right into the middle of it. Northwest Airlines was still operating the former Republic Airlines as a separate entity. (Even though its airplanes were painted with Northwest's colors, the pilots joked that the new paint job Northwest had put on the airplanes made them look like a bowling shoe, with grey on the bottom and red on top.) The seniority lists and the flying schedules within the companies were still separate. Only former Northwest pilots (called "Redbook" pilots) were flying the old Northwest routes, and only former Republic pilots (called "Greenbook" pilots) were flying the old Republic Airlines routes. The upshot of this was that former Republic pilots were flying only with their former colleagues from Republic. The "Red" and "Green" pilots never mixed, and so never flew together.

The strategy to separate the pilots continued until sometime around February of 1989. Up until March of 1989, all of my Captains were former Republic employees. I had never flown with a Captain who was a former Northwest, "old employee" from prior to the merger. The former Republic pilots treated me with great respect, and all of my probationary reports were excellent. I was sure to get off probation by the end of March. My wife and I were looking forward to the substantial increase in pay.

Follow These Signs to Hell

Northwest Airlines had an outdated, archaic way for the pilots to select their schedules for the next month of flying. Every pilot was assigned a five-minute window during a given day during which the pilot was supposed to get in touch with a crew scheduler over the telephone and submit a "bid" for a "trip," a schedule of flying for the next month. Based on relative seniority to other pilots flying your respective airplane, you were able to pick from the trips still available. If you were lucky, there were many trips to select from and you might be fortunate enough to get a special day off for some time with your family.

The senior pilots always got their first choices. The junior pilots with the least seniority ended up with what was left at the bottom of the barrel. Usually those trips were less desirable to fly, as was the case when I bid for the month of March 1990. I wanted some particular days off that month to go steelhead fishing with my brother on the Pierre Marquette River in Michigan.

I happened to be on a ski trip in Colorado when my five-minute window arrived in mid-afternoon. Earlier in the day I had scoped out a payphone, and I planned my skiing so I would end up there at the appropriate time to call the crew scheduler. I came off the slopes just in time to make the call from the top of the mountain.

To my surprise, the crew scheduler informed me that I would have to fly a five-day trip in order to get the days off I wanted. Worse still, I had no idea which other pilots I was being paired with for this five-day flight schedule.

A Stroke of Bad Luck—or Fate?

Before my five-day trip began I commuted home to Nashville on a Northwest flight. Seated next to me was "Scott," another Northwest pilot. Scott had flown with Republic Airlines, but now flew for Northwest because of the pending merger. We chatted about all the usual things pilots do, and then the conversation turned toward other pilots and the working environment. "Watch out for an abusive Captain who claims to be part Indian and wears a turquoise and silver watchband," he cautioned. Apparently, this Captain was a "Redbook," an old Northwest Airlines officer known for giving other pilots he flew with a hard time. After listening to Scott's horror stories about this guy, it was obvious he was not someone I wanted to be cooped up with in a cockpit for several days.

I made a mental note of Scott's warning, but really did not think too much about it after that because I would be finished with my one-year, new-hire probationary period in a few weeks. The Greenbook pilots had only flown a single month with this man, and so the stories about this pilot's behavior were only just beginning to circulate among the former Republic Airlines pilots now flying for NWA. The merged groups had been flying together for such a short time that the pilots from one group did not know many pilots from the other group.

So, although I had been cautioned to be on the lookout for a Captain with a silver and turquoise watchband, the odds were that I would never even see this guy, let alone fly with him.

Chapter 10

The Five-Day Trip From Hell

When I showed up for my next trip I was on top of the world. I had a big smile on my face and was looking forward to flying. After years of hard work, everything was going my way.

But when I introduced myself to the flight's Captain, a shock went through my body: he was wearing a turquoise watchband. It took less than a minute to confirm that he was the same one Scott had warned me about. What were the odds that, of all the Captains I could have flown with, I got the guy with the silver and turquoise watchband! It was simply a matter of the luck of the draw that the First Officer, a nice fellow named Bob, and I were scheduled to fly with this particular Northwest Airlines Captain.

One of the most important responsibilities for an airline Captain is to set up a good rapport with his fellow crewmembers. Most Captains are adept at this skill. A few, however, are tyrants who destroy trust and rapport with their fellow crewmembers. Fortunately their numbers are relatively few, because conflict in the cockpit can trigger unsafe flying procedures. Officers who are tyrants and bullies make team cohesion impossible, which is never a good thing. I decided that this guy could not be as bad as the stories portrayed him to be, and that I would make the best of it no matter how obnoxious he really was to his flight crew.

Within a few minutes after meeting him I knew we were in trouble. The tension was already heavy, and this was not a working environment I was accustomed to flying in. Frankly, I thought the Captain was the biggest jerk I had ever flown with in my life. I couldn't figure out what was making him so miserable. He enjoyed spending most of his time criticizing and making demeaning comments about his fellow crewmembers. He acted as if he knew all of the answers, and he spat out orders like some kind of demented drill sergeant. I had flown with more than a hundred different Captains during my major airline career, and I had never encountered anyone as domineering and arrogant as this man. And I had just met him! A sinking feeling settled into the pit of my stomach. This was going to be a long, long five days.

The Captain was not only upsetting me. His actions and his mouth were also upsetting the First Officer. The way he commanded an aircraft was downright abusive. Almost everything Bob or I did was wrong in his eyes. He criticized us nonstop and without mercy. I had never been so uncomfortable with another pilot in my entire flying career. I could tell Bob felt the same way just by looking into his eyes.

This was particularly disheartening to me, because as a new Northwest hire and a probationary pilot still in my first year, I was extremely vulnerable. The Captain of the ship could get a new pilot fired for just about anything. It had happened to others in the past, and I was afraid that it would happen to me if I opened my mouth to complain. Every evaluation I had ever received from every Captain I had previously flown with at Northwest had been excellent.

I decided to work overtime to get this Captain to accept me. He said he was an American Indian, so I showed him an interesting book I was reading about Indians penned by one of the most knowledgeable and respected writers and researchers of our time.

The Captain rolled his eyes. "That book is a joke. It is so grossly inaccurate I can't believe you are reading it."

As I was putting it away, he took a shot at my luggage, boasting that he got his "at a better price." A few minutes later, when he spotted me studying the aircraft manual he jumped all over me for doing so.

"I'm getting ready for a probationary test in a week," I replied, trying to smile and make peace with this man. "I really want to do well, so—"

He cut me off in mid-sentence. "On my last trip I had a female second officer read the manual the entire trip, every chance she got!"

"What in the world could be wrong with that?" I wondered. Surely the airline would want its new pilots to be ready for their exams! Somehow I managed to keep my mouth shut.

Timing is Everything

The newly-hired pilots in my class had their probationary periods with the company extended by two weeks. Without this new contract provision, I already would have passed my probationary check rides and been off probation.

If I *had* been done with my probationary period, I could have told this Captain that I was going to get off the trip. It would have been a no-harm, no-foul situation, and the company would have found another second officer to pick up the rest of the legs. I could have made sure to never fly with this particular Captain again. Sure, there might have been some explaining to do in the Chief Pilot's office, but, based upon what I had learned, I would have been justified in taking such action because of this Captain's reputation for giving second officers and other pilots an unnecessarily hard time.

But I *wasn't* off probation, and I didn't think my position as a probationary, new hire pilot afforded me the luxury of choice. As far as I was concerned, I was trapped. And I didn't have the emotional tools to do anything about it.

What is He Doing?

During the trip, the Captain left the cockpit in flight on what seemed like every leg. What was he doing? Knowing what I do now, I have a hunch he was drinking in the lavatory, but I can't be sure. At the time, Bob and I just assumed he had a weak bladder.

His absence from the cockpit, however, relieved the tension up front and allowed us an opportunity to discuss the Captain and his nasty attitude toward us. We both agreed he was an ass. We also agreed that eventually we would let the Captain "screw something up" (as long as it did not jeopardize passenger safety) so he would be embarrassed and humiliated by a mistake we were sure he would make. When he did, we thought he might be a bit more humble and stop his unwarranted criticism of us. We could not have been more wrong.

The Wrong Course!

During one of the first legs of the trip, when Bob was flying the airplane, the Captain, in a very loud and critical voice, cried out, "You are flying the wrong course!"

Bob checked the instruments and calmly replied, "The course looks good to me Captain. What do you mean?"

"You are flying the wrong course, damn it! Turn to a 180 degree heading and get back on the airway, now!"

Fortunately for us, Bob did not react. Instead, he remained calm and held the course he knew to be the correct one. "What course does your map show for this airway?" Bob asked the Captain,

"What course does your map show?" the Captain yelled back.

"My map shows a course of 182 degrees."

The Captain's face was turning red. "My map shows the course is 180 degrees," he barked in reply. "Turn back on course, now!"

Bob, somehow maintaining complete professional calm, replied, "My chart shows the course as being 182 degrees."

"Your map must be out of date, and you are wrong!" insisted the Captain.

"What is the date on your map?" asked Bob.

By this time the Captain looked as if he was about to explode. But he hesitated for a moment, then checked the date. I thought his eyes were going to bug out of his head: the Captain's map was out of date. Bob had the most current edition and was using it to navigate our flight. The Captain had failed in his responsibility as a crewmember to keep his maps up to date. He had not done his revisions, which were issued by the company every two weeks. Airways and navigational aids change on a regular basis, and professional pilots are expected to keep their own houses in order.

Bob did not say another word, and the Captain never apologized for yelling at him in the cockpit—even after the Captain realized he was wrong.

Hot Debate in Tucson

Before the leg from the Tucson airport, while performing my preflight inspection of the airplane, I noticed that the hydraulic reservoir in the tail section of the aircraft was short on hydraulic fluid. It had been a standard procedure at Eastern Airlines to check the accumulator in the tail section of a

Boeing 727 because the gauge in the cockpit on the Flight Engineer panel was just a repeater gauge, and could give a false indication. The true hydraulic quantity could always be read off the gauge on the actual reservoir. My duty was to notify the Captain of any discrepancies with the airplane. Low hydraulic fluid could be a major safety issue: a Boeing 727 has a very complicated hydraulic system, and the landing gear, flaps, slats, and brakes all depend on the system working properly. A failure of any of these components might result in a disaster.

The quantity in the main hydraulic reservoir was not sufficient for the flight to be dispatched, or to fly safely under the company policies of either Northwest or Eastern Airlines. Any other Captain would have thanked me for checking the fluid level in the tail section, which involved pulling back a protective curtain in the aft air stairs and looking at the gauge. During one of my pre-flights at Eastern Airlines, I had noticed this same problem with the hydraulic quantity, and the Captain, who was also a supervisory pilot in the training department, wrote a letter to the Chief Pilot. "Eastern needs to hire more pilots who are as vigilant as Flight Engineer Balzer," was how part of his letter read. I was also on probation at Eastern at the time, and a "feel good" letter and a nice comment from a Captain to a new-hire probationary pilot really goes a long way. Kind words put a spring in your step and inspire anyone to keep doing a good job. They make you feel like part of a winning team.

"You don't know what you're talking about." With these six words the Captain cut my legs out from under me. "It isn't a Northwest procedure to check the gauge on the reservoir," he continued in a raised, irritated voice, "and the cockpit gauge on the Flight Engineer panel reads fine—we have enough hydraulic fluid to take off and fly all the way to Detroit or Minneapolis or wherever we are going!"

"Sir, I think we might—"

"Why in the hell are you looking behind the curtain in the aft stairwell, anyway?" he continued.

"Because it was a standard procedure at Eastern, and the gauge on my FE panel is showing the needle right on the absolute minimum amount for dispatch, and my gauge was reading accurately." He just glared at me. "Besides," I continued, "it would only take a mechanic a few minutes to replenish our hydraulic fluid, and we will be one hundred percent safe for flight on that score."

As Flight Engineer, I was responsible for pre-flighting the airplane, and I was just trying to do a thorough job. What I didn't fully realize at the time was that I was also trying to please the Captain and to impress him with my attention to detail. I was just looking for some approval from a man who had been abusive for the last few days. But nothing I ever did was right, and this event was no different.

"You are not notifying maintenance," he shot back, "and you have no business checking the reservoir in the tail."

His words cut through me like a knife. This guy is a Captain for Northwest? Wasn't safety our primary concern? He was totally discounting my suggestions as a professional flight engineer.

I was sick to my stomach, and contemplated walking off the airplane, but I was on probation. I reluctantly stayed on the trip. For the first time in my life I climbed into the cockpit of an aircraft that I did not feel was completely safe. There wasn't any upside for a probationary pilot to complain about a Captain being abusive, whether he was being abusive to himself or others.

An Indiscretion

When there are no available seats in the cabin, pilots often get to and from work riding on a cockpit jump seat. I had a friend and classmate, a former Air Force fighter pilot, who was riding the jump seat the day we left Tucson. He immediately sensed something was wrong. It never takes long for another pilot to notice things like that. He also knew I was upset with the Captain about the hydraulic quantity indicators and fluid levels.

On climb out from Tucson, I was so upset with the Captain that I told my classmate he was acting like a real ass. At one point when the Captain made a derogatory and demeaning comment about me, I gave him the "finger" behind his head. My friend thought that was funny, and for just a moment I felt better. But my childish action distracted me from what I was doing, and I allowed my fuel to get out of balance. I noticed my error and took immediate corrective action. This is just a small example of how a bad cockpit environment can get out of hand. Frankly, I had a hard time concentrating around this man.

Unfortunately for me, the Captain noticed my error because he was flying sitting nearly sideways in an effort to try to find anything I might be doing wrong. He overreacted and tried to make a big deal out of it. My classmate could tell things were bad; he could feel the emotional friction in the cockpit. My mistake was not a big deal, and I fixed it quickly, but it was embarrassing, and it proved to me that, at that moment, my head was not focused on doing my job. If I allowed myself to become engaged in emotional crap with this Captain, then I would not be completely present as the Flight Engineer of this jet. I had let my professional guard down. I was enmeshed in this dysfunctional three-man dynamic, while piloting an aircraft with passengers through the sky.

I am not proud of my actions on that day. It would have been best for me to refuse to leave Tucson with insufficient hydraulic fluid, but I did not have the emotional tools to deal with the problem at that point in my life. Today I would handle a situation like this one completely differently. I would have refused to fly, contacted maintenance, and let the chips fall where they may. Passenger safety is the rule—first, last, and always. I had no idea that my lack of knowledge and wisdom during this five-day trip from hell was about to cost me in ways I could not even imagine.

[Note: Several years after our incident, a person from Northwest showed me a training tape for pilots. The purpose of the tape was to train airline Captains on building rapport with other crewmembers. Three pilots were in a Boeing 727 simulator. The flight session was being videotaped for training purposes. The Second Officer (Flight Engineer) and the First Officer were being "set up" by a check Captain who would be intentionally abusive and abrasive. To my amazement, the agitated second officer gave the Captain the "finger" behind his head, just as I had to our Captain, with my classmate sitting on the jump seat. And the second officer had only been with this Captain for twenty minutes.]

The Leader and his Shenanigans

As the five-day trip dragged on, the Captain bragged to me about being thrown out of every Officers' Club he had ever visited for being a jerk while under the influence of alcohol. As far as I could tell, he was proud of his misbehavior and bad reputation. He also told me he had his own La-Z-Boy lounge chair delivered to the Chief Pilot's office because he spent so much time there defending himself! He was *proud* of it. He also boasted about all the fistfights he had been in. During one of the Captain's many trips to the aircraft lavatory, Bob turned to me and observed, "It looks like we're flying with the heavyweight champion of the world!" We both laughed, but neither of us thought the situation was funny.

All this man did was talk about himself. He never took an interest in anything related to us. I so desperately wanted to get away from this man.

Ho-Ho-Ho and a Bottle of Rum

The Captain began the trip with what looked to me, at least, like a half-gallon bottle of rum in a bag. He stored this in the cockpit, and he would take it with him when we left the plane after each flight. It was gone by the third day of the trip.

"I have never seen anybody drink like that in my entire life," Bob confided to me on the morning after the Grand Rapids layover. Those words should have been a giant red flag for me, but I hadn't had my own personal "alcohol education" yet. I missed this opportunity to identify a very serious problem. I didn't have the educational tools or the required training to fully understand what was happening, or what all of this meant. I know that seems difficult for non-drinkers to understand, but it's the simple truth.

I just didn't put two and two together.

Broken Beyond Repair

Bob and I went out to lunch together to discuss the problems that we were having with the Captain. We were both very frustrated, and both very angry. We didn't like the way the Captain was treating either of us. "Being on probation with a tyrant like this guy is about as unfair as it gets," grumbled Bob.

During this conversation we discovered that both of us had called the crew schedulers to ask that we never fly with this Captain again. Bob was determined to let the Captain screw something else up to teach him a lesson in humility, as long as it did not endanger the aircraft. I was not sure what that would be—but I was about to find out. I really trusted Bob and his judgment. He was a good man and a good pilot.

By this time I feared for my job, especially after having screwed up the fuel. When I told Bob I was concerned the Captain might write me an unfavorable probationary report, he acknowledged the possibility, so he suggested that we might have to meet with the Captain later in the trip to try to work some things out.

The Flight That "Missed" the Airport

We were flying into Grand Rapids, and it was the Captain's leg. He was approaching the airport way too high to be landing on the correct runway. Both Bob and I realized his error. The Captain believed we were supposed to land on the opposite side of the airport, going in the opposite direction. Bob looked at me and we both thought the same thing at the same time: *This guy has done nothing but criticize us for the last several days; let's just let him screw up.* We had saved him from himself before, but he didn't see that. All he did was point out to us what he thought *we* were doing wrong all of the time. Now it was his turn.

Bob and I nodded in agreement. Normally, airline pilots back each other up and work as a team. After what we had been through, however, Bob and I were not about to save his butt unless his actions were an obvious compromise to the safety of our passengers. We both knew there wasn't a threat of interference with any other air traffic, so the passengers would not be in any danger. That, of course, was the primary concern.

We let the Captain over-fly the airport, several thousand feet above the altitude at which he should have been to land on the correct runway. He was deep into it now, well beyond the point of no return. His glaring screw-up was obvious to everyone in the system now.

"NWA XXX, where are you going?"

Bob hesitated to key the mike, wanting instead to wait for a response from the Captain.

Suddenly, the senior officer realized something was wrong. "Ah . . ." Only Bob and I heard his mental confusion.

"Ah . . . ," the Captain grunted again. "Didn't he tell us we we're landing in the other direction?"

Bob still hesitated to say anything on the radio.

"Damn it!" snapped the Captain. "Did he tell us we were landing in the other direction, or didn't he?" His voice was angry, but it was also filled with panic.

Bob could barely contain the smile trying to break across his face. Finally, as sweet as could be, he replied, "What would you like me to tell him, Captain?"

"Hell . . .a . . . oh . . .ah . . . " His face was turning red, and his eyes seethed with anger and embarrassment. His veneer of perfection had shattered in just a handful of seconds. He now knew he'd made a major screw-up, and it was finally dawning on him that we had been feeding him the rope.

Bob smoothly took charge. "Grand Rapids tower, we have over-flown the runway," he calmly replied to the controller. "We will need radar vectors to come around and make another approach for the correct runway."

The controller acknowledged the error and turned us away from the airport so we would not be a factor to any other traffic in the area. He knew airline pilots rarely make errors of this magnitude. Bob and I felt a certain vindication. During the short conversation, the Captain turned several shades of red. He had to know we had led him down the primrose path.

"This wasn't . . . ah . . . not my . . . They didn't give us the right . . ."

He was trying to justify his actions, but could not find the right words to do so.

Throughout this ordeal I did not say a single word. And about this time, as the aircraft was circling around to land, it occurred to me that a man with his personality would not learn a lesson; instead, he would seek revenge.

Chapter 11

Nightmare in Fargo

We arrived in Fargo the next morning and were not scheduled to leave there until early the following morning, at 6:30 a.m. We grabbed an early lunch and I went back to my room to read a book my brother had given me at the end of our fishing trip, about Dick Rutan and Jeana Yeager flying around the world nonstop in the aircraft known as *Voyager*. Jim had written some inspirational words on the inside cover of the book:

> "Joe, Thank you for all of your love and patience over the years, my friend. I truly admire the dedication you have shown in pursuing your personal and career goals in life; you set a good example for all. Love, Jim."

I was reflecting on what my big brother had written to me when the room phone rang. It was Bob. "How about we grab some dinner?" he asked.

"Sure," I replied, "sounds like a great idea."

"Look, this might sound crazy," Bob continued, "but I think we should invite the Captain to join us."

I could not believe my ears. "Why would we do that?"

"Look, Joe, if we invite the Captain out for dinner and spend a little time with him away from the cockpit, maybe we can talk about some of the tensions we've been experiencing. Maybe we can get something resolved."

"I don't know, Bob. I hate that guy, and the last thing I want to do is spend more time with him."

"I know," Bob acknowledged. "But after his screw-up, maybe we can work things out to at least make them bearable, and maybe we can make sure you don't get a bad report while you're still on probation."

I had to admit his plan made some sense. "Ok," I sighed, "let's give it a shot."

I had only one week to go on probation. Bob was doing this as a gesture of kindness, as an ambassador of good will. Looking back, that made the entire situation even more tragic for him. Bob's intentions were good; he was only trying to help out a fellow pilot who might be in a jam with an abusive Captain. Bob himself, as an established pilot, was untouchable.

But we did not know with whom we were dealing, and I did not have a good grip on all of the fear I was feeling inside, nor on the interpersonal dynamics that were unfolding right before my eyes. We started out with good intentions, but we were about to become a part of something that would change our lives forever.

We arrived at the restaurant at 3:30 in the afternoon. I remember the place was dark and did not have any outside windows. I had forgotten to put on my watch, so I could not easily keep track of time. This would pose a real problem for me later. But I wasn't planning to drink heavily anyway, and went in thinking we would be there an hour or two at the most.

However, we had barely taken our seats at the table when the Captain blurted out to the server, "We are going to run a tab a mile long!"

At the time, I didn't think he was serious. But those ten words still ring in my ears today. No, I was no longer following my earlier, strict-avoidance regime; I had slid back into some imbibing. But I did not really enjoy drinking, and would have preferred to not drink now. It just goes to show the strong grip of the disease of alcoholism, and the insanity of the accompanying denial, that I thought good intentions in this case would be enough to keep things under control.

Normally a Captain will offer to buy the drinks, but this time the Captain did all of the ordering, and Bob did all of the paying. Pilots traditionally buy beer and dinner for a pilot who is on probationary status, as a gesture of kindness. Beer was brought to the table faster than we could drink it. As soon as a pitcher was two-thirds empty the waitress arrived with a fresh one.

As it turned out, our attempt at good will was a complete waste of time. Being in the restaurant bar didn't change any of the interpersonal dynamics of our threesome. The Captain still dominated the conversation, he had little or no interest in our lives or backgrounds, and he spent all of the time talking about himself. He was loud, obnoxious, and rude—just like he was in the cockpit. It was as if he wanted other people in the bar area to hear him, and they did.

One patron, a man named Charlie, met me in the restroom. "The guy you're sitting with, can I ask you a few questions about his time in Vietnam?"

As I stood there washing my hands at the sink, I thought to myself, invite him over to the table and let him find out for himself. So I said, "Charlie, I don't know much about it, but you're welcome to come over to our table and ask him, if you like."

Charlie proceeded to do just that. He followed me back to the table, introduced himself, and sat down next to the Captain. Bob and I had already had enough of the Captain's conversation.

"You guys talk for a while," I mumbled as we took the opportunity to slip to a nearby table. We decided to keep to ourselves.

Charlie and the Captain spoke for only a few minutes before the Captain yelled, "Get the f**k out of here!" He yelled it over and over again: "Just get the f**k out of here!"

Other patrons turned to stare at the Captain, who was beet red and looking as if he was ready to pick up a chair and crown this poor guy.

Charlie lifted his hands up, palms out, as if to say "Easy, man;" the look on his face was one of complete bewilderment and embarrassment. He left the table for a seat at the bar. Once there, he ordered a pitcher of beer for us and a drink for the Captain, and had them sent over to the table with his apologies for whatever it was he had done. I could tell he felt really bad about what had just transpired.

Charlie walked back to the table, offered to shake the Captain's hand, and said he was sorry. The Captain angrily screamed, "Get the f**k out of here Charlie, hit the road! I don't want to shake your f**king hand, there is the door, use it!"

The waitress later told us that the Captain was being so loud and obnoxious that if the bar manager or owner had been there they would have thrown him out. That would have been a real godsend to us, but things just didn't play out that way.

Our Fatal Mistake

At our table, Bob asked me, "You want to leave?"

I shook my head. "I haven't eaten yet. Let's grab something and then get out of here."

That was a huge mistake.

Since we weren't really talking to him any more, the Captain shot us a scowl, then joined other patrons at their table. This would have been perfect—except for one thing: he decided to badmouth me to those complete strangers. As I later found out, he told one of them that I thought I was "really hot shit" because my wife had been a Dallas Cowboys cheerleader. (That was in 1986, before Deborah went to work for Eastern.) Bob and I were sitting far enough away that we couldn't hear normal conversation. But one of the men turned in my direction, stared at me, and said something. At first I could not make out what he said, but he repeated it several times. Each time he said it, the Captain broke into a hearty laugh.

And then I heard it. "Hey! Hey! How many of those football players did your wife have to hose to become a Dallas Cowboys cheerleader?"

The tables were almost ten feet apart, but I finally realized the stranger's comments were directed at me alone. How many people in a bar in Fargo, North Dakota, are married to a former Dallas Cowboy cheerleader? I could not believe my ears.

Anger was rising inside me. "I can't believe this," I said to Bob.

Pushing my chair back, I stood up and looked at the guy shooting his mouth off. The Captain was also in my line of fire. "You guys are a bunch of low-class hicks."

I didn't use a single swear word. Bob put his arm around me and sat me down. I couldn't believe that a Captain from a major airline would say something like that to complete strangers about me or my wife. He was one very vindictive and sick individual.

Bob called over the waitress, paid the tab, and we left. As Bob and I walked into the parking lot I said through clenched teeth, "I should go back in there and kick their asses." I was getting madder by the second.

"You can go back in if you want to, but I am going to the hotel," Bob replied. "Getting into a fight on probation—or at any other time—doesn't seem like a good idea to me. But have at it if you want to."

I took a deep breath and exhaled, letting common sense seep back into my consciousness. Bob was right. That would be a stupid thing to do. Instead of reentering the bar, I followed him back to the hotel.

After settling into our respective rooms, I walked down the hall and knocked on Bob's door. When he appeared, I said in my best imitation of

Dustin Hoffman's little *Rain Man* voice, "You are my main man, Bob; you are my main man"—just like Hoffman had in the movie. The tension broke completely, and we both enjoyed a good laugh.

Unbeknownst to us, it would be the last time we would laugh at anything for a very, very long time.

Meanwhile, Back at the Bar

While Bob and I were at the hotel sleeping, the Captain was out drinking with the local guys who had harassed me in the lounge. They even went to another bar together. Later, the guys claimed that when the Captain got up from the table to leave, he fell down onto the floor. On the way down, the Captain hit his head on the table and gashed his left eyebrow. He managed to stand and stumble his way out of the bar in search of his hotel. He was so smashed he couldn't find it. Frustrated, he returned to the bar and announced, "I am a Northwest Airlines Captain . . . I have to fly early in the morning . . . and I can't find my hotel." According to later witnesses, the sign was at least partially visible from the bar.

And that is when the you-know-what really hit the fan. After all they had witnessed, the guys he had been drinking with decided to call the FAA hotline. One of the tipsters had a relative booked to fly the next day, and he was justifiably afraid for her safety. They reported that pilots were drinking into the early morning hours.

Chapter 12

The Worst Day of My Life

I wish with all my heart that the next morning never happened. But I had had too much to drink the night before. I didn't even realize how much I'd had to drink. It was this non-realization, added to the unpredictability of some earlier drinking incidents, that—later—helped to convince me I was an alcoholic.

I know that at some point in the night I threw up into the sink. I remember the bed spinning around, and I know I didn't even bother to take my clothes off when I crawled onto it. Looking back now, after many years of sobriety, it is obvious to me that I was in no shape to fly. Was I about to compromise my own personal value system and the safety of my passengers? I really didn't understand what was happening; so, the overriding fear of losing my job or getting into trouble made me press along, trying to get the job done.

To my knowledge, what was about to happen was unprecedented in aviation history.

Tragedy in the Making

On the following morning, March 8, 1990, Bob called my room around 5:30 a.m. He and the Captain were downstairs and it was time to leave for the airport. I wasn't even close to ready. I had a bad case of diarrhea, and had barely slept. "Sorry," I mumbled. "I'll catch the next van out and join you at the plane."

What none of us knew was that an FAA safety inspector was already at the airport. He was waiting to meet the pilot who was the subject of the anonymous report fielded at about 2:00 that morning. He didn't have any specific names or even a description of the pilot, other than that he flew for Northwest and that he had been out drinking into the early morning. The FAA inspector didn't have the Captain's real name because he had given his drinking mates the fake name of "Lyle Pseudo."

Northwest headquarters had been notified by the FAA in the early morning that one of its pilots had been out drinking all night. No one at Northwest, however, notified anyone in Fargo or tried to contact any of the pilots still on the ground there. Fargo was a small station, and Northwest had only two crews there that night. If the Northwest station manager had been notified, he easily could have prevented the terrible incident about to ensue.

I've often wondered whether authorities at Northwest wanted this Captain to fly under the influence so they could catch him red-handed. After all, the airlines canceled the next leg of the flight out of Minneapolis before we even *arrived* in the Twin Cities. Why not just cancel the outbound flight in Fargo and get on with an investigation there? I just don't know the answer to that question. Also, I was told after the incident that people inside the pilots' union as well had been trying to get this Captain to seek help for alcoholism.

Suffice it to say, lots of mistakes by many people were made that morning, including by me. And we pilots were about to pay an enormous price for our roles in the incident.

You would think that sleeping in my clothes and throwing up the night before would have been a huge warning sign to me. It was just so sad that I was still losing my battle with alcohol, that it still had its self-destructive grip on me, and that I was still ignoring or not recognizing the situation. It was getting the best of me now, and, as it had only a few times before, it was about to interfere with my duties as a pilot. My drinking the night before had already kept me from showing up, in the lobby, on time, ready to fly an airplane. Bob had to send the crew van back to the hotel to pick me up. While awaiting my arrival, he ordered the plane de-iced and performed the walk-around of the aircraft.

Only in the future, after several months of recovery, would I fully realize and remember the previous incidents I had been involved in as a crewmember. There was a time during my recovery when so many things from the past came to light in my consciousness. During this moment of clarity I began to recall when I had lost control in the past. There had been two other instances at Eastern Airlines: the one in Aruba, and another in West Palm Beach. Now I know that someone who drinks does not have to experience a large number of similar episodes to be an alcoholic; a couple of blackouts will do the trick just fine.

So there I was, out of control again, yet in a position where I believed I had to go fly an airplane despite having too much alcohol in my system to be a safe airman. We were three airline pilots, all with alcohol in our systems, about to enter the same cockpit, poised and ready to fly. As I had in times past, I gritted my teeth and plunged forward in order to complete the mission. I convinced myself that everything was going to be all right. But I can only speak for myself; I don't know what the other two pilots were thinking.

I know this will shock readers, but the subject of alcohol never came up that morning. Bob, the First Officer, had observed the Captain drinking heavily while they were out together during our earlier layover in Grand Rapids. The following morning at the Grand Rapids airport, while I was performing my pre-flight duties, Bob told me, "I have never seen anyone drink that much at one time in my entire life." Sadly, on this morning in Fargo, no questions that I am aware of were asked about the night before. I do know that the First Officer saw the cut above the Captain's eye and asked him how he had gotten it. The Captain lied, telling him that he had hit his head in his hotel room. He never told Bob how late he had been out drinking.

The crew's ability to communicate openly and honestly had been severely damaged during the previous four days by this overbearing "taskmaster" Captain and our own weaknesses. It was just like a dysfunctional and unhealthy family. Now silence was the order of the day. As a crewmember, my opinion was never solicited by the Captain that morning. The pilots never came to any collective decisions. When we did speak, our focus was on unimportant things, such as whether the flight was going to leave on time.

Unknown Territory

Verle Addison, the FAA Safety Inspector alerted at 2:00 a.m. by the anonymous tip-off, showed up at the airport and was waiting for the two Northwest Airlines crews flying that morning. He was there prior to our departure, and spent up to twenty minutes talking with the Captain of our flight. As I later learned, Addison told the Captain that he wanted to have a meeting with the entire flight crew before the plane left the airport that morning.

Looking back, that was a great idea. It would have allowed Bob and me to talk in front of another individual who had some authority, and perhaps the flight never would have left the airport. But the Captain never told us that the FAA Inspector, who was himself a professional pilot, wanted to have a crew meeting with all of us before our departure. Did he blow off the inspector the same way he had blown off Bob and me over the previous four days? I don't know; I was not present for any conversations that the Captain or the First Officer had with the Federal Safety Inspector.

A Plea for Help

But prior to boarding the airplane, I had my own conversation with Addison. It was conducted out in the hallway (in the gate area) in front of some large glass windows—in the clear view of the Captain and First Officer. A person at the security checkpoint notified me upon my arrival that a Federal Safety Inspector was looking for me and wanted to speak with me before I got on the airplane. When I spotted him walking behind me, I stopped next to the window in the terminal for him to catch up. As luck would have it, I was positioned directly in front of our airplane.

When Addison arrived, I introduced myself and we shook hands. Looking over his shoulder, I could see through the front of the cockpit windows; the Captain and the First Officer were already in their seats, where they could clearly see that I was having a conversation with the Federal Safety Inspector. Both pilots were waving at me like they wanted me to hurry up, beckoning me to come down to the cockpit. I thought to myself, what is the big hurry here?

A Northwest ramp agent walked out of the jet bridge door just as the inspector reached me. He witnessed the entire conversation that followed.

"Are you the flight engineer for this flight?" Addison asked.

"Yes, sir, I am."

"I received an anonymous tip about a Northwest pilot being out into the early morning hours drinking. I think I smell alcohol. Did you have anything to drink last night?"

"I was out last night and had some beer," I replied honestly, "but I did not break the eight-hour rule." The rule I was referring to was the FAA regulation about not drinking alcohol for a minimum of eight hours before a flight. Although he would later testify that I had denied ever having a drink, that is not correct. I emphasized that I had not broken the eight-hour rule.

"Have you had a chance to talk to my Captain yet?"

The inspector eyed me coolly. "Yes, I have talked with the Captain."

I swallowed hard and continued. "Sir, since you are out here questioning this flight crew, I think it would be a good idea to give the entire crew a blood-alcohol test." When he did not immediately respond, I continued. "I don't know how late the Captain was out, but I would like you to give *me* a blood-alcohol test. Blood, breath, or urine—your choice, sir." I paused, but he did not immediately respond. "I think it is important that this crew be blood-alcohol tested before the flight leaves Fargo," I added.

I was begging for help—literally *begging* for help. I wanted him to save me from myself. My gut told me to run like hell out of this airport. If I could have put it into words, my instinct was shouting, "Do not board this airplane!" But at the same time, my head was telling me just the opposite: "You have to get on this flight or you will lose your job." I was looking for a savior. Unfortunately, this inspector did not fit those shoes.

The Captain, meanwhile, was gesturing to me for all he was worth, waving at me to get down and onto the airplane.

"I am not requesting blood-alcohol testing," the FAA Inspector finally answered, with a shake of his head. "Just so you know, officially there is no violation of any regulations until the aircraft moves." He had just given me a very valuable piece of information—". . . *until* the aircraft moves . . ."—but I was not quite quick enough to act upon it. Of course, I was totally unaware that he had previously made a request to the Captain to have a meeting with his entire crew.

"I would like to see your pilot's license," he continued. It was not a request, but a demand put politely.

"Sure," I answered, pulling out the documents and handing them to him.

As he was examining the papers and jotting down some information, I again asked him to give me a blood-alcohol test. He handed back my licenses. "I am not requesting a test," he replied.

That was it. He turned and walked away from me, heading for a restricted area to write up a formal report. "There were no signs of inebriation or intoxication," he wrote in his report. "Therefore, there was no reason to prevent the flight from leaving." But the inspector would admit later in Federal court that I—as a crewmember, and the only crewmember to do so—requested blood-alcohol testing, and *prior* to leaving Fargo.

I looked up; the Captain and Flight Officer were still waving frantically at me. I sighed aloud and thought, "The inspector didn't ask for an alcohol test. The other guys must be ok. I'd better board."

As I entered the door of the airplane and walked into the cockpit, the Captain was sitting with his body half turned in his seat. This position hid the left side of his face from my view.

No sooner had I stepped inside than he snapped at me, "Sit your ass down and finish your pre-flight!"

This demand was consistent with his management style throughout the entire trip. He didn't ask me a single question about my conversation with the Federal Safety Inspector. He didn't care about my input, even though I had come up with the best idea of the entire morning: getting our blood alcohol tested.

And I was just not healthy enough to do anything about it. No matter how uncomfortable I was in this situation, I was powerless to do what was right and step off the familiar, self-destructive path I was traveling. My inner alarms were clanging like bells in a convent on Sunday morning, shaking my soul and rocking my head, but I felt as if I did not have the strength to do anything about it.

So, instead of standing up, telling the Captain what I thought of him, and walking back into the terminal to seek out the inspector, I began to fulfill my pre-flight responsibilities.

Looking back, it is obvious now that my sickness of co-dependency helped keep me in this boiling pot. I had not been comfortable with this Captain from the beginning of our five-day trip, but I never made a constructive attempt to do anything about it other than talk in a bar, where the beer flowed freely. I paid nothing but lip service to the issue, talking to Bob about it at lunch a few times. And where had that gotten me? The conversations had blown up in our faces.

The Captain was only interested in covering up what had happened the night before. I, too, was incapable of being honest with myself, of really understanding the dynamics of this crew and my role in allowing this tragic event to unfold as it did.

But I knew I was full of fear, and it made me sick.

Chapter 13

The Calm Before the Storm

Somehow, we managed to take off without incident, fly without any issue, and land safely in Minneapolis.

Ironically, it turned out to be the smoothest and most uneventful flight of the entire five-day trip. The Captain just sat in his seat and talked on the radio to Air Traffic Control. Except for yelling at me when I walked in, he never spoke a word to me during the entire flight except to pull the voice recorder circuit breaker. Bob flew the airplane without a hitch from Fargo to Minneapolis. As the Flight Engineer, I ran all of the aircraft systems, including fuel, electric generators, hydraulics, air conditioning, and cabin pressurization, to name just a few. I did my job in my usual, methodical manner. I operated all of these systems without incident or error.

Airline pilots do not like surprises; we like to be in control. Perhaps this is why the profession had appealed to me so much. As a child, I was constantly on guard against surprises and constantly trying to be in control. Flying was predictable. You flip a switch on and something happens, and if it doesn't, you have a well-developed procedure to fall back on. Safety is implied in all this.

The flip side is that nothing strikes fear into the heart of an airline pilot like a total surprise or things out of control. And nothing represents that more than an authoritative figure from the FAA. As the old pilot adage goes, when you hear, "I'm from the FAA, and I'm here to help," you know your world is about to fall apart.

After arriving at the gate in Minneapolis, I remained in the cockpit and had a brief conversation with a Northwest mechanic who met the airplane. It was routine for a mechanic to meet a flight early in the morning in Minneapolis.

What I did not know was that during this time the Captain was against the wall inside the terminal being questioned by law enforcement officials. The FAA safety inspector in Fargo had called the FAA office in Minneapolis and told them about the anonymous report of a pilot drinking late at night and into the morning hours. He told the field office that he had interviewed the crew members individually, and that we had left Fargo before he could have a meeting with the entire crew together. He also told the inspector in Minneapolis that the Second Officer (me) had asked to be blood-alcohol tested before the flight left Fargo. Armed with this information, the inspector in Minneapolis decided to meet the flight at the gate. He would not have been doing his job if he had not done so.

While awaiting our arrival, the inspector struck up a conversation with the gate agent assigned to meet the flight. As he would later testify, when he mentioned the Captain's name the gate agent knew who he was, and told him that he had a reputation for drinking. According to court testimony, she told the safety inspector that she had "been involved in a case whereby she had to testify concerning a crew member in an alcohol-related situation." [Court transcript, page 208, lines 21-24] When asked who it was, she named the Captain: Prouse. This Captain's reputation had even crossed over into other departments of the company: a remote gate agent in the Twin Cities knew of him by name *and* reputation. The cards were stacked against this guy—but he had set them up himself. He had even bragged about his bad reputation to anyone who would listen. Now it was finally going to catch up with him in a big way.

I realize today that I was tied to the Captain. He was the "father figure" I allowed to pull me into the uncontrolled, no-security, no-sanctity place that capped a lifetime of absolute terror. I was weak, and I did not, could not, resist it.

When I finally left the plane and entered the terminal, I was met by a law enforcement official and the FAA inspector who had met the flight. They instructed all three of us to follow them to a different area of the airport for questioning. I couldn't believe it. *Now* someone wanted to do something about all of this—*after* we had flown the plane full of passengers? I had requested and been denied testing in Fargo, and *now* we get the serious treatment?!

Even though I was standing there in my official capacity as an airline pilot, panic surged through me. My inner voice was screaming at me to get out of this situation. "Run, Joe! Run anywhere for safety," the little voice shrieked inside my head. "This place is not safe." The idea of being found out, of having the world know I had done something terribly unprofessional, made me sick to my stomach. No pilot wants anyone to know he may have done something that endangered the lives of his passengers.

The law enforcement officers in Minneapolis did not want to make a big scene, so they led us to a private room. They really didn't know what they were allowed to do or supposed to do, since no one at the airport had seen any of us commit a crime.

The officers would not allow us to call an attorney. I don't recall exactly how that issue arose, but I do remember one of them refusing a request. That struck me as unusual, and probably against our rights. Yet, surprisingly, none of us—neither the Captain, nor Bob, nor I—insisted upon our rights. I don't know why. As events would aptly demonstrate, this was a terrible mistake on our part.

After about thirty minutes of stalling and lots of little private conversations among themselves, the FAA Safety Inspector in Minneapolis decided that he could make a citizen's arrest. He also threatened to press criminal charges if we did not submit to blood-alcohol testing.

Again I thought: "What the heck is the matter with you people?" I wanted to shout at them! I had pleaded to be tested in Fargo *before* we took off, and *now* blood-alcohol testing is suddenly a good idea? And it took several law enforcement types and an FAA Safety Inspector more than thirty minutes to come up with this idea?

I considered turning down the test on principle alone. At the time, that would have been a smart thing to do, because I had asked to be tested in Fargo before the flight left. Now, someone else was calling the shots.

A Sword Piercing Through My Heart

As we stood there in that room at the airport, my mind raced as if I had downed four cups of coffee in the space of ten minutes. I looked at the Captain's face, and for the first time that day noticed the left side of his head. He had a large gash above his eye. The discovery almost knocked me down; even though I remained standing, my knees were buckling, and my stomach had the weight of solid lead in it: not only heavy, but toxic. Here I was again, in an unpredictable situation, with an unreliable authority figure.

I asked him in a hushed tone, "What happened to your eye?"

He shrugged. "I hit my head on the circuit breaker panel inside the airplane when I was getting into my seat."

I knew that he was lying, and a feeling of betrayal overwhelmed me. Pierced by this sudden thrust of the liar's sword, my heart sank. Something very bad had happened the night before, and now the situation was out of control for all of us.

Children are easily manipulated because they have few or no options except for survival. Right then I switched into survival mode; the feeling of being manipulated, lied to, and let down was a heavy one. I understand today that the "survival" option is one of the strongest "emotions" for the adult child to experience in this situation. To try to make myself secure, I could pick fight or flight. Fight: take on the whole world alone. Flight: "I have to get away from a father (Captain) who is more incapacitated than I am as an adult child." This is no excuse for my actions. It is just my way of making sense of the tragedy of it all and the role I played. The Captain was in denial of his reality, and I was in denial of mine.

When they threatened me with criminal charges if I did not submit to a blood-alcohol test, I decided to back down and cooperate. Thus, I did exactly what I had done as a child: when things were out of control and the person who was supposed to be present and cognizant was not, I resorted to trying to please everybody. I was trying to maneuver so as to make the situation work for an adult who was less present, less cognizant, and less capable than a young child. As it is with every child in this situation, the true answer was, "There is nothing I could do," but rather than turn for help from anyone in the outside world, set up a boundary, and get good legal advice, I tried to survive by pleasing those in authority around me. I turned on my child-like response: "What can I do to make this OK?"

It had been at least twelve hours since my last drink, so I figured I would not have any alcohol in my blood when the results came back. The last thing I wanted was to be suspected of trying to cover anything up. The idea of being charged with a crime terrified me, but I thought I would be ok. And so I made another terrible decision: I agreed to a blood-alcohol test, without so much as waving in the direction of an attorney. It was shortly after 9:00 a.m.

All three of us pilots piled into the back of a squad car with two airport police officers, who drove us to a hospital in Minneapolis for blood-alcohol testing. Unfortunately, someone from the hospital alerted the media, and things began to take on a life of their own.

While we were waiting to be tested one of the officers who had driven us to the hospital said, "I cannot believe someone would make a prank phone call like this on some pilots." I am not sure whom he was speaking to, but I understood what he meant: he hadn't observed anything out of the ordinary about us during the ride to the hospital, or while we were waiting there. But he would change his story later—when it was time for trial.

After the medical staff drew our blood we talked briefly with some attorneys from the pilots' union, who had finally shown up on our behalf. None of them had any experience dealing with anything like this, and they proved it by the bad decision they made at Northwest's headquarters, which is where we went after the blood draw: the union attorneys allowed us to provide recorded statements to a Northwest company attorney. At the time it seemed like the thing to do. Unfortunately, the statements would be used against us in the criminal trial.

Official Mess

The company attorney and chief pilot acted as if what I had to say was completely unimportant. The Captain kept going back into the room where the company attorney was taking his statement and changing his mind about what he wanted to say. He was also trying to get me to agree to some acceptable storyline. The company men didn't care about the dynamics or relationship of the crew; they were just trying to establish some facts.

After the statements were taken we had nothing left to do but wait anxiously for the results of the blood tests. Frankly, I was looking forward to mine, because I was sure it would come back negative. But a few hours later the union attorney walked into the room with a puzzled, sad look on his face. He sighed before saying, "The blood-alcohol results came back positive for all three of you."

I stopped breathing, literally. It was as if someone had given me a body blow with a baseball bat. I felt as if I was falling from a high cliff into a bottomless abyss. After some fourteen hours my blood-alcohol content was still .08; the First Officer's was .06, and the Captain's reported as 0.13.

Point zero eight. I kept thinking that to myself as the implications of that number sank in. Federal aviation regulations limit blood-alcohol content to .04. I had compromised my own personal value system by flying a commercial jet with alcohol in my system. As the initial shock wore off, the shame became nearly overwhelming.

The Captain and First Officer talked with the company about their future and what the results meant. I was not really included in those talks. I was a second-class citizen because I was living the "automatic" probationary life of a first-year pilot again. The Captain and First Officer caught airplanes home that night. But they had taken up so much time talking to the company that I was not able to fly home that evening. A union representative drove me to a hotel by the airport and dropped me off. On the most tragic and emotional day of my life, I was stranded in some hotel room.

Chapter 14

Stranded and Alone

My world as I knew it was careening toward an end. I had been just one week away from successfully completing my probationary period as a "new hire" pilot with Northwest, and now I was almost certain to be fired. I was also afraid the FAA would yank my license to fly, known in the business as an "emergency revocation." My wife and I were not going to get the house on the lake we had been saving for and dreaming about for so long. The nightmare I had stepped into was getting darker and scarier by the minute.

There was proof positive I had flown a commercial jet as a pilot for a major airline with alcohol in my bloodstream. If only I could wind the clock back and get tested in Fargo, as I'd requested; I would never have been allowed to fly.

I turned on the TV, only to discover that the media was already reporting the story on the local news channel. Several major newspapers in the country were getting ready to print the story the following morning. Even Jay Leno got in on the act, manufacturing laughs at our expense on The Tonight Show.

The pressure and stress were coming down on me hard and fast. I had allowed alcohol to get the best of me, again. I had ruined my airline career. I had ruined my life. My actions would call negative attention to professional airline pilots, especially pilots from Northwest Airlines. The shame was nearly too much to bear.

Endless Pain

I had to end the pain.

I was sitting on the bed staring at the window in my seventh floor room when a solution to all of my problems arrived. I didn't want to live any more. I thought about running through the window for one last flight in the air. I slowly paced off twenty or so steps and turned to look at the glass. The short but fast run would probably give me enough speed to crash through the window and plunge to my death. But when I walked back up to the window to look out one last time before smashing through, I hesitated. Sure, *my* pain would end; but I would end up hurting terribly all of the people who loved me, including my family and close friends.

Then, standing in front of the window, I completely broke down and cried, from the deepest part of my being. The sobs welled up from places so deep inside me I did not know they even existed. I don't know how long I stood there, but the tears rolled down my face, down my neck, then down my chest. It was a long, hard cry.

Finding Courage

When there were no tears left to cry, a calmness descended upon me. There was no peace in the way I felt, but I had a desire to accept some responsibility, realizing how difficult my life was going to become. I had just lived the worst day of my life, and many more bad days would follow—I was sure of that. I knew I had to be strong, that somehow I had to face the pain, shame, and disappointment.

It was then that a level of anger flooded into my consciousness. I was so angry that I had let alcohol back into my life. I was very angry with myself, and completely demoralized by my unprofessional behavior.

But one important thing was about to change for me: I was finally willing to ask for help. In one of the hardest calls I ever made, I picked up the phone and rang my friend Tommy, a Northwest mechanic. I didn't say all that much on the phone, but he knew it was important. He drove over right away, and we spent a long while together at the hotel.

When he was ready to leave, Tommy looked me squarely in the eyes and demanded, "Joey, you have got to promise me you are not going to do anything stupid."

I knew exactly what he was talking about. He had perceived the desperation in every part of my being. Tommy was looking at a young man whose life and dreams were falling apart around him.

But as images of my family and friends danced through my head, I realized again how selfish suicide would be. "Okay, Tommy," I answered. "I promise that I won't do anything stupid, tonight or ever—no matter how bad it gets."

Tommy gave me a bear hug and asked me to give him a call first thing in the morning. As he left, I was hoping I could keep my promise. It's incredible what bizarre thoughts go through your head at a time like that. Sitting in that room, alone, a hundred thoughts raced through my mind. One I can't forget was my concern about the mess I would make on some innocent person's car if I jumped out of the window into the parking lot below. Someone would find me in the morning lying in a puddle of blood on top of his car's smashed-in roof, and the image would remain with him forever. Now, how selfish would that be?

Confessing to the Folks

I was unable to immediately contact my wife. She was traveling as a flight attendant somewhere in the United States, and I didn't know her exact itinerary. Besides, I was very ashamed of myself, and I couldn't bear the idea of telling her over the telephone what was happening. It was the number one call I didn't want to make. I had blown everything we had built together, and the news was going to shake her to the core. I knew it would be so difficult, so painful for her to hear, and I just wasn't ready to rip her dreams away from her.

Instead, I made a phone call to my parents in Fort Lauderdale. They were in bed asleep when their phone rang. There was no easy way to break the news to them, so I decided to level with them. "I just flew a commercial jet with a positive blood-alcohol level," I said, doing my best to keep my voice from breaking. "It was a low level, but enough to violate the Federal Aviation Regulations. I tried to get a blood test in Fargo before we left, and I explained that I was flying with a Captain who never listened to anything I said."

The shock and sadness in my father's voice was palpable. "This is terrible, Joe, after all of your hard work!" replied my father. "What's going to happen?"

"I don't know for sure," I answered, "but I'm probably going to lose my job and my piloting licenses."

I clearly remember my mother's deep cry of anguish when she heard that: "Oh Joe!" Those two words are still painful to recall.

This news crushed my parents. My mom and dad were the two people who knew firsthand the many personal sacrifices I had made to become a pilot. They were the ones with whom I had shared my passion, and they were the people who had always encouraged me to pursue my dream of becoming a pilot. Throughout the conversation I could not stop thinking about my father's warning to me about drinking during layovers.

We hung up at the end of the call, but something strange happened: the connection remained open on both ends of the line. When I realized I could hear my parents, I stayed on the phone, listening as they both cried on the other end of the line. It tore my heart out to hear them in such pain. What had I done to them? They didn't know I could hear them, and I never told them.

My father's words that night still ring in my head: "He worked so hard . . . He worked so hard."

My mom responded in a melancholy, monotone voice: "It's going to be all over the news."

I decided I couldn't listen any longer, and quietly hung up the phone. Stranded in that lonely hotel room in a strange town, it was time to face the future—alone.

Chapter 15

Media Circus

When I arrived at the Minneapolis airport it was obvious that the people in the news media knew I had been stranded overnight in Minneapolis and would be trying to go home the next day. I don't know how they found that out, but someone must have been feeding them information. People with news cameras were trying to find me in the terminal. They had camped out by the gate of the flight bound to my hometown of Nashville, Tennessee.

Even though I had woken up that morning determined to face the rest of my life, I was *not* ready to face anyone in the media. I knew I couldn't handle the news reporters in the state I was in, so full of shame and guilt. So I walked to the other airline terminal and got a ride on an American Airlines flight to Nashville. Although there was comparative peace on the journey to Nashville, I didn't know what was waiting for me on the other end of the flight.

When we landed in Nashville, I discovered members of the media camped out at the Northwest gate; that was no surprise. After I got off the American Airlines flight, I walked right past all of the cameras at the Northwest gates. I was in hide-and-seek mode again, a game I had played since my early days. Tension–relief, tension–relief; someone is sober and the world is wonderful; someone is not sober, and all hell is going to break loose.

A Northwest gate agent who was a friend of mine told me that the media was searching for me at the airport because they knew I would be coming home that day. These people were relentless in their hunt for me; I felt like a fugitive on the loose. This came on top of feeling so full of shame; I still couldn't believe what I had done. Luckily, the media didn't have a picture of me yet, so I narrowly escaped, walking right past several reporters throughout the airport.

Relieved at the easy evasion, I began to think I was home free. But, having little or no experience with the media, I had no way of knowing how cunning and ambitious reporters can be. Their next move left me stunned: they were so bound and determined to talk to me and get me on camera that they found out where I lived, and had a news crew camped out in front of my apartment when I drove up.

Tempted to Spill my Guts

As I walked from my car to the front door of my basement apartment, I spotted a familiar face. I had taken a few steps more before it dawned on me that she was a local television reporter. I quickened my pace and trotted down the steps into the entryway of my apartment. She trotted right down after me.

"Mr. Balzer! Cheryl Mason, Channel Three News!" she announced. "Can I speak to you about what happened during your flight to Minneapolis?"

Bob had wisely cautioned me not to talk to the media under any circumstances. Yet I desperately needed *someone* to confide in, if only for the comforting feeling of having someone, anyone, to talk to. It was the same comfort I had longed for during my early years of existence. So, after I put my key in the lock, I hesitated, then turned to face her. I nearly invited her into the apartment. With my insides ripping apart, I wanted to tell her about the hell that my life had been for the last five days—the hell that I had had to endure as a result of this abusive airline Captain. I wanted someone to listen to me; I needed someone to know how desperate I was.

But the look on her face stopped me cold. Reporters have their own agenda, just as a drinking adult has his or her own agenda. The perky smile on her face could not mask the shark-like, hungry look in her eyes. A voice in my head sang out to me: *The media is not the safe haven you need.* So instead, I kept it all inside.

"I can't talk to you," I finally spat out. "I'm very sorry."

I quickly turned the key and opened the door. I could still see the determined look in her eye as I gently closed the door behind me.

I was in the apartment, but it sure didn't feel like home. The isolated, dark and lonely world of my basement living quarters rushed up to smother me. Since my wife and I had both been out of town, all of the blinds were closed. I was afraid to open them in fear that hordes of strangers and media types would be peering in at me.

Who's There?

Across the dark room I could see the red message light flashing on my answering machine. (This was long before cell phones were a necessity of daily living.) The last thing I wanted to do was listen to the messages on my answering machine, especially since the blinking light indicated the tape was full. But listening to them seemed like the right thing to do.

I walked over to the machine and stared at it for at least a full minute. By pressing the "play" button, I was inviting the outside world into my own. I took a deep breath, held it a second, and pressed the button while exhaling.

To my pleasant surprise, the first message was from my little sister. "Hello, Joe, this is Barbie," she said in her sweet, calm voice. "I am so sorry about what happened to you. Forgive yourself. I love you. Call me when you can. Bye-bye."

The thought of forgiving myself was totally foreign to me. "Forgive yourself." I could hear her soft, loving voice telling me that over and over. *"Forgive yourself."* What a perfect message. I really didn't fully understand it at the time, but the relief it gave me was the first comforting thing that had happened in the middle of this firestorm.

Barbie is a leader in our family. She had entered recovery a few years earlier. Her courage eventually led our entire family into recovery. She had done the hard work of self-examination that people in recovery must do. She was in her second year of sobriety, and she was offering me some outstanding advice. People in recovery who have a family member already in recovery have a real advantage.

I flashed back in my mind to a night when she was in treatment called "family night." I attended family night, but nobody emphasized that alcoholism is a family disease, and I probably wouldn't have listened anyway. Most people who have someone in the family suffering from alcoholism don't listen, and thus don't get into recovery to repair the damage. I remembered reading Claudia Black's book, *It Will Never Happen To Me,* and trying to convince my sister that she might be an alcoholic. But now I was the one in trouble, it was my life that was going down into a deep, dark spiral, and I was the one getting a heavy dose of reality. It was a real blessing to have my sister, who was already in recovery and doing a great job of staying sober, as a resource to me as I experienced this devastating set of circumstances I'd gotten myself into.

I then listened to the remainder of the messages on my machine. It had a large recording capacity. The next several messages were not as enlightening as my sister's had been. They were all from the news media, wanting a piece of my story. It was *big* news. We were already being reported on CNN and every news channel in the country. There were several messages from CNN and other television networks. Other messages were from the Associated Press, United Press International and *Newsweek* magazine, to name a few. Everyone was interested in this story. I just stood there, overwhelmed and embarrassed with the magnitude of it all. Then the phone rang. I dared not answer it in case it might be more media. I screened the call and it was, of course, another reporter, so I let him too talk to my answering machine.

She's in the Dark

I walked into the bedroom and turned on the light. I saw a beautiful sweater on the bed, with a little note from my wife, waiting for me to discover it. She was good about leaving surprises for me. She was still out of the country, and probably had yet to hear about the incident that involved her newlywed husband. Her note said that she loved me and missed me and could not wait to get home to see me. As I read this note, the remaining parts of my heart that were not already broken began to shatter. I fell to my knees next to the bed. I realized the hurt that my actions were going to cause my wife. She was an innocent bystander in all of this, and the pain of this event was going to be overwhelming for her. All I could think of was her innocence, and how my actions and "loss of control" while drinking would affect both of our lives from now on.

I knew I had to do something, but what? I didn't look forward to the first phone call from her, when my words about the previous day's events would rip her innocence away forever. My wife was about to become one more victim of the persistent march of alcoholism.

I waited in that dark apartment all through the next day for her arrival. The last thing I wanted to do was hurt her, but it was too late for that. How was she going to react? I realized many, many women would be out the door in an instant.

That night, after spending the day alone in my apartment, I listened to the song *Shattered*, by Linda Ronstadt. The song described exactly how I was feeling at the time: there were shattered pieces of me all the way from Fargo to Minneapolis to Nashville.

The Possibility of Jail

I didn't get any sleep that first night at home by myself. My head felt as if electrical impulses were shooting up the sides, and my body as if someone had beaten me with a rubber hose.

The next morning my friend Kurt, who was also an airline pilot, came directly to my apartment. He said he'd seen me all over the news. He asked me what had happened, and I gave him all of the details. I told him that I was very concerned about becoming a criminal and being sent to jail. I told him that the Federal Government had recently made it a felony to fly while under the influence of alcohol.

I will never forget what Kurt said next: "Man, you are never going to jail for this. Think of all the horrible things people are doing, and they never go to jail. Don't even think about that!"

I so wanted him to be right.

Chapter 16

Tragic Homecoming

The next day I continued to sit in that apartment. I waited for what would become a horrible, head-on, tumbling collision with reality. I had been able to track down my wife, and her company got a message to her. In Deborah's own words, this is what transpired:

I was on a trip, having to get up early that morning. I didn't turn on the TV while getting ready. We were in flight when the pilots received a message for me on the satellite communication system. It said that after I arrived in Raleigh-Durham I should take the next flight directly home. They said it was a family emergency and nothing else. I ran to my flight, so I had no time to stop and make a call from a payphone. I cried all the way to Nashville, wondering what was wrong.

Once I arrived in Nashville, a close friend of ours, Kurt, met me as I got off the flight. He told me that Joe was OK, but he had to tell me something that had happened. While he drove me home Kurt explained that Joe had been arrested after a flight, and that he had been out drinking the night before at a bar. He said one of the pilots had been turned in to the FAA for drinking, and he didn't know any other details. I didn't know what to expect, because Joe has always been a really happy person. I was not ready to encounter what waited for me at our apartment.

When I first saw Joseph, he was sadder than I had ever seen him in his life. As I hugged him, he told me, 'I can understand if you want to leave me.' I told him that everything would be OK. 'I am not going to leave you,' I assured him, 'we will get through this together.'

I was very upset and angry when he told me that he'd requested blood- alcohol testing from the FAA inspector before the flight even left Fargo, and then they decided to arrest him after the flight landed in Minneapolis. Being a flight attendant, I also realized that everyone would have known if he wasn't OK to fly, and the flight attendants had said they thought the pilots were fine.

We cried together and prayed together. We felt attacked by the onslaught of calls from television, newspaper and magazine reporters. Of course, we ignored all of the calls from the media. There were potential criminal charges hanging over Joe, and we were afraid of something backfiring on us.

Everywhere we looked the story was being treated as 'the biggest news item of the century.' It all seemed so surreal. But I had no doubts about how difficult our lives were going to be.

Waiting Out the Inevitable

I was tormented with the possibility of losing my pilot's licenses. Thoughts of how hard I had worked and all the sacrifices I had made to become a pilot raced around in my mind, as I awaited news in the form of an official letter from the FAA. Each day I would walk out to our mailbox with dread for what might be awaiting me in the mail. It was a potential emotional bomb that was waiting to drop on me, and it was only a matter of time before it hit.

I remember that it was a beautiful spring day, and the sunlight shone on the front of the envelope that read, "Federal Aviation Administration." I knew how bad the news would be, and I didn't want to open it. But as difficult as it was, I slit the envelope and pulled out the letter, which informed me that all of my pilot's licenses and flight ratings were being "emergency revoked" by the FAA. I think my heart stopped momentarily. It was official now, but that didn't make the pain of it any easier. The letter stated that I had broken FAA regulations—something I never dreamed possible—and reiterated that I was involved in an alcohol incident.

At that time in my life, even in the midst of the turmoil and destruction, my *denial* allowed me to still be convinced that it had been okay to fly in the shape I was in on the morning of March 8, 1990.

The next day, I went out to get the mail and found a small white postcard in my mailbox. The entire postcard was taken up with the words, "Boeing 727s do not fly on ethanol!" Some stranger had gone to the trouble of finding out my address and sending me this hateful card. Talk about kicking someone when he is down. I figured the mail would be full of all sorts of new and excitingly dreadful things in the days and weeks to come.

And I was right. Next to come was the formal letter from Northwest Airlines telling me that I was being fired from my job. Of course, no official people from Northwest ever did any investigation of my personal experience; they just wanted to get rid of me in a hurry.

A Chance to Get into Recovery

I spent the next several weeks making trips to Minneapolis and talking with one attorney at the pilots' union. He asked me one afternoon if I had ever considered getting into a treatment program for alcoholism. He made it clear that I had the right to keep my insurance benefits after being fired from Northwest, and the insurance company would pay for me to go to a thirty-day treatment program.

Based on my limited and skewed idea of what an alcoholic was, I told him that I didn't think I needed to go to treatment. After all, I thought that you had to drink every day to be an alcoholic. I also thought that true alcoholics behaved like the Captain, drinking to tremendous excess all the time. I also thought that alcoholics really didn't function well in society. Up until this event, I had always been a good employee. I didn't have an abusive sick-leave record with any company I had ever worked for. I just didn't think that I could be a bona-fide alcoholic. There was so much social shame attached to the label "alcoholic," and I knew I couldn't handle any more shame.

Chapter 17

Criminal Charges

I t didn't take long for the government to file criminal charges for flying under the influence of alcohol. They charged the Captain with a criminal felony. The government offered First Officer Bob and me misdemeanor plea bargains. They said if we pled guilty to a misdemeanor charge of flying under the influence in the state of North Dakota, they would not pursue felony charges against us.

My wife and I had saved about $50,000 to put down on our dream house on a lake outside Nashville. I used all of this "home equity" to retain legal representation from a criminal defense attorney in Minneapolis. The other two pilots also hired criminal defense attorneys. My lawyer's advice to me was to give this plea bargain offer *serious* consideration.

I could not believe what I was hearing: a choice between two convictions, a felony or a misdemeanor. That was not the answer I had expected to hear. Trust me here. I had absolutely no legal savvy at this stage of my life—none. Now, you and I both know that hindsight is 20-20. But at that time, in my infinite wisdom, I turned down the misdemeanor plea bargain. I could not comprehend myself as a criminal. In my ignorance, I had no idea how devastating a felony conviction would be compared to a misdemeanor. My attorney tried to tell me, but I just couldn't get it through my head. Knowing what I know today, I never would have gone to trial. Back then, I didn't want to be labeled as a criminal in any way, so the plea bargain was out of the question for me.

There was another factor. When my attorney told me, "Joe, we can avoid going to trial and you can avoid a felony conviction," I asked, "So, if we don't go to trial, how much of your $50,000 fee am I going to avoid paying?"

He replied, "The fee is the same whether we go to trial or not."

I thought, if I'm paying for a trial, then, by God, I'm going to get a trial! That's how out of touch with reality I was in those days.

In addition, one afternoon Bob spoke to me on the telephone. "The best thing we have going for us in this trial, Joe," he said, "is that you asked that Federal Safety Inspector for a blood-alcohol test before the flight ever left." Those words too influenced my decision to go to trial.

But in reality I had no idea what I was getting myself into. I was facing a year in prison and a $10,000 fine in North Dakota if I took the misdemeanor plea bargain; by going to trial, I faced up to 15 years in prison and up to a $250,000 fine if I was convicted of a felony.

Looking back, I realize I was still very sick, yet saw myself as part of a functioning "crew." Going to trial, somehow, in a very sick way, fulfilled my need to continue to be accepted as part of the "team." But we really had not been a healthy crew at any time during the trip; dysfunctions in our personalities overlapped. On some level we as a crew had been destined to fail. Yet now, when I needed to be taking care of myself and going for the plea bargain, I was still trying to seek approval and validation instead. This confusion in my own mind would lead to tragedy yet again. It was a very difficult and costly lesson to learn.

More bad news arrived in the mail. A letter from the government included the criminal petition filed against me. When I read "UNITED STATES OF AMERICA vs. Joseph Balzer," I realized anew what a big mistake I had made.

The United States of America?

The weight of the universe settled on my shoulders, making my steps heavy and difficult as I slowly walked down the path to my apartment. Who in his right mind is going to take on the United States of America, and expect to live to tell the tale?

Surrender

In the midst of all this trouble and turmoil, my sister made the correct and timely recommendation for me. She said that I should consider again what the Eastern Captain, my friend Al, had told me a few years earlier: I would benefit from going to some twelve-step meetings. I was finally desperate enough to seek help, and I wanted some answers; I was ready to see what they had to offer. I spent the next several weeks going to faraway places around Nashville, trying to find a meeting that I liked or was within an hour drive of my apartment.

One day I was at a meeting attended by just one other guy, who was an adult child raised by an alcoholic parent. He told me of a recovery bookstore down the street that was run by an addictions counselor who had a really good reputation in the recovery community. Was it time for me to get the professional help I needed? My life was in a shambles; I had nearly hit bottom. I decided to go there directly when the meeting was over.

I walked into the recovery store and introduced myself to a young lady behind the counter. She gave me a warm smile and said her name was Coby. I didn't know it at the time, but she was also a person on the road to recovery. It took her about five seconds to see I was a real mess. I told her a little bit about my story, and after sympathizing with me a little, she added, "You're in the right place, Joe." She told me to wait around and a man named Buddy would be there in an hour or so.

When Buddy showed up, I introduced myself and began to tell him my story. He told me he could help me if I really wanted his help, and that he was going to have a private recovery group that night he would like me to attend. I did, and, in a word, this group was *awesome*. Coby became my friend and mentor. She had a rock-solid program of recovery, and to this day is helping people in recovery as a health-care professional.

Buddy helped me to see inside myself. He gave me a lot of learning materials and things to read, which helped me get through my web of denial. Over the next few months I read every recovery book I could get my hands on. It was the time in my life for the struggle with alcohol to end and the surrender to sobriety to begin. For the first time in my life I was willing to listen to other people and try to learn from their experiences and struggles. I wanted to learn about this dysfunctional engine that had been driving my life for so many years.

I learned about enmeshment in dysfunctional systems, and became willing to face some very painful things that had occurred in my life. This was not about blaming anyone for anything that had ever happened to me; instead, this was about healing shame and damage from a turbulent past, including the Northwest incident.

No, I didn't go to a thirty-day treatment program for alcoholism. Fortunately for me, I didn't need to. When the Fargo incident occurred my faith was stronger than it had ever been; then the tragedy of the incident and the hard work of recovery exposed me further to God's possibilities. Twelve-step programs teach people to surrender to a power greater than themselves, to learn to depend on God. I had badly needed professional intervention and help, and now—because God put the right people in my life at the right time for me to get the help I desperately needed—I was getting it.

Of course, I had been sincere to my friends several months before when I told them, "I just do not understand it, but I cannot drink like other people." I didn't understand alcoholic blackouts and what they meant. My denial had kept me from going to any twelve-step meetings previously. Now, with Buddy's and the group's help, I was growing and learning about the dynamics of families with alcoholism.

I attended twelve-step meetings twice a week. In addition to reading the materials made available to me through these meetings, I read a series of books by a well-known author and recovering person named John Bradshaw. In them he describes the Adult Child of an Alcoholic Parent syndrome and offers many healing solutions. He encourages action on the part of the recovering person, so he or she can come to grips with the shame and other things that have kept him locked in self-destructive behaviors and attitudes.

After several weeks of meeting with Buddy and his group in an old brick house in Nashville's West End, Buddy decided it was time for me to read the book *Under the Influence,* by Dr. James Milam. Up to that point in my recovery I knew I had problems with alcohol, but was not convinced I was an alcoholic. After reading Dr. Milam's book, however, I was sure I was a "stage one" alcoholic. It was a true "Aha!" moment for me, a real milestone in my life. The book explained to me in detail the three stages of alcoholism. It became crystal clear to me. It was as if someone had reached above my head and flicked a switch; as we say in recovery group, a light bulb went off in my head.

Chapter 18

"Under the Influence"

A brief summary of the main things in Dr. Milam's book that really jumped out and grabbed me will be helpful in understanding what I was experiencing. I relay this information with his permission and blessing. My hope for you is that you will want to read his book and get a great education about alcoholism, or, if you know someone who could use the help, that you will recommend it.

Dr. Milam's book changed my life because it made me see for the first time that alcoholism is a *disease*. This educational experience was a turning point for me. Until I read the book, I didn't know that alcohol is harmless for 90% of people who drink, and addictive to the other 10%; thus, it is a selectively addictive drug. It is addictive to those who are physiologically predisposed and do not possess enough of a certain liver enzyme to break alcohol down when it enters the liver. This causes the liver to convert alcohol into a very dangerous chemical called acetaldehyde. When acetaldehyde goes back into the bloodstream, it ends up in the brain and stimulates the "opiate receptor," which begins the addiction process.

I found this fascinating. It is not heavy drinking that causes alcoholism; nor is it psychological problems. It is the liver enzyme malfunction that is the culprit. So, when my friends and I proceeded to drink in college, the ones who had the proper enzyme in their livers were going to drink normally, while I was destined to develop alcoholism because of my lack of the liver enzyme.

What an education!

I had experienced blackouts (alcohol-induced amnesia) within a few weeks of my first drink. While I had thought that blackouts were normal behavior, Dr. Milam's book made it crystal clear to me that they are not: blackouts are an indicator of early-stage alcoholism. They were a sign that I cannot drink responsibly because my body will never have a normal reaction to alcohol, so I can never safely return to drinking—my body is not set up for it. I just wanted to drink normally like everyone else, but I was physiologically set up for failure from the get-go. My genetic predisposition made that so, and the only thing that could ever save my life was to break the addiction and achieve a lasting sobriety.

In the laboratory, researchers have bred teetotaler rats that will not consume alcohol. Yet when they are injected with THP (a product of acetaldehyde), suddenly they want to drink everything in sight. They also suffer from withdrawal symptoms—another sign of addiction.

The World Health Organization classifies addictive drugs. Since heroin, crack cocaine, and nicotine are addictive to 90% of the users, they are classified as addictive drugs. Alcohol is only addictive to 10% of its users, and so is not classified as an addictive drug. But for those individuals who are genetically predisposed and lack the liver enzyme to process alcohol, developing alcoholism in its early stages is inevitable if they drink. This fact is what made me decide once and for all that I had no business trying to learn how to drink like "normal" drinkers. For me, drinking always spelled disaster. Not because I was weak, stupid, or irresponsible; I had a *condition.* I had not understood that before, but now it was my responsibility to understand I could never drink again.

Dr. Milam also explained the gradual, inevitable progression of the disease of alcoholism, in three stages. Sadly, our society is fairly uninformed about these stages (as was I), so society rarely recognizes alcoholism until it has already reached the later, catastrophic stages.

I myself, of course, had observed the addictive behavior in other family members, particularly my dad, for most of my life, but I was not going to blame anyone for anything. It was not about that at all; it was about understanding what alcoholism is and what alcoholism is not. It was all just a matter of education.

Chapter 19

Getting Real

A tremendous weight lifted off of my shoulders after reading Dr. Milam's book. The mystery and confusion about whether I was really an alcoholic were gone.

The *Alcoholics Anonymous "Big Book"* describes the alcoholic's reaction to alcohol as an "allergy." When the AA *"Big Book"* was first written, the state of the art aircraft was the DC-3. But tremendous leaps have transpired in aircraft technology since the 1930s; and similarly, tremendous research regarding the physiology, neurochemistry and biochemistry of alcoholism since the 1930s has shed new light on this powerful and devastating disease. In the 1930s, calling alcoholism an allergy was an honest attempt at explaining what alcoholism was—a very misunderstood physiological disease. But to continue calling alcoholism that today would be a mistake.

For me, I needed to read Dr. Milam's book to gain a modern-day, up-to-date, physiological explanation. This included the neurochemical and biochemical details of what was going on inside my body. I found all of this fascinating. I am certain that if the founding fathers of Alcoholics Anonymous had knowledge of this state-of-the-art information back in the 1930s, they would have included it in the *Big Book*. It simply didn't exist at that time; the research had not been done.

On the other hand, the spiritual principles in the *"Big Book"* are timeless and powerful. I owe a tremendous debt of gratitude to the fellowship of twelve-step programs. Some of my closest friends are members, and they have taught me how to live a healthy and productive life. Twelve-step programs have inspired millions of other people to have sober lives as well.

As I drove to my next twelve-step meeting in the spring of 1991, I felt that I had made a quantum leap in my recovery process—a *real* lifestyle breakthrough. I could not wait to make my big announcement to Buddy and the group. Most other aspects of my life were falling apart, but on the level of recovery I felt that I was right where I belonged, and that I was hitting on all cylinders. I was already grateful to Buddy and the group for all the help they had given me in the previous weeks, but now things were even clearer to me.

I arrived a little early that night. I sat on the couch in our large room and waited for everyone to arrive and the group to begin. The grin on my face gave me away to Buddy, and the others in the group were wondering what I was so happy about. After all, my life had become a giant pile of crap, pain, and failure, so what did I have to smile about?

That night Buddy let me share first. I looked around the room at these wonderful people who all had the inner courage to look at themselves. The people in my group had the desire to heal the wreckage of their pasts and were willing to do something about it. After making eye contact with everyone in the room, I announced with assurance, "My name is Joe, and I am an alcoholic!"

The room erupted with cheers and laughter. I had never been able to bring myself to utter those nine life-changing words.

For several weeks now these people had listened to my "line." In actuality, they could both see and hear the denial, but they understood it was part of my struggle with alcohol. And now they got to witness the miracle moment when I acknowledged I was sick, that I suffered from a disease that could be fatal if it was allowed to follow its course. When people understand how ill they are and are finally willing to go to any length of self-examination, self-discovery, and education to "heal up" from their illness, their lives can begin anew. I now had a new clarity, a new focus to my recovery. I know today that Dr. Milam's book saved my life and changed it in a positive way forever.

And in early August of 1990, the week my trial began, I truly realized that I was going to need all the help I could get.

Chapter 20

Trial—and Errors

The success I experienced overcoming my alcoholism, as described in the previous chapter, unfolded before, during, and after my criminal trial. So now it is time to turn back and face that very difficult time of my life.

The attorneys from the Airline Pilots Association helped each of us find our own legal counsel to defend us against the potential charges we faced. My attorney was an experienced criminal defense attorney named Bruce. As I explained earlier, Bruce ended up charging me $55,000 to represent me. This surpassed my net worth, eventually exhausting the majority of the home equity from the house my wife and I had sold in Florida prior to this mess. [Ultimately, when I was released from prison, Bruce forgave almost $20,000 of the debt I owed him. He knew I had a rough road ahead of me. This was a very gracious act on his part.]

Recall that the government charged the Captain with a felony, and offered Bob and me a misdemeanor plea bargain. My attorney thought the plea bargain was the way to go. As he explained to me, "The government would not offer you this plea bargain if they felt they had a strong case against you." However, he left it up to me to make the decision about going forward with a trial.

For a time I had leaned toward the plea bargain—especially since my hope was that it would save me the large legal fee he was about to charge me. But when I learned the fee was hard and fast regardless of whether I went to trial, I decided to fight the charge. My wife and I were quickly running out of our money. My ignorance of the magnitude of the difference between a felony conviction and a misdemeanor conviction didn't help in the matter.

At the time, I figured I was paying out the nose for a full-blown trial, and the government's case against me was weak, so why not put the money toward trying to get my name cleared of the criminal conviction I dreaded so much?

Bob's earlier words rang in my head: "You know, the best thing that you and I have going for us is that you told the FAA safety inspector before the flight left that you wanted to be blood-alcohol tested." He made a very convincing point. Would a jury really convict a pilot who had tried to not be on the plane in the first place?

Bob also said, "The government is going to try to make us look like the Captain's merry little men." I knew nothing could be further from the truth. We were anything *but* that Captain's merry men. Being with him had been a miserable experience, and my hope was that all of these facts would come out in the trial. We desperately needed to separate ourselves from the Captain.

After deciding to move forward with a trial, all three of us met in Minneapolis with the attorneys. My heart sank when I realized that the negative dynamics of the crew and the abusiveness of the Captain were not going to be a part of the story presented to the jury. I never learned why; the attorneys made this decision. But it meant that the Captain's abusiveness never made it into the record; instead, he was portrayed as merely a strict taskmaster.

In addition, the government waited until I committed to going to trial before it decided to not give us separate trials. I really didn't like that idea; I didn't want to be in the same courtroom as the Captain. So the trial had not even begun, and already I was wondering if this would be the beginning of the end for me.

My wife was also very upset about the way the pre-trial dynamics were shaping up. It appeared to us that everything was being set up to the Captain's advantage. For example, the Captain's attorney made a motion to the Judge to have the jury instructions changed. The law was written such that a person had to have a blood-alcohol level (BAC) of .10 or greater to be considered under the influence of alcohol. With this presumption in place, it would mean an automatic conviction for the Captain, because his BAC had been very high (reported as high as .18 and as low as .12 and .15), much higher than the government would need to convict him. The Captain's attorney's motion was to have the .10 assumption deleted from the jury instructions. This meant the Captain's BAC could be *above* the legal limit (which it was), and he still could get off! The removal of this .10 requirement for guilt left the legal door wide open against Bob and me, who could now be convicted with a BAC *below* .10. This made the government's case against us infinitely easier, because our BACs were below the .10 level. In other words, the jury would not have a benchmark to determine whether Bob and I were under the influence. The government no longer had to prove a BAC above .10, which left the jury free to decide we were under the influence with *any* alcohol in our systems. The change left me stone-cold with fear.

"Can we go ahead and take the misdemeanor plea bargain?" I asked my attorney.

"It's too late to get out of the trial, Joe," he answered with a shake of the head. That was hard for me to grasp, because the trial date was still several weeks away.

It was at this point that we learned for certain that the government was not going to allow separate trials. I dreaded the idea of being tried with the Captain.

A few weeks earlier I had traveled back to Minneapolis for the motion hearing in front of a Federal judge. When I arrived at the Federal courthouse I was handcuffed for the first time in my life. The sense of humiliation took over my emotions. I sat in the courtroom, cuffed and embarrassed, listening to the testimony of some of the witnesses the government would be calling to testify against us in the trial. The government witnesses could not get their stories straight, and much of their testimony was contradictory.

It quickly became obvious that the prosecutor wanted it to appear as though all three pilots had bloodshot eyes, when in fact only the Captain's eyes were red. The FAA Safety Inspector's reports as to our physical condition didn't agree with the testimony, and he had come face to face with all three pilots that morning.

"How far away from these pilots were you standing when you noticed that all three of them had bloodshot eyes?" the judge asked the FAA Safety Inspector who met the flight in Minneapolis.

The FAA inspector replied, "I was standing thirty feet away."

When the judge heard him say that, he almost fell off the bench! (Unfortunately for me, this judge was not our trial judge.) He caught himself with his arm and rested his head on his open palm for a full minute. He could not believe what he had just heard. Our attorneys sat there and shook their heads in disgust. It was obvious to everyone that this man was not telling the truth. But he would get away with it during the trial.

My biggest fear was that this deliberate changing of the facts to suit the prosecution was just the beginning of what we could expect in Federal court.

After the hearing, I told my attorney Bruce that I wanted to have a meeting with the trial judge and tell him about my struggle with alcohol, and that I was already doing something about it by getting into a recovery group. I wanted the judge to know what I had learned about myself, and that I was taking positive action.

"This is not the time to get on a soap box and talk to the judge," he answered with a shake of the head. "Besides, it's not allowed."

I didn't understand what harm it would do, nor did I grasp how the court system worked. I sank deeper in despair. The train was moving too fast to jump off.

When the trial began, the Federal judge who handled the case ordered our attorneys to stay away from the news media. But every day after court the prosecutor held a meeting with the media and presented the government's side of the case. Friends and family members were even more astounded by the unfairness of the judge's actions in the courtroom itself.

The police officers who had escorted us to the hospital the morning after the flight were called to testify. One of them had said to me in the hospital, "I can't believe that someone would call in a prank like this on a flight crew. You guys look fine to me." During the trial this same officer told the jury something different: that he believed we were under the influence of alcohol that morning. I could not believe my ears. I scribbled a note to my attorney about the officer's comments in the hospital, and slid it across the table.

My attorney leaned over and whispered, "Police officers lie all the time on the stand." I couldn't believe what I was hearing; I felt as if I'd been gut-punched. The deck was clearly stacked against us.

At lunch that day I shared my disappointment with my family and attorney. The growing consensus was that the prosecution was going to do anything, at any cost, to win this trial. I wanted to hang on to some glimmer of hope, but each passing hour made that more difficult. Watching my family struggle through the trial was excruciatingly painful.

The only hard evidence the prosecution had—the blood taken from us at the hospital—had "disappeared;" apparently, it had been destroyed in their lab. So the government didn't even have the blood that it was trying to use to convict us! But to the defense's dismay, the judge didn't seem to care.

Making matters worse, the first thing the jury members asked for when they were dismissed for deliberation was a calculator. They were going to use a procedure called retrograde extrapolation to "project" what "might" have been Bob's and my BACs at the time of the flight. Even though this is not allowed in Federal Court, they did it anyway—without admonition by the judge, and over the objections of my attorney.

I will never forget waiting over the weekend with my family for the jury to reach a verdict. The tension was indescribable. The media continued to pound away with sensational reports of three pilots flying an airliner stone drunk. Only the prosecutor's side of the case was being reported.

When the members of the jury didn't look at us as they filed back into the courtroom, I knew for certain we were doomed. The tension in the courtroom was heavy.

The first verdict was for the Captain: guilty. This came as no surprise to anyone. I sucked in a deep breath and exhaled slowly. There was still hope for Bob and me.

Bob's verdict was next. I held my breath as the jury foreman read the decision: guilty. I exhaled and closed my eyes tightly. When I opened them, I shot a glance at my family. We all knew the world would soon come crashing down on top of us with the certainty of the legal system behind it.

Now it was my turn. "In the matter of Joseph Balzer, we find the defendant . . . guilty as charged."

I looked at my wife, and then my dad and mom. Their bodies had gone limp, their eyes swollen with tears. My attorney's daughter, a sweet girl who had befriended me during the trial, cried loudly with deep sobs when the verdict was read.

Time stood still. For what felt like the longest time, everything in the courtroom seemed frozen in the moment. And then it hit me. *I am going to prison.* I sat there gasping for breath; I had not been breathing for quite a while.

The families of the other two pilots were as devastated as my own. Losing my wings, my career, my life savings, and my home equity was almost more than I could handle. Watching my wife and family suffer so much from my actions was unbearable.

What was it going to be like to go to prison? And for how long? What was it going to be like to live the rest of my life as a convicted felon?

More Bad News

A few days before Deborah and I went back to Minneapolis for my sentencing, I was standing in the living room of our apartment when Deborah returned from outside with the mail. In the stack was a letter from the judge who had presided over our trial. She opened the letter and a few seconds later screamed.

"What is he trying to do! Haven't we suffered enough already?"

"What is it?" I asked, grabbing the letter from her hands so I could read it myself.

The words swam before my eyes when I finally grasped their meaning. The judge was considering departing *upward* from the mandated sentencing guidelines. In other words, he wanted to give us longer sentences than first-time offenders. As my attorney would later explain, he might sentence us to as much as five years in prison.

I tried to console Deborah, but it was useless. I had never seen her in such a state. She wailed, cried, and otherwise expressed her anger for ten minutes before she would even come and sit next to me.

In all honesty, she had been a real trooper through all this ugliness. And what was her reward? Her unemployed, criminal husband was facing five years in Federal prison. Wave after wave of bad news had washed over us for months, and there seemed to be no end in sight. Why would a judge want to put us through so much? Even the judge's clerk thought something was amiss. "You guys are getting a raw deal," he confided to my wife over the telephone one afternoon. The uncertainty of it all overwhelmed us both as we prepared to fly back to Minneapolis for the sentencing hearing.

Sitting in the courtroom, we nervously waited for the judge to pronounce the sentences. The judge pontificated for several minutes about our crime. One thing he said I will never forget: "You are good men who have done a bad thing." But he also talked about how we had let down people who had trusted us. Today I agree with him absolutely.

Then something completely unexpected happened. The judge stopped talking, took a deep breath, and lowered his head until it rested upon his open hands. The courtroom was silent for several minutes waiting for the judge to do something, but he remained deep in thought. I was already feeling devastated, crushed like a bug on the windshield of life, with little fight left in me. My fate was in his hands as I helplessly awaited his decision.

The tragedy and sadness of it all overwhelmed me, and for a moment, perhaps, my heart turned to stone for its own protection. I was awaiting doom and a prison sentence which, as the judge had already expressed in a letter, might be much longer than I had thought possible. I feared the worst: that the judge would depart *upward* from the sentencing guidelines.

The waiting ended when the Judge finally raised his head. My body went numb. He sentenced the Captain first. "You will serve . . ."

The Captain thought he heard the judge say he was going to prison for *sixty* months, or five years. Hearing the news, the Captain's head dropped down and shook slowly from side to side. However, what the judge had really said was *sixteen* months in prison, and that is what I thought I heard.

Bob and I were next. The Judge sentenced us both to twelve months in prison.

I should have been ecstatic at that sentence, but the strangest feeling came over me. I was relieved not to be sentenced to five years, but was simultaneously devastated by the prospect of spending any time in prison at all.

My attorney urged me to appeal the sentence, which would give me another ten months or so before I would have to report to prison. Deborah and I really did not know which way to turn. My wife and I had struggled daily to cope with what our lives had become. Just six months before we had been on top of the world, getting ready to buy a new home and start a family. Now we faced insurmountable uncertainty, chaos, pain, and tremendous financial loss. The only way we could deal with it was by taking it one day at a time. In the end, I filed an appeal and we spent the ensuing weeks and months getting our affairs in order and getting right with ourselves.

The Captain, however, elected to go into prison right away. He was sent to the Atlanta Federal Prison Camp, which is right next door to the Atlanta Federal Penitentiary. The Camp has no fences or walls to keep the inmates inside during the day. Someone sent me a copy of a letter the Captain had written while in prison. In it, he mentioned how glad he was that he didn't have to go "behind the wall"—inmate slang for being inside the penitentiary. "The wall" was a massive thirty-foot structure surrounding the cell houses and grounds of the maximum-security prison. He was doing the best he could, and had gone to a thirty-day treatment facility for alcoholism prior to going to trial. I hoped—for him, but especially for his family—that it wasn't a ploy to get leniency, knowing what a miracle it is for anyone who suffers from alcoholism to get sober and stay sober.

I don't know Bob's exact feelings after the trial, but he asked his attorney to tell mine that he didn't want to have any contact whatsoever with me ever again. Hearing that honestly hurt me, but I honored his wishes and continue to do so. To this day I don't know how things have gone for him. I do know that he served his sentence in a minimum-security prison close to his family home, as did the Captain.

*   *   *

Bob, if you ever read this book, I want you to know a few things. I was not expecting to be cut off from you so suddenly. I know you are a good man and I have always deeply appreciated that you stuck up for me throughout our trip. I'm sorry I didn't have the courage to stand fast and refuse to let our plane leave Fargo that day. Certainly things would have turned out differently if I had. My prayer for you is that you are happy today and are doing well, in spite of all the difficulties you have had to endure. I hope you will find it in your heart to forgive me some day for my part in what happened to us.

Chapter 21

A Brief Reprieve

While out on bond during my appeal, I decided to pursue a Master's Degree. Mine was in Supervision and Administration, with a concentration in Aerospace Education; my thesis was on Cockpit Resource Management, studying effective leadership in the cockpit. (No surprise, right?) I enrolled in a program at Middle Tennessee State University, and worked my tail off to complete my degree in eleven months. It was a great diversion for me from the pain of the rest of my life.

During a summer aviation seminar, one of the guest speakers was a local airline pilot named Skip. He is a very intelligent and funny man, and his seminar was hilarious. I approached him after his talk and introduced myself.

"I know your name from somewhere," he replied.

"I was one of the pilots involved in the Fargo drinking incident."

"Excuse me? What did you say?" he asked, taken aback by my identity. I repeated what I had said.

It was a small world. Skip was a pilot for a major airline, and was also in charge of the Cockpit Resource Management department.

"We need to get together. Are you available for dinner?" he asked.

We talked through our time together. All he could say after I told him certain parts of my story were, "Good night!" or "Holy Cats!" He proceeded to become one of the best friends I have ever had, and he nurtured my soul by teaching me fly-fishing. Forgive me while I diverge for a couple pages and share a story with you. I think you will find it worthwhile.

Today, on my living room wall above the fireplace, hangs a mounted rainbow trout. It is a very special fish. Each time I look at it I recall the feeling that day when a man reached out to me and let me find that trout in my own way. On that hot August day when I was transformed into a fly fisherman, I also found, finally, some hope that there was something I might enjoy by continuing to live. My life then was overflowing with disappointments. My heart and soul needed the stimulation this man and his wonderful art—and, in its own way, this fish, in its glorious environment—had to offer me.

The Caney Fork River is a thing of beauty. It winds through the Tennessee countryside, over hill and dale. Its banks are lined with hardwood trees and an occasional steep cliff or deep cave. As spectacular as the scenery is, the fishing could be much improved. The Caney Fork is tail-water from a dam, and when the generation of electricity begins and the water flow increases, the insect population becomes doomed. I can't imagine what these trout must do to survive the onslaught of floodwater when millions of gallons of water rush downstream during a full electrical generation schedule. Yet they are amazing creatures: hardy enough to survive this deluge, but so delicate that any tiny bits of silt in their gills can suffocate them.

You won't see many people dry fly-fishing on the Caney, but when Skip Swift fishes, he *is* dry fly-fishing. The artistry of the purist comes naturally to this man who has dedicated so many years of his life to his art—one that he freely shares with individuals who show an interest in learning more.

I needed to catch a fish for selfish reasons. My life was in such a shambles. I needed this day in the country, in the stream, in order to touch something really important to me. And so I was determined to catch a fish that day. My fishing arsenal included worms, fresh corn, fresh salmon eggs, and an array of colorful and shiny Panther Martin and Mepps spinners. I was armed for bear.

As a light breeze blew through the trees, the arcs of Skip's rhythmic casting set against the background of Tennessee splendor was a sight to behold. He managed to entice four fish to rise to his fly and strike. I watched him play each fish, then carefully release it before it became too exhausted. On such a hot day, the fish on the end of the line could be stressed to death, a condition I could easily relate to in my own life. Skip is extremely fond of these fish, and they are in good hands. He is always careful not to handle them when he releases them, touching only the barbless hook as the fish wiggles free.

For my part, I spent more than two hours trying to catch a fish, casting spinners into deep pools, dropping worms into slow water, bouncing eggs along the bottom—all to no avail. The only thing that kept my frustration level down was watching Skip. He would take a calculated, stealthy approach to an area, he would make a pinpoint cast, his fly would gently land on the surface of the water—and a trout would come up and take it. He had offered earlier in the day to help me learn fly-fishing, but I was determined to do it my way—which, of course, was not working.

But something was about to happen that would change my life. I was standing in front of a narrow, ten-foot-wide chute of water near the bank. The water was running faster and whiter than the main body of the river. Skip walked over to me and said, "I'll bet there might be a fish in there; would you like to try him on this rod?" I looked down at his beautiful, hand-crafted, split-cane bamboo fly rod, soft yet very strong.

A few short casts of the fly into the air, and I laid the fly right at the head of the pool. The fly drifted rapidly on top of the foam. As it passed about a third of the way down the run, I thought I saw a huge fish rise in the fast water but miss the fly. I yelled, "Skip, did you see that?!" He had seen something, but thought it might be a stick.

"Go get 'im, Joe!" he said. "Cast it in there again."

I had never caught or raised a fish on a fly rod; but the second cast was as good as the first one, right at the head of the run. The fly drifted along just past the spot where the "phantom" had appeared earlier. Slowly, rising out of the depths, I spotted a huge rainbow trout. It was turned around, drifting with the current as it watched my fly slip downstream.

"Whoooa! Baby! Whoooa! He is going to grab it, Skip. Skip! He's got it!" I screamed. I set the hook, being careful not to break the delicate tippit. All of this was very unfamiliar to me: the fly rod, the line, and the very idea of having a trout on the other end. But my years of lake-fishing experience and instinct kicked in. I let the fish run, and he took advantage of it. I was just hoping that he would not break the line. He did take almost all the line off the spool.

Skip excitedly hollered, "Do you have him, Joe?" Then, trying to be helpful, he asked, "Do you want me to take him for you?"

I waved him off. "I'll either land him or lose him on my own, Skip, but thanks."

"Wow! Wow! Joe! Gosh, Joe! What a fish! Careful!" Skip exclaimed.

I was laughing loudly at his reaction and the chain of events. Here were two grown men, laughing and tripping along in cold water, trying to keep up with a fish which was determined to escape, as it must have a time or two in its past.

After several minutes the trout finally stopped running, and so did we. Where he was holding now the river was thirty yards wide and two and a half feet deep in the middle. I decided to try to walk him in to the shoreline, into calmer water, so I could land him. Skip and I were walking and stumbling along as if we were joined at the hip. The fish lunged in one direction, then another, and Skip and I bumped heads several times as he did so.

"What a big fish, Joe!" Skip continued to say.

The fish was in warmer water now, and I was thinking he was exhausted. Still, he made a few more runs, one of which was way up the river. Then, he clearly was tired. I took him in my hands. In fact, it was as if we three stood there, Skip and me in thigh-high water, and all looked at each other. The fish gave me that opportunity to let him go.

"I wish we had a camera," said Skip. "Are you going to let him go?"

Skip loves trout, and never does anything to harm them. But he and I were only in the early stages of what would become a tremendous friendship. I don't know now if I had fully realized then how he felt whether my actions would have changed that day. But looking back, that trout was going to fill a hole in my life at that time. It would stop the hurricane-force winds ripping through my heart, if only for a short while.

So, I worked the fish to shore and quickly ended his life with a rock blow to the head. How this must have hurt Skip; the trout may have been the prettiest he had ever seen on the Caney. I'm sorry I made him a part of killing it.

However, I took that fish to a taxidermist whose artistry won him the championship in the state of Michigan. That fish is the only one I have ever mounted in my life. It represents to me a day in my life when a man was willing to share something with me that he truly loves with all of his heart, even if he did end up watching me kill it.

However, life does get complicated sometimes, and, as hard as this end was for him to witness, Skip knew there was a major void in my life, an indescribable helplessness and sadness. He knew I was a man whose life's dreams had been shattered, a man really struggling to make any sense of the world at all. He knew that sooner or later I was going to prison for something

I really hadn't wanted to do, but wasn't able to change; I had gone along and done it anyway.

That day on the Caney, the pain and the hopelessness vanished, if only for a short time. Skip and I laughed and talked like schoolboys as we drove back along the ridges, with the sun setting, the evening sky and stars dropping in, and the breeze cool on our wet clothes. It was a day I will never forget. Skip and I have become the best of friends. I cherish his counsel, wisdom, and compassion. He brings to our friendship the most wonderful things anyone can.

A Celebration of Joy on the Hard Road of Reality

One of the proudest days of my life was the day I received my Master's Degree. My wife, family, and friends experienced a myriad of contrasting emotions. I was supposed to enter prison on December 1, 1991, and would have missed my graduation if the Federal Judge who handled my case had not graciously allowed me to remain free for another two weeks so I could graduate with my class. I am grateful for his kind gesture.

On Saturday, December 12, 1991, I walked across the stage at Middle Tennessee State and received my Master's Degree with honors from the President of the university. More than forty people, all friends and family, stood and cheered for me as the President called my name to walk across the stage. Some of the people in the audience, along with many of my graduating classmates, were aware of my personal struggles; together they rejoiced with me. Their love made my heart soar. Afterward, everyone drove to our house for a celebration—and to say goodbye to me. One gift I will never forget was a beautiful hand-planed, split-cane, bamboo fly rod. It was one of Skip's favorite rods, but he wanted me to have it. I was deeply touched by his thoughtfulness, and the rod gave me something to look forward to on the other end of my prison sentence. We all had a wonderful time, but with each passing moment I could feel my impending incarceration drawing closer.

The next day I looked at my wife before we went to bed, realizing this would be the last time I could kiss her good night for a very long time. I really hated the idea of leaving my wife alone as I went away to prison. My heart was breaking, and I knew she was terrified about what might happen to me while I was incarcerated. She really didn't talk to me about her fear, but I know today that she was very scared and lonely during this difficult time.

We said our prayers together, cried together, and held each other as we both tried to go to sleep. But peace and sleep eluded us that night.

A Rare Gesture of Kindness

A week before I went to prison the U.S. Marshal's office in Minneapolis contacted me. I was directed to voluntarily surrender on December 14, 1991, to the prison at Maxwell Air Force Base, which was where I was supposed to serve my twelve months. Like paying taxes, however, my surrender was not really "voluntary." Do it or else, was the clear message the letter conveyed. I knew I was helpless in the situation; it was not exactly as if there were any choices on the table.

One nice thing a Marshal did was to warn me not to turn myself in to the local county jail in Nashville. "Avoid the jail system at all costs," he cautioned. "You will be much better off driving or flying down to Alabama and turning yourself in directly." It was great advice. I could have turned myself in on December 14 to the county jail. That would have begun my Federal sentence immediately; but if I had, it would have been up to the government to transport me down to Montgomery, Alabama, to the Federal prison there. There was no guarantee how long that would have taken, and it was not uncommon for Federal inmates to sit for weeks waiting for the move. County jails are not known for their hospitality or safety, so the advice made sense. My wife and I agreed I should heed this counsel.

Chapter 22

Turning Myself In

The morning after our virtually sleepless night we caught a flight from Nashville to Montgomery. We had three or four hours to spend together before my incarceration was to begin at noon. According to Federal authorities, I could bring my own tennis shoes, toothbrush, glasses, some recovery books, and my Bible. We prayed together, bought a few last-minute provisions for my prison stay, and engaged in the kind of small talk both of us knew was more to pass the time than anything else.

To kill some of that time, we decided to try to find the prison so we would know how to get there when it was time for me to turn myself in. The last thing I wanted was to be late. We arrived well before noon—well in advance of my turn-in time. Our plan was to make sure of the directions, then find a quiet place to really say our good-byes: to visit and talk with each other, to pray together—and for me to try to allay Deborah's fears.

I drove up to the gate, only to discover that the speaker system at the entry gate was broken. Unsure what to do, we decided to drive inside. Several inmates were sitting around, while a few others were raking leaves. But to us it was rather surreal, as if we had gone behind some invisible barrier, and were now hidden away from the real world. Deborah shot me a "I can't believe we're here" look. I couldn't believe it, either.

We climbed from the car and walked into what appeared to be a gymnasium. Inside, we found a friendly man, an inmate, who pointed me to the building where I was to turn myself in. I walked inside and introduced myself to the man behind the counter.

"I'm here early to make sure I could find the place." The man nodded in reply. "I'll come back in an hour," I continued. "My wife and I are going to a local park to say good-bye."

"That's fine," he answered. "See you then." By the look on his face, it was obvious he had heard these same words more times than he could remember.

We were walking back to our car in the parking lot when a uniformed female ran down the sidewalk toward us. She lifted her arm and pointed a finger at Deborah. "You're not supposed to be here!" she yelled. "You're going to have to leave right now!"

The unexpected verbal barrage caught us both by surprise. Deborah nodded that she understood and began to speak, but the female guard cut her off. "Leave the parking lot immediately!"

Deborah took a few steps backward. "We're here to find out where my husband needs to turn himself in," she began again, as the guard glared at her. "We're early, so we were just going to say our goodbyes at a local park."

"Did you hear me?" the guard shot back. "I am going to arrest you if you do not leave right now!" The guard turned her fire in my direction. "Step away from your wife!"

Deborah burst into tears as she climbed into the car. I was frozen in place, unable to act as I watched through my own tears as my wife drove away. By this time Deborah was crying hysterically. All I could imagine was her driving alone back to Nashville, all the while thinking of me being in a place where the people in charge are out of control.

Welcome to Federal prison.

Are You Serious?

Even though I was two hours early, the guard inside told me I was not allowed to leave the facility. I later learned that was a lie, but you discover quickly that some prison personnel lie to you all of the time, and if you go along with what they say, they will take tremendous advantage of you every chance they get. The guard who had just lied to me ordered me to take a place in the holding cell until he could get to me. I did as I was told.

I was early, my wife was gone without a good-bye, and I was devastated.

The holding cell was at the far end of the entry room. It was the only cell in the entire place. The sound of the bars closing is one I will never forget. I spent the next few hours sitting on a wooden bench, watching other soon-to-be inmates enter the same door I had. The difference was that they were processed into the system. The entry guard went through their personal property, inventoried it, and returned it to them so they could take it into the prison with them. He also gave the men jump suits and assigned them to their living quarters.

By this time I was completely confused. I finally got the admission guard's attention. "How come I'm not being admitted into the prison like everyone else?" I asked.

"This is an Air Force base," he replied. "You're a pilot, so you're not allowed to stay."

"What? Why?"

"The warden doesn't want you here. He told me, 'This Balzer guy might steal one of the Air Force's planes and fly away!' That's what he said."

My jaw fell open. Why would a guy like me ever want to steal an airplane and ruin the rest of my life? The stupidity of that way of thinking left me dumbfounded.

"So . . . where I am going to stay?" I asked.

"Marion, Illinois."

The words hit me like a ton of bricks. *Marion, Illinois! That was far away from my wife and my family. They will rarely if ever be able to see me.*

"Someone from the Montgomery City jail is coming to transport you to their jail until the Federal transporters can take you to the Atlanta Federal penitentiary."

"WHAT?" I shot back. "You're going to send me to the *penitentiary*?"

"That's what I said." He smiled, clearly enjoying the agony this was causing me. "And you're going to have to stay there at least six months because it's the holidays, and things are going to be slowing down for a long while as far as transporting prisoners goes." With that, he turned away and greeted another arriving inmate.

When I asked the guard about my personal property, he shot back in a mean voice, "I'm giving it to the Salvation Army."

I love giving things to the Salvation Army, but at that time I felt I really needed to have my underwear, socks, toothbrush, Bible, and recovery books— not to mention my address book with all the numbers inside for my family, friends and support group. I even had a new pair of tennis shoes with me because I was told by another pilot doing time for income tax evasion that you could bring in one pair of shoes. "Make sure to bring your own," he had warned me, "because the shoes they issue you in there are really bad." He wasn't kidding.

Three hours after I turned myself in I was led to a van that took me to the Montgomery City jail. I had never seen the inside of a jail before. I left Maxwell, a minimum-security prison, labeled a "dangerous" man, a potential airplane thief. Now I was heading into unknown territory at the city jail in Montgomery. What troubled me most was that not a single person in my family knew where I was, or where they were going to send me.

Chapter 23

Wrong Turn?

W hen I originally turned myself in, I was mentally prepared to stay
at the Maxwell Federal minimum security prison camp. There
were no bars there, no fences, no visible guns, not even guard towers. The
inmates were mostly white-collar criminals or, to put it another way, the
non-violent variety of felons. I vividly recalled the fellow at the U.S.
Marshal's Office in Minneapolis telling me, "Whatever you do, don't turn
yourself in to a county jail." Jails, he continued, were very different from the
minimum-security prisons. "Avoid the jail system at all costs." And so my
wife and I had flown down to Maxwell expecting to find the minimum
security prison so I could turn myself in and avoid the hard-core jail
experience. Obviously, things weren't unfolding as we had intended.

I was on a path to experiencing the entire system the Federal Bureau of
Prisons had to offer, including what's referred to as "doing hard time." Of
course, at that time I didn't know that. If I had, who knows what scenarios
my mind would have conjured up. Knowing preparation is the key to
success, I had taken the opportunity to speak on the phone with several
professional criminals and inmates before I turned myself in. One fellow had
been a criminal all his life. He provided me the crash course on prison and
jail survival—nearly seven decades of jailhouse wisdom. I had done
everything I could to soak it up and assimilate it into my psyche.

So there I was, Mr. Former Northwest Airlines pilot, climbing out of a
van at the Montgomery City jail. Anyone who has been to jail and is used to
it would not have been affected by any of this. But I was recalling the rest of
what that Marshal in Minneapolis had told me. My thoughts reverberated in

my mind: "Each time another row of bars or steel doors locks behind you, you are being paraded deeper and deeper into the system."

Naked in the Laundry Room

The first thing I noticed was that most of the guards were behind some kind of thick, bullet-proof glass or bars—for their protection. This definitely was *not* a minimum-security facility! In fact, I could not help but conjure up images of prisons in the 1920s. It was as if I had stepped back in time or was playing a movie role. Except this was real, and I was playing myself.

After they had me behind several layers of "security," the guards took me into the jail's laundry room, where I changed into a jumpsuit with no underwear. By now I really had to urinate; the guard at Maxwell had refused to let me use the restroom before I left. The person guarding me told me to pee down the hole where the washing machine hose was draining.

"Where's your property?" asked the guard at the entry clothes checkpoint.

"It was confiscated at Maxwell. I don't have any property to check in."

Later, when I asked the warden of the jail where my property was, he said the jail didn't have it, and the people at the Maxwell prison apparently didn't have it, either. I didn't see any of my property for many months. Deborah had to make countless frustrating phone calls and write a dozen letters before anything was done about finding and returning my belongings to me. When the Federal government finally moved, it sent my personal property to our house—two months after it was seized from me. Deborah then had to begin the entire process over again to have it all returned to me in the new prison, which turned out to be next to impossible.

Once in my jumpsuit, they walked me through several sections of the jail. This place had brick walls and large cages built to hold twenty or so inmates at a time. The jailkeepers were cleaning the inside of the jail with a big hose by simply shooting water on the floor and letting it drain out. The place was sopping wet, the floor was slippery, and the air was foul.

Cell Hell

I was shocked to see where they were going to put me. The cell was very wide, about twenty-five feet, but it was only about twelve feet deep. Inside, twenty-five metal bunks were crammed into this small area. Occupying them were twenty men. I was number twenty-one. There was a single metal toilet without a lid at the front of the cell. Everyone used the same toilet. Every inmate was black except for me, an old fellow named Jack, and a mean-looking perpetual convict named Ronnie.

Ronnie was huge and scary. He probably tipped the scale at 245 pounds, and some of his teeth were filed to a point. I found out he was dong a long sentence in jail because he had put seven people in the hospital, some with serious injuries. He never said anything to anyone. He grunted or sometimes growled—literally—more than he spoke. A few times I made the mistake of catching his eye. When that happened he would issue a wild grunt or groan. I made a point not to bother Ronnie.

My First Friend in Jail

I had to walk past all the other inmates to reach my bunk, which was on the far side of the long jail cell. Thankfully, most of the inmates were asleep. In fact, the only ones awake enough to know there was a new kid on the block were Jack and Ronnie. Jack greeted me with a handshake and a semi-toothless grin. "Welcome to this giant shit hole."

Jack was a career criminal who had been in and out of jail his whole life. This time he was in for growing pot plants on his farm. Jack was a mess. He was white as a ghost from a lack of sunshine, and his fingernails were falling out. When I asked him why, he explained he had not seen any real sunlight or had any rest and relaxation for more than six months, which I later found out was against federal law. He was giving the warden a hard time by writing lots of letters.

"I'm supposed to be doing my time in Federal prison," he explained. "They were supposed to transfer me there." When I heard those words, my heart sank.

"Listen, you said your name was Joe, right?" He lowered his voice and whispered, "You look really scared. Never look scared. Never. If you do, the other inmates will take advantage of your fear and treat you pretty rough." He paused before adding, "Know what I mean?" I swallowed and nodded my head. I knew what he meant.

Over the next few days, Jack taught me how to play chess and how to be a good inmate, minding my own business and not complaining to any of the other inmates about anything. He also told me that an inmate had hanged himself in that cell the previous week. All of us had been locked up for a wide variety of reasons; however, most of these men had violent backgrounds and showed their anger routinely. Only a few were passive. All of these men were poor, and had some sad stories to tell.

Old Man in the Hole

There was a punishment cell, what the inmates and guards called the "hole," in the Montgomery City jail. When I arrived an elderly man in his seventies was in there, sleeping on the hard, concrete floor. His bed consisted of a few filthy towels. The small cell had steel walls and a thick steel door. The door had a small space about two inches tall at the bottom. Jack bought candy bars and shoved them under the door so the man inside would have a treat. It was the first time I directly observed inmates taking care of one another. I was under the impression that this old man was suffering from some kind of mental illness.

Most of the inmates, however, were like vampires. They slept during the day, then smoked, played cards, and raised hell all night. It was very difficult to get any sleep. I prayed all the time for God to give me the ability to sleep in this chaotic environment, the strength to persevere, and the good sense to always do the right thing.

Drive-by Shooting

In a short time I got to know every inmate in our cell by his preferred name, be it his first, last, or something made up. It turned out that many of these prisoners had a decent sense of humor and a very carefree attitude about life in general. Most of them had experienced traumatic lives and didn't have any education. One of the young inmates, a fellow in his late teens, had large scars on his arms and legs. One day I asked him about them. His story floored me. When he was a little boy playing on the street with his friends, someone he didn't know drove by in a car, rolled down his window, and shot him. I can't begin to describe the look on his face as he told me that story. I'd never met anyone before who was the victim of a drive-by shooting.

Another fellow named Otis was in jail for nine weeks for not paying his alimony. He had a very odd sense of humor that sort of got to you after a while. He did all sorts of crazy things. One day he passed gas and uttered, "The great toothless wonder has spoken!"

Two other people were in the cell awaiting trial for bank robbery. They had been certain that was the best way to get a lot of money at once. Instead, it was going to get them a long, long prison stretch.

"How long is your sentence?" one of them asked me one morning.

"One year," I replied.

"What? One year? Maaaaaaaaaaaan . . . I could do that standing on my head!" he answered, before he and his friend began to laugh long and loud at my expense.

Bored out of our minds, one day I decided to start teaching several of the inmates how to play drum rhythms with their hands. They really enjoyed it, and so did I. By the time I left that jail, they were all giving me high fives and calling me by my first name.

Chapter 24

Heavy Metal

Not long after I arrived in Montgomery, the jail officials told me that I would be spending at least six months there. The news left me depressed for days. So it was a total surprise when Federal prison transport guards showed up unexpectedly a few days later to take me away. (As I was quickly learning, prison was always full of surprises.) That afternoon I was being escorted back to the laundry room. A man was waiting for me there who described himself as a Federal agent responsible for transporting prisoners. "I am here to take you to the Atlanta Federal Penitentiary," he intoned dryly.

During his body search he discovered a new little address book I had made in jail. The address book they had stolen from me at Maxwell had been all I had, so I started making a new one. And I was not about to give it up; I snatched it back. "You are not allowed to take my personal property," I said emphatically—something I never would have done a few weeks earlier. If I had let him, he would have taken anything and everything. Many of the guards, like many of the prisoners, will take complete advantage of people who do not know their rights. I was learning quickly how to survive in prison. Inmates who do not are run over by abusive guards, staff, and fellow inmates.

After the search, I was led into another room where I was shocked to see a man holding chains and shackles. While one man guarded me with a sawed-off 12-gauge shotgun, another put shackles around my wrists and ankles and around my waist. Thick chains were connected to all of the shackles. I was bound like an animal. "Start walking down the stairs," ordered one of the guards, tilting his head toward a flight of stairs. When I got down into the secured parking lot behind the jail, two more guys were waiting for me with sawed-off shotguns. Talk about overkill! I stood there for a second, happy just to be outside. Ten feet in front of me was a Greyhound-size bus. "Get into the bus," barked another guard.

I was about to climb on when Jack hobbled out of jail behind me. I breathed a sigh, happy he was finally getting a ride to the Federal pen. Three other inmates were already in the bus, being transported from other maximum-security facilities to the Atlanta Penitentiary.

I had never seen a prison bus before. It was yet another unique experience that my other co-defendant pilots would never share. The driver was in a cage all his own. The only way into the driver's compartment was from the outside of the bus. Another guard sat in a separate cage at the front of the bus next to the driver's, with his shotgun at the ready. A third guard sat at the rear of the bus in his own cage. He, too, carried a shotgun.

Looks Like We're Going to Die

I found out later that these guys drive for hours and hours straight so they can make enormous amounts of money collecting overtime. The downside is that it compromises safety because they are very tired much of the time. We had been on the road about an hour when I noticed the man behind the wheel seemed to be having trouble focusing on the road. I was sitting close to the front, so I could see his eyes in the rearview mirror. My attention was divided between a couple of bank robbers on board the bus who were bragging about having kicked some guards' asses at their last prison, and the fatigued driver who had my life in his hands. The bank robbers were also talking about the riots in the Atlanta prison where these guards and drivers were taking us.

I couldn't believe how fast we were traveling. This Greyhound was flying along at 80 m.p.h., weaving in and out of other traffic on the road. A veteran inmate told me that these guys drive like this all the time, and the Highway Patrol lets them get away with it.

Speed wasn't the only thing bothering me. The bus was beginning to weave along the road, causing my chained body to sway to and fro in my seat. Every few seconds the bus would cross the outer lines bordering the highway and run onto the shoulder of the expressway, bumping along for a few moments until the driver jerked the bus back onto the pavement. I looked in the driver's mirror and noticed his eyes slowly closing before snapping open with a start. This guy was falling asleep! A minute or two later his head went down and stayed down.

At the top of my lungs, I yelled, "Hey, the driver is going to sleep!"

Suddenly, the bus swerved off the road doing more than 80 mph, bumping along the shoulder again. Thank God for the shoulder!

"The driver is asleep!" I screamed a second time.

This time my screaming caught the attention of the number-two man at the front of the bus, sitting next to the driver. But he was in his own little cage, unable to reach through to grab the wheel; he was nearly as helpless as the rest of us.

With his eyes wide open, the caged front guard yelled at the driver, "Hey! Hey! Wake up, wake up!"

The driver abruptly snapped awake and jerked the wheel to the left, correcting the bus' trajectory toward the ditch at the last possible second.

"Pull over so one of us can drive!" the guard yelled. He was obviously worked up over the whole affair, as afraid as we were. The startled driver pulled the bus over and slowed to a stop. The fellow in the rear cage got out and walked to the front of the bus to drive. He must have been fairly well rested, because the rest of the drive was uneventful from an emotional standpoint . . .

. . . until we crested a hill and I laid my eyes on the Atlanta Federal Penitentiary for the first time.

Chapter 25

The Big House

The sun was just beginning to set in the west when I spotted the ominous, large, cold, dark, granite building. My heart sank faster than the sun. On cue, bright lights snapped on, illuminating the interior. Before me was a massive stone complex surrounded with razor wire and an impassable thirty-foot-high wall, with a machine gun guard tower in front.

My mind flashed back to a time when I was an Eastern Airlines pilot. I remembered flying over this prison when Castro's prisoners, the mob of criminals he let out during the Mariel Boatlift in the early 1980s, set the place on fire. The smoke, flames, and riots went on for several days until the guards, in an armed intervention, regained control of the prison. Someone told me that several thousand of these men were still in this prison. Many of these inmates were serving long sentences for violent crimes such as rape, murder, and armed robbery.

If I had ever had any doubts, I knew then and there the Atlanta penitentiary experience was going to test me to my utmost limits. This was no lightweight, minimum-security camp or two-bit county jail. The guards in this place were ready to use lethal force at the drop of a hat, the inmates were among the worst in the world, and I was going to be dropped in the middle of them.

By the time the shotgun guards were in place, it was dark. As the other inmates shuffled off the bus, I kept staring at the machine gun tower guarding the front of the prison. I hoped and prayed that none of these inmates would do anything to incite the guard in the tower to open fire on us. After all, some of these guys had been talking crazy all the way from

Montgomery, and one of them was an absolute nutcase. Was he going to get me killed?

I was the last one to get off the bus and was trailing way behind the other inmates because I just didn't have any expertise in walking while chained and shackled. It was very cold (in the low twenties), and I was still naked under my jumpsuit because the guard at the Maxwell minimum-security prison had taken all of my personal property from me except for my address book.

The other inmates pulled way out in front of me, about twenty feet or so. The guard in the rear said, "Man, you've never done this before, have you?"

"No," I said, "this is the first time in my life that I've ever tried to walk anywhere chained up like this." I was just quietly asking God to give me strength, and to guide me through this ordeal one moment at a time.

As we approached the thirty-foot walls from the outside of the prison, he asked me, "What are they putting you in here for?"

"I'm one of the airline pilots who flew a commercial airliner under the influence of alcohol."

He looked at me in disbelief. "Are you joking? They don't lock people up in here for that, do they?"

"Well, maybe I am the first one to go 'behind the wall,'" I replied.

I will never forget what he said next. "Man," he said shaking his head, "you are really in the wrong place."

After passing in front of the prison into the darkness, I followed the other inmates down a stairway that led to an underground chamber. A thick, steel door slammed and locked behind me. We hobbled into another area with more doors made out of thick bars. People in here were meant to stay, and would never have the opportunity to just walk away. I continued to lean heavily on God. I prayed, asking for His peace and protection from evil. I had a feeling there was plenty of that inside.

Searching the Dangerous Pilot Inmate

"Remove all of your clothes."

In my case, that wasn't demanding much. The basement entry to the prison was cold, and shivering while standing there naked with other prisoners—with whom I otherwise had absolutely nothing in common—only added to the humiliation that followed. We had to remove our clothes so

Me as a baby (left), with my brother Jim and sister Brenda (below) in 1956. All four Balzer kids pose in 1961 (bottom), with Brenda holding Barbie, the latest arrival.

Grandpa Balzer and me on my seventh birthday (top). We celebrated at the French River in Sudbury, Canada. That same year I enjoyed my first airplane ride. Here I am standing next to a classic Ford Tri-Motor in 1962 (above) in Sandusky, Ohio. We ended up flying in a Cessna 206 because the Tri-Motor had mechanical problems.

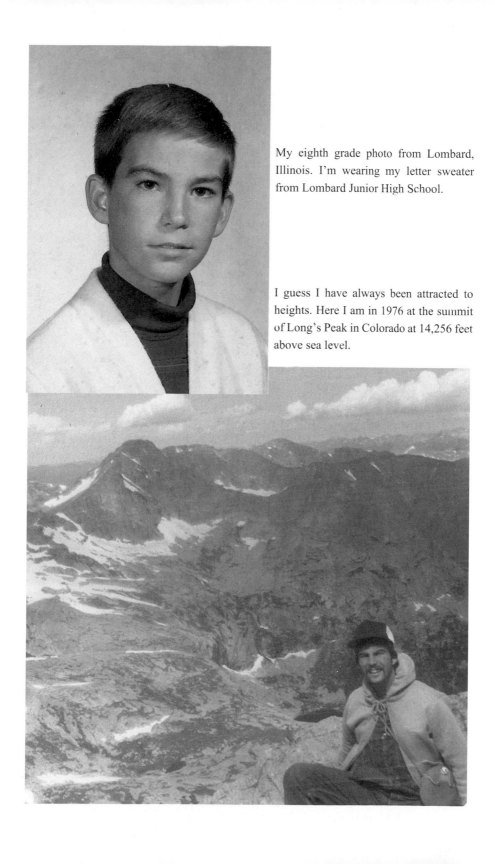

My eighth grade photo from Lombard, Illinois. I'm wearing my letter sweater from Lombard Junior High School.

I guess I have always been attracted to heights. Here I am in 1976 at the summit of Long's Peak in Colorado at 14,256 feet above sea level.

Standing next to a Convair 340 airplane, which I flew in the Bahamas when I was 25 years old. Look at the giant R 2800 engine!

Inside the Convair 340 cockpit (above). Just two years later I was flying a Learjet for Harvey Hop (below), a big jump up from my exciting prop days over the Bahamas.

Music has always been an important part of my life. Here I am as a Cavalier snare drummer in 1975 (right), one year after winning the AYOP National Rudimental Snare Drum Solo Championship. A few years later, I was having fun playing percussion in the play "It's a Wonderful Life" (below), at the Majestic Theater, Dallas, Texas.

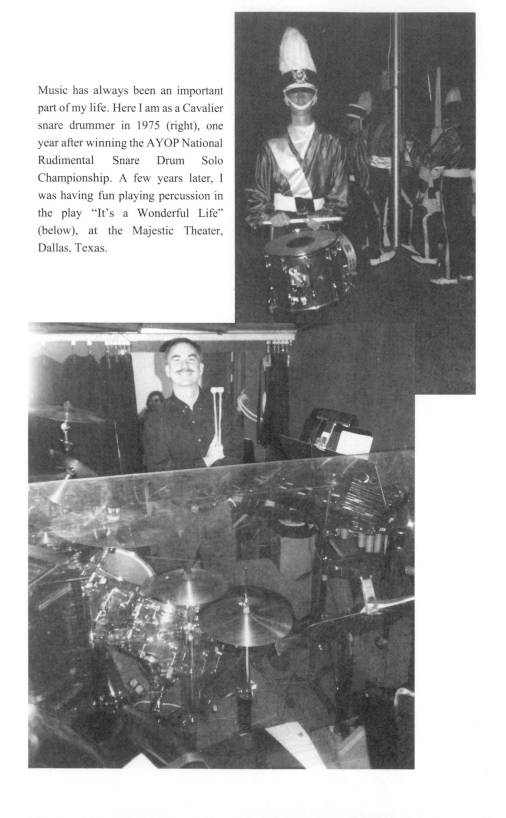

One of the proudest days in my life was when I was hired by a major airline. Here I am in Florida (above), a happy new hire with Eastern Airlines in 1985. My dad was always proud of my achievements as a pilot. We celebrated together (below) by raising our beers into the air at a party my family threw for me and my classmates.

"Taking them alive!" My dad, Bob Balzer, and me hunting alligators in the Everglades in 1985. I am pointing at the duct tape I put on the live gator's mouth.

I've always loved fishing. Here, my nephew Tim and I were fishing for Steelhead trout on the Pere Marquette River in Michigan in early March 1990, just three days before my life fell apart. The temperature was cold, but the fishing was hot!

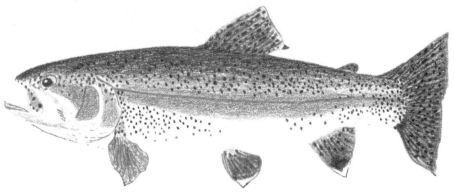

Just before going to prison in the fall of 1990 I caught this rainbow trout (top) on the
Caney Fork River in Tennessee using a handmade, hand-planed, split cane bamboo fly
rod. This is the rainbow trout I drew from memory (above) while in prison in 1991. My
drawing was eventually published in the *Art of Angling Journal*.

Finally, flying again! Here I am dressed in my uniform in front of the lovely dogwoods in Tennessee in 1995 (right), and inside the cockpit of a Corvair 600 at Kitty Hawk (below).

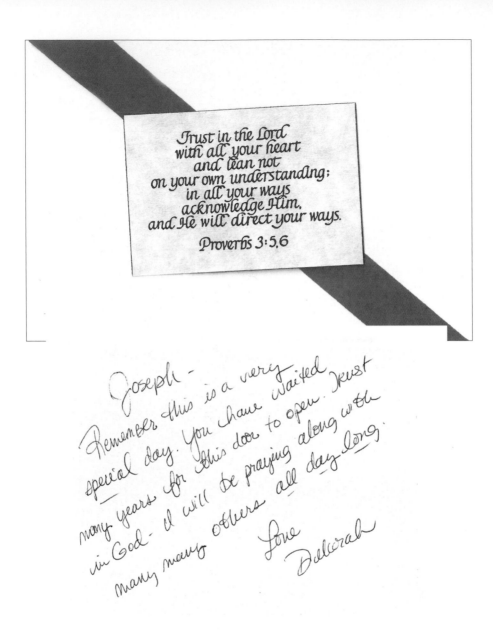

Trust in the Lord
with all your heart
and lean not
on your own understanding;
in all your ways
acknowledge Him,
and He will direct your ways.

Proverbs 3:5,6

Joseph -
Remember this is a very special day. You have waited many years for this door to open. Trust in God. I will be praying along with many many others all day long.

Love
Deborah

My wife Deborah gave me this card (top) on the day I interviewed with American Airlines, one of the most emotional experiences of my life. This was the note my wife wrote inside the card (above).

Hired by American Airlines. In the cockpit (top) of an MD-80 for my IOE (Initial Operating Experience), and with my check Captain Gary Luders (above), a real prince of a guy and one heck of a pilot.

Our first Christmas photo (top) as part of the American Airlines family, with Deborah, our son and daughter, and me at the C. R. Smith Museum in front of the DC-3 "The Spirit of Knoxville." My parents (above left), Bob and Rose Balzer, in 2000. My brother and best friend Jim (above right) in March 2007, catching crappie at Lake Fork, Texas.

Welcoming our newborn son (top) in 1997 with our 18-month-old daughter by my side. My family in 2000 (bottom) in Cades Cove, Great Smoky Mountains National Park.

Deborah and me at the Dallas Arboretum in 2005.

the guards could check our body cavities to see if we were trying to smuggle weapons or drugs into the prison.

Prisons (as I was soon to learn) are full of homemade weapons anyway, so the procedure is largely a waste of time. This is a place where a toothbrush can be converted into a lethal weapon by simply filing the end into a point. A jab in the right place will kill a man fairly quickly. The prison was full of killing experts. They knew what they were doing, with the capacity to inflict lethal damage quickly and quietly. So nobody was going to have a toothbrush stowed up his behind; he could get a toothbrush on the inside eventually through normal, more comfortable, channels.

As we were being checked, a guard named Maxie seemed to sense I was different from the rest. "What are you here for?" he asked me. "You don't fit the profile."

I didn't want to say I was supposed to be in a minimum-security camp, especially after inmates on the bus had been bragging about killing and beating guards in a prison riot. In a quiet voice, I told him why I was there.

He raised his eyebrows, then frowned. "You are in the wrong place, man," he replied, adding, "Let me know if I can do anything for you."

I appreciated the human gesture of kindness and understanding, but I never saw or heard from him again. I still don't know if he was just jacking with me or being sincere. What was a prison guard going to do for me? Talking to a guard is a fast way to lose favor with fellow inmates. I had learned that in the crash course on Prison Survival 101 I had gotten over the telephone. Jack had given me a mini-course, too. I was grateful for both. The rules were pretty simple: don't talk to anyone; don't accept any favors from anyone; if confronted, quickly defend yourself, or you will be preyed upon as a weakling for the rest of your time in prison.

In addition, as a "short timer" (which includes any person with a one-year sentence), many inmates serving much longer sentences resent you from Day One. It's all relative; trust me, one year is plenty long when you're the one doing the time. It seems like it will never end, but you find a way to just keep going. When writing these words some sixteen years later, it dawned on me that many of those guys with whom I had the unfortunate luck to rub shoulders in prison are still in there; a few who became friends behind bars just got out a few years ago. My prison buddies were missing everything that mattered in life, such as raising their children. The pain in their eyes when we talked about these things was clearly evident.

In this regard I especially remember an inmate named Conrad. On visiting day, his little boy would come into the front row of the chapel and watch his daddy and me sing together in the choir. He was two years old, and Conrad had another nine years of time ahead of him. Every time he talked about his son the tears would well up in his eyes.

My first journey into the bowels of the prison was emotionally overwhelming. I had never been inside a real prison before. They walked us from one set of steel bars, which went from floor to ceiling, to another set some distance down the hall. Each set had its own lock and door, which separated it from the previous corridor and secured each one we entered from the next. The sound of each steel door slamming shut behind me echoed down the long corridor as if mocking me. We passed through three or four of these before arriving at a large steel door on the side of the wall. When the guard opened it, the cacophony of voices yelling and jabbering on the inside blew past me like a wall of hot air.

The first thing that came to mind was that this looked like pictures I had seen of the inside of Alcatraz. I don't know if my mouth fell open as I gazed up at the rows of cells and railings lining each floor five stories high, but the shock was enough to nearly stop me in my tracks. The floor was so crowded with inmates that I could hardly get around without bumping into someone. The men were practically standing on top of each other. I'd heard about prison overcrowding, but the sights and sounds of so many dangerous men compressed into such a small space was overwhelming and beyond my imagination.

When my mind began to adjust to the new surroundings, I realized there was a small cage with a desk in it to the left of the entry door. This was where the cellhouse guard was stationed. The house guard checked me in and told me where my cell was.

"Can I get a light jacket or something to keep me warm?" I asked.

"We don't have any," he answered gruffly, without looking up. "You're on your own to find one. And your cell might not have a mattress to sleep on."

Jack from Montgomery City jail was standing next to me. I sort of stumbled around on his coattails; I followed his lead. I found my cell up on the third tier. The people running the prison had to put up steel mesh above the railings on each floor. The mesh ran all the way to the ceiling and served as a fence. When I asked Jack why, he explained that prisoners threw their enemies off the upper levels, hoping to kill them.

Jack, of course, was assigned to another cell. Inside my five-foot by nine-foot cell was another inmate. He was asleep, and I was not about to wake him up. I sat there on my steel bed without a mattress for what seemed like several hours. Finally, he stirred, stood up, stretched, and noticed a stranger in his bedroom.

"So, you're staying with me, huh?" he asked, in a not-unfriendly way.

"Yup," I answered as stoutly as I could muster. "This is where they stuck me."

Damian was a big guy, about six-foot-four, and had been a body builder on the outside. He would later tell me they locked him up for money laundering. He and his dad had been getting away with it for years before being caught.

"Where is your stuff?"

"They took it all away from me."

He shook his head and reached into a satchel, pulled out a thin jacket, and handed it to me. "Here, take this, it will help keep you warm." I thanked him, and breathed a sigh of relief as I slipped it on; maybe I had lucked out on my cellmate.

My prison cell had been designed in the late 1800s, with old, thick, steel bars and sliding, steel-bar doors, similar to the ones you see in movies and on television. Someone told me these cells were originally used for punishment because they were so small.

It was freezing cold in there because many of the glass windows at the very top of the building were broken. Cold winter air made life in the cells challenging, especially if you didn't have a coat or a hat, and I didn't have either one. Pigeons also found it easy to fly inside the building and crap on the inmates. It was an absolute pig sty. The noise level inside the cellblock was unbelievable. Turn up the volume on one hundred TV sets, each set on a different channel, and you will get an idea of what the inside of a prison block sounds like. There was no real quiet time, day or night. The inmates smoked and yelled, or at best talked loudly, during every second of daylight. When darkness descended and we were "locked down," the inmates on the cleaning crew turned on the TV set and blasted the volume so they could hear it all the way across the cellblock.

I sat back on my bed, thankful I now had the thin jacket, but finding it difficult to come to grips with what I was seeing and experiencing. "My God, what am I doing here?" I kept asking myself. This has to be a nightmare, and I will wake up any second. For a while I actually believed that. All I could think about was that the people who loved me didn't even know where I was. What if I am killed in here? That thought was never far from my mind. So I didn't smile; I didn't look at anyone; I didn't shave; I tried to look mean—and I minded my own business.

The house guards didn't seem to care that I didn't even have a mattress to sleep on. Someone else had taken the mattress, so it was up to me to find one, or sleep on a piece of cold steel. They didn't care about me being cold, either. No one cared about anything.

The third day I was in there, my cellmate Damian ran up the stairs to our cell on the third tier and whispered to me in an excited voice, "Come on, Joe, come with me! I have a bed for you, but we have to hurry before any of the guards see us!" He had noticed an open door on a storage closet on the first floor, and he wanted me to have a new mattress—but it was right under the guards' eyes.

I hesitated. "What am I getting myself into, here?" I wondered. "What if we get caught taking prison property?"

It was then that I realized the guard had been lying to me. They had extra beds all along, and my cellmate was trying to get me one. Together, we walked down the steps slowly, so as to not draw any attention to what we were up to. When we arrived at the storage room, I stood there and stared for a few seconds. Inside were dozens of brand-new mattresses stacked along the walls. Why didn't they just give me a mattress when I checked in? But nothing was easy here.

Damian grabbed a new mattress and passed it to me. "Hightail it up to the cell before the guards see what's going on."

The thin, floppy mattress was hard to handle, and I struggled to get it up the three flights of stairs and into our cell. My heart raced faster with every step I climbed. Would the guards see me with my loot? The mattress was wrapped inside a tough nylon bag that we couldn't open with our bare hands. By the time we had it inside the cell, the guards were beginning the evening inmate "count." Our time was limited. We used the razor blades on Damian's shaver to cut through the nylon and get the mattress out and onto my bed just seconds before the guards arrived outside our cell door.

Who knows what the penalty would have been if they had caught us.

Rumors Abound

Prison inmates invent and spread rumors even better than airline employees. Every one of them wants to tell you what is going to happen to you—especially if it is bad. Even the guards told me I was going to be stuck in the maximum-security system for six months before a transfer to the minimum-security prison camp in Atlanta. They all reaffirmed, "We don't transport people between prisons over the holidays." They also repeatedly told me they were sending me to a place called El Reno, which, according to the inmates, was a very bad place to end up. Actually, what the guards told me was that I *was* going to get to Marion, Illinois, but I had to pass through El Reno prison to get there. El Reno, every inmate told me, had a horrible reputation for poor living conditions, terrible treatment from the guards, and worse treatment from the inmates. It had the absolute worst reputation in the Federal maximum security system.

Several inmates said that if you piss off the wrong person, you'll get what they call "Diesel Therapy." The Bureau of Prisons puts inmates in buses, like the one I had been on, and transports them from prison to prison. According to the rumor, these inmates never get a break, and are forced to ride around in buses for weeks or even months on end. After my firsthand experience, the thought of riding around endlessly while chained and shackled, bouncing along the highway system, would constitute a form of slow torture.

Is Death Around the Corner?

One afternoon Damian and I went to see a film in the prison movie house. There were hundreds of inmates in the theater, because inmates will jump at any opportunity to get away from the cellblock. Without thinking about it beforehand, there I was sitting in the old theater, right in the middle of a mass of prisoners.

But right about then I remembered Jack telling me to try to stay away from crowds of inmates, because bad things often happen in packed places. And in fact, most of the violence I witnessed in prison took place in the middle of a crowd of inmates. I think the attackers do this intentionally because it is difficult for the guards to single out who the perpetrators are. Beatings, stabbings, and rapes happen all the time in prison, and they are largely hidden from the authorities. The question you ask yourself as a fellow inmate is not whether there are perpetrators, but just who the perpetrators are, so you can avoid them. The mysterious, and therefore stressful, part is: you never really know. On this particular day, in this crowd, was someone a target? Did someone have a shank (homemade knife) at the ready, waiting for the right moment to strike?

As it happened, the movie itself proved uneventful, and I breathed a sigh of relief as we exited the theater and walked down the stairs. Then, without so much as a shouted warning, someone stabbed a man with a homemade shank. Someone later told me it was a toothbrush filed down to a point on one end. One stab deep into the kidneys and you bleed to death before anyone can do anything to help you. I had never been in the midst of a man's death being delivered in such a cold, merciless fashion. It wakes you up in a hurry.

Naturally, I also witnessed untold numbers of fights. They erupted without warning and were usually brutal in nature. Some men died of their injuries from prison fights fought with just fists and feet. The vigilance required to survive in prison took a heavy toll on my psyche. Each night I prayed to God I would survive another day.

Dreaming of the Smoky Mountains

The constant stench of stale cigarette smoke, urine, and other bodily fluids made it difficult to breathe. There were no plants, flowers, or trees for enjoyment, no lakes or streams to dream of wading or fishing in. When I was in the prison exercise yard, all I could ever see were the clouds and sky. The wildlife consisted entirely of the pigeon population that lived in the rafters of the prison.

After praying at night, I imagined myself in the Smoky Mountains. I usually fell asleep dreaming about wading in a beautiful stream, fly-fishing for trout. I learned to tune out the noise inside the prison and replace it with the rushing, musical sound of flowing, ice-cold, mountain water. I imagined the fresh mountain air in my nostrils and a soft breeze on my face. The image of wildflowers growing along the stream calmed my soul, and the sun glistening on the water eventually put me to sleep.

A Dangerous Wait

On Christmas Eve I got to use the phone. In order to make that call, I had to stand for seven hours in a line of hundreds of inmates, many of whom had friends in line and worked a system so they could cut in and use the phone again. When I spotted one particularly large guy in the line behind me, I made him aware of the scam. He put a stop to it, and it was only afterward that I was able to move ahead in the line and eventually use the telephone.

My mail had yet to catch up to me in the prison system, because the Bureau of Prisons had already moved me twice in my first week of incarceration. Thus far, I hadn't had any contact with family or friends.

I knew my wife would be at her parents' house, suffering through a tearful Christmas Eve that night. I pictured them crying as they opened gifts in my absence, thinking I was still in the jail in downtown Montgomery. I couldn't bring myself to call them on Christmas Eve and tell them that I was in the penitentiary. I don't think I would have been able to keep myself together, frankly, and I didn't dare risk losing it in front of the other inmates. Instead I desperately needed to speak with someone in recovery, and since my sister had the experience and training of recovery under her belt, I called her.

"Hello?" she answered.

I was greatly relieved to hear Barbie's voice. That single word seemed like a giant calming hand placed upon my heart, a feeling that had been utterly foreign to me for a long time.

"Hi, Barbie," I replied.

"Joe? Is that you? How are you? Where are you?"

"I love you, Barbie," was all I could muster at first. I couldn't even truthfully tell her I was "okay," because there is nothing okay about being behind bars in a penitentiary. But I lied to her anyway. "I'm okay."

I was even more afraid to answer her other question. If I told her that I was in a real prison, "behind the wall," I knew it would cause alarm, especially to my wife and my mother when they found out. At the same time, I knew that I had to tell *someone* where I was. I hesitated, and then continued. "Look, they stuck me in the Atlanta Federal Penitentiary, but it's—."

"What!" she shouted into the phone. "You're where? What are you doing in there? I thought you were going to the prison camp at Maxwell Air Force Base?!"

I did my best to explain what had happened to me, even though it made no logical sense to my sister. Heck, it didn't even make sense to me. For the remainder of our short conversation I could hear in her voice her terrible concern for my safety.

What a pitiful set of events. Here I was on Christmas Eve, alone in this ugly prison. This would be my only opportunity for me to have any communication with any of my family members who loved me.

"Barbie, I need you to do me a favor. I need you to break the news as gently as possible to Deborah, mom, dad, and the rest of the family."

"Okay," she hesitantly replied. "How long are you going to be there?"

I explained that the guards told me it would be at least six months. I could get family members onto a visitation list; however…. "I'm a transferred inmate," I tried to explain. "It's going to take another six weeks or so before anyone will be allowed to visit me." The truth was I really didn't want anyone in my family to see me in this horrible place. It was just too scary, and it would give people in my family nothing but nightmares.

When I hung up the phone, my heart sank as I considered the tears and pain I had caused and would continue to cause my family. It was surely one of the saddest days of my life. Once my wife found out I was in this type of prison, her journey would be even more difficult and challenging. Knowing Deborah, her imagination would run wild because of the way she had been abused at the prison camp on the day I turned myself in. I really worried she might fall apart for a while when she heard the bad news.

A Precious Gift

During the count it was standard procedure for inmates to stand at the front of their cells to make it easy for the guards to see us. So just before lockdown that Christmas Eve, I was standing alone in our cell. (Damian, as one of the helper inmates, was elsewhere.) It had been a really gloomy day for me, and I was missing my family terribly.

But as we were waiting to be counted, I noticed something out of the ordinary: several large boxes being hauled into the common area below my cellblock. The boxes were large enough to hold a refrigerator. As the guards locked us into our cells, a few hand-selected "helper" inmates began opening the boxes. Inside were red and white plastic bags. As the guards walked by each cell, they handed each inmate through the bars one of the little red and white bags. Each bag had "Salvation Army" printed on one side, with "Merry Christmas" on the other.

I slowly opened mine and peered in. The first thing I saw was a wad of material. I reached in, and as I pulled it out it took on the wonderful shape of a wool hat. Wow! What a gift! Finally, something to keep my head warm in this icebox of a prison. Deeper in the bag was a pencil, a pencil sharpener, toothpaste and a toothbrush, spiritual literature, and a tiny address book.

Something happened to me that night. For the first time in my life I was on the receiving end of some much-needed charity and compassion from complete strangers. I reflected back on when my father had explained to me how important the Salvation Army had been to him during his childhood. I realized that now I was the one receiving these simple gifts. It really was all about kindness and caring.

Tears streamed down my cheeks as I went through the reading material, and for the first time in several days enjoyed the feeling of warmth about my head. These were truly wonderful gifts that touched my heart and helped to heal a troubled soul.

Real Snail Mail

Al Capone had once been in this prison, and I was told that he had special speakers installed so he could listen to ball games on the radio. He also bought some beautiful, brass mailboxes as a gift for the warden. One of them was still attached to the wall by the current warden's office.

It took weeks for my mail to catch up to me because it was addressed to the minimum-security camp at Maxwell. Finally, a letter reached me. It was a Christmas card from one of my former neighbors in Fort Lauderdale. Everyone encouraged me to hang in there and let me know that many people were praying for me. My spirits lifted when more of my mail began to catch up with me. This was the beginning of the support my soul received from hundreds of friends and family members. It would continue to fill my heart with joy for the duration of my stay in prison.

Saved by Jack

One afternoon I was standing in the crowded common area on the first floor in the middle of a large group of black and Hispanic inmates. Jack was on the third tier above me, and spotted trouble a few seconds before it erupted into the open. Just before the mini-riot broke out, he yelled, "Joe! Get out of there!"

I looked up at Jack and saw the urgency on his face. I had no idea why he was urging me to leave, but I knew enough not to question or hesitate. I scooted away from the middle of that group as fast as I cold—just in time. Within seconds, punches and kicks were being thrown, and men were falling down behind me. But I made it up the stairs and into my cell area unscathed, thanks to Jack and his watchful, experienced eye.

They were fighting over what channel the TV set was turned to. People actually get seriously beaten up in prison over stuff like that. Jack advised me, "Joe, stay clear of the TV set! It is always trouble there. Guys get hurt most often trying to change the TV channel!"

Drugs and Alcohol

I quickly discovered two things in prison: nearly every inmate was sick, and illegal drugs and alcohol were readily available behind bars. Everyone all had the same sinus infection and cough, and all the smoking in those close quarters only made matters worse. The physician's assistant who worked for the prison system constantly handed out antibiotics to sick inmates. Whatever germ was floating around eventually got me, too. And it was a bad one. It took me eight years to completely get over that sinus infection!

Ample supplies of drugs and alcohol made the rounds in the prison. The guards largely ignored it. They knew inmates were making their own hooch from fermented fruit smuggled out of the chow hall. The food in the pen was lousy. I lived on bread and fruit because I heard about some of the disgusting things some mentally sick inmates did to the cooked food. But I had to smuggle my fruit out of the chow hall because occasionally the guards cracked down on the hooch makers and tried to catch them at the door with their stashes.

Much later, when I finally made it to the Atlanta prison camp, I discovered that not all prison food was horrible. In fact, the food there was unbelievably good. I went out of my way to tell Mr. Johnson, the man who ran the cafeteria there, how much I appreciated him and his staff of inmates. They were like world-class chefs by comparison.

Chapter 26

Happy New Year!

On New Year's Eve I was sitting in the penitentiary chow hall wondering when, if ever, I was going to get out of this place. And would I get out in one piece? Over the past several days, I had noticed one particular inmate casing me out for something, and it made me very uncomfortable. As I was sitting there pondering my fate, a guard walked up to me and said, "You might be getting out really soon."

I looked up, a frown of obvious confusion plastered on my face. Was this just another guard lying to me? I had been told just the opposite by everyone else in a position of authority. "For real?"

"Yeah," he answered. "If there is anything in your cell you want to keep, I will give you a minute to run up and retrieve it, because I am ready to take you out of here right now."

The shock was so great I nearly fell off my seat, but I managed to stand up. "I would like to go back to my cell and get my address book."

"Ok, go get it. But keep the fact you are leaving to yourself."

He escorted me down the hallway past the Marielitos (former Cuban prisoners) inmates' cells. These men were disgusting, and often spat and threw feces at other inmates passing by. All I could think about at that moment was that I would never have to put up with that again. Once on the third tier I grabbed my things, including my coveted blue cotton hat (the one the Salvation Army had given me at Christmas to help survive the cold). Damian was not there, so I left him a quick note, thanked him for his help, and wished him the best.

I was about to look for Jack when he stepped out of his cell. We made eye contact. He had a strange smile on his face, and was obviously glad to see that I was getting out of this place. He winked at me, but never said a word. I felt deep gratitude for all the help and pointers he had given me. I hope my look communicated that to him.

The guard escorted me back through row after row of barred-off, secured corridors. I felt a bit more free each time we passed through another set of bars. Within a few minutes we passed through the final guard post inside the prison, walked beyond the bulletproof glass, and stepped out the large door at the front of the prison. I cannot begin to describe the feeling of relief I experienced when I walked away from that ominous granite structure into a beautiful sunny day. It was as if I had stepped out of a black and white nightmare into a world of wonderful color. I took a long, deep breath, letting the fresh air rush into my lungs. I was doubly elated because they didn't chain me up this time. I just climbed into a car and a guard drove me a short distance to the Atlanta prison camp, which was right next door to the penitentiary.

As we approached the camp, the first thing that struck me was that it was similar to the camp at Maxwell. There were no walls around it or guard towers or wire. Inmates were walking around from building to building, and there was an outdoor area with a baseball diamond and a track around it for jogging. Was some level of sanity about to re-enter my life?

After being admitted to the camp, I went for a walk on the track. It was very peaceful and quiet. I had forgotten what that sounded like. Walking in silence in the sunshine was a double treat. The change from the overcrowded and dangerous prison was palpable.

But I was too blown away to realize why there were no other inmates in sight. Without warning, two angry guards trotted up to me. "Who are you?" one yelled.

The sudden verbal assault set me back on my heels. "I'm Joe Balzer," I answered, as matter-of-factly as possible.

"What are you doing out here? You're late for count!" shouted the second guard.

Being late for count is not a good thing. In the penitentiary, inmates are counted at least twice a day, and are locked down in their cells when it happens. You can't miss count unless you have escaped, and, of course, I had no intention of escaping. When I had checked in at the prison camp, no one told me about a count that afternoon, so I was outside enjoying the fresh air—something I had not done in a long time.

The guards finally figured out that this was my first day in camp. "Wait, you're new here, right?"

"Yes," I replied with a vigorous nod of the head. "I just got here an hour ago."

Thankfully, they let me back into the lockdown dorm in front of all the other inmates standing at attention in their small cubicles, which were their minimum-security cells. The guards and the inmates thought my late arrival was funny.

A Nice Place to Rest my Head

When they first transported me to the camp I was assigned to a vacant cubicle—one picked clean by the other inmates: the mattress and blanket were substandard, and there was no pillow. As inmates everywhere do, they had taken it upon themselves to hoard whatever they could, whenever they could.

When I arrived, most of the inmates were working at their jobs in other areas of the camp; those who did not have jobs simply milled around the dorm area all day. I decided to go shopping for a pillow (I had been an inmate long enough to know how to take advantage of a situation like this). All the way across the dorm from mine there was a cube with only one inmate but two complete bed setups. I knew I was risking assault, but I didn't want to go without a pillow. Walking over as nonchalantly as possible, I reached down, grabbed the pillow and, while no one was looking, launched it across the room into my cube. Satisfied that the theft had gone unnoticed, I walked back and picked up the pillow off the floor of my cubicle. I decided to sit down in my cube and wait for the inmate to return and discover the pillow missing from the other bed.

The inmate returned a few minutes later. The first thing he noticed was the missing pillow. His face turned red and he became visibly angry. After making sure it was really gone, he set off on a stalking mission around the dorm in search of it. To my dismay, he was a very large and well-developed dude. Suddenly, I began to regret my impulsive action. I watched as he stopped at each cube and cast a look inside for his cherished pillow. I stretched out on my bunk to wait for him to pass. My heart pounded with dread as he approached. When he stopped outside my cubicle I caught my breath and held it. He looked inside, looked at me, narrowed his eyes, hesitated—and continued down the corridor. I exhaled quietly. I had dodged a real bullet.

Now that I think about it, this guy must have thought I was the culprit. After all, I had just arrived that day and did not have a pillow when I arrived. But he had been an inmate for several months, and his "connections" on the inside were good. He had a new pillow the next day.

Gambling, Anyone?

Getting a decent night of sleep is one of the biggest challenges in a prison camp. The person in the cube next to me filled his limited space every night with inmates who loved to smoke and gamble. That made it difficult to get any rest, but I just kept to myself, because you do not get into other people's business in prison. Shooting off your mouth is a sure-fire way to get hurt.

Even so, I was pretty naïve about so many things that were transpiring right under my nose. One afternoon a couple of inmates I had made friends with explained them to me, and after a few days of careful observation it became clear to me they were telling the truth.

The person in the dorm who controlled the drugs was a guy nicknamed "H." He was one mean dude. I witnessed several guys get beaten within a breath of death for doing something he didn't like. One day he walked past me, and, with no provocation whatsoever, said, "I would like to kill you."

Then and there I started planning a way to get out of that dorm and as far away from H as I could. He was the kind of guy who made prison life miserable for everyone else. People convicted of violent crimes are not supposed to be in minimum-security prisons. But violent people are often arrested and convicted of nonviolent crimes, and they flood these camps across the country. It was wise to keep your head on a swivel.

Chapter 27

Stayin' Alive

Word travels quickly in prison. It didn't take long for certain inmates to hear that I was a pilot. One of them, a guy named Bobby, wanted me to do him a favor. He asked a buddy of mine to set up a meeting. We sat down in my cubicle and he launched right into his spiel.

"Joe, man, your life, as you know it, is over, got it? No one ain't gonna ever give you a decent job again. Got it?"

He had a point, even if he could not articulate it very well. I sensed he was about to make me some kind of a proposition that involved illegal activity.

"My best friend, see, he's an untouchable drug dealer, man. He was busted after years of dealing, see." Bobby stopped talking and looked me in the eye. "I got this plan that will make you a rich man. All you got to do is do everything you are told, see? That's it. Got it?"

The last thing I would ever do was get involved with this creep, but I wanted to stay alive and stay on his good side. I nodded. "Yeah, sure."

He nodded vigorously. "Cool. I got connections. I can send you to helicopter school in California, man, and you can learn how to fly the Hughes 500. This bird is super maneuverable, man—a really fast copter."

I nodded like I was seriously interested. "Ok. . . . ok. What's in it for me?"

Bobby smiled. "Man, what's in it for you? How about thirty thousand dollars a month and three million dollars in a Swiss bank account, man, when you finish school and earn your helicopter rating?"

"Ok," I answered slowly. "So you want to pay me to learn how to fly a helicopter. . . "

Bobby shot me an irritated look, lowered his voice, and continued. "See you keep a low profile after that. Real low, man. When the time comes, you fly into a prison and pick up my friend the drug dealer, see? Then you fly him out. When you do that, I pay you another million bucks."

I have to admit the offer floored me. *This guy was serious.* I had heard a few stories in prison about people who had tried to pull off stunts like this. What was I going to do when I got out of prison, other than struggle like everyone else and go through rejection and poverty? I thought, *"This wasn't an opportunity that came along to everyone every day. Only a sharp pilot could pull off something like this. . ."*

Then I did a mental shake of my head to clear it. *"What if this guy is some kind of undercover government agent in prison trying to set me up on some conspiracy charges?"* That would ruin my life forever. And even if this guy's offer was real, was I really going to risk going back to prison—real, hard-time prison—if things didn't work out? What if these people decided to try to kill me after I got their friend out? This idea was not only nuts, but dangerously so.

I mustered up a tough, no-nonsense look and replied. "Look, Bobby, I appreciate the offer, but I'm not interested in any plan that involves illegal activity. There is nothing I like about being in jail, and no amount of money will ever convince me to risk coming back here."

That did not sit well with Bobby, who pressed his lips together tightly, stared hard at me, stood up, and walked away.

Daring Rubin

I met several helicopter pilots in prison. One was a fellow named Rubin. We actually knew many of the same people in the aviation community. He loved to brag about all of the risks he used to take flying airplanes in south Florida. When giving flight lessons, he often had taken a twin-engine Beechcraft Baron out over the Atlantic, then cut off both engines. He would do loops and aerobatics, scaring the crap out of the foreign flight students on board with him. There was no end to Rubin's crazy flying stories.

A few years ago, while spending the night in Miami, I was watching the local news. A breaking story was unfolding about a midair crash involving two helicopters. One of the helicopters had a news crew on board. An eyewitness, a woman watching the helicopters fly above her neighborhood, observed the collision. According to her, it looked as if the helicopters were flying erratically—"hot-dogging it"—before they collided, broke apart, and hit the ground in a fiery crash. The way the reporters portrayed it, this woman didn't know what she was talking about. Why would two helicopters be flying erratically, as if playing a game of cat and mouse at high speed so close to the ground?

The news channel showed the photo of the innocent news photographer—with his wife and children; luckily, they were not on board when the helicopter went down. On the screen was footage of smoldering, twisted metal burning under a plume of black smoke.

The next image was of the pilot. I thought to myself, "*I know that guy!*" It was Rubin. He had been the pilot of one of those helicopters. The instant I recognized him I knew the woman's eyewitness report was accurate.

Everyone aboard both helicopters had been killed in the crash. My heart sank. I felt especially sorry for the innocent photographer and his family. But I even felt bad for Rubin: he had some growing up to do, but he ran out of time before he could do it. May they all rest in peace.

There is a well-known saying in the flight school business: "There are old pilots, and there are bold pilots, but there are no old, bold pilots."

Going for a Long Swim

Another pilot in the prison camp bragged about how he would hire young men to load and unload his DC-3 when it was full of dope. He made those guys feel like kingpins for several weeks by renting sports cars for them to drive and paying for hookers. These young guys thought they were on top of the world.

According to the convicted pilot, when they had been "used" enough, he would stand next to them as the airplane flew high above the ocean, talking about how great everything was—next to the open back door of the plane. Then he would suddenly shove them from behind, right out of the plane. Their term as a "kingpin" was short-lived, and they were never seen again. Later I learned enough about this guy to believe he was telling the truth.

Pilots in Prison

Most of the pilots I met in prison were in for drug crimes. One of them was a former airline pilot caught smuggling cocaine into the country in his flight bag. Several were former helicopter pilots who flew dope off ships in the Caribbean. One smuggler I met from Texas made four more drug runs to raise money for his family while he was out on bond awaiting the beginning of his prison sentence. He knew his wife was going to have difficulty supporting their children, and he did what he thought he had to do to make sure she could feed and clothe the kids while he was in prison.

Listening to these guys, I was just happy I had never flown drugs when I was younger. The opportunity had presented itself several times, but I was never willing to risk going to jail. At that time I just couldn't imagine what it would be like to lose my freedom. Now I knew the answer, up close and personal.

A Run to the Liquor Store

The guards in the prison camp were well aware that a few inmates "escaped" for a short time to obtain liquor. The guards sometimes acted as if they wanted to catch them, but they rarely did. They easily could have every time, because inmates who wanted alcohol simply walked across the street and bought it at the local liquor store. The craving for alcohol can get people to do some crazy and risky things. Inmates who *were* caught leaving the premises usually spent the remainder of their prison sentences "behind the wall" inside the penitentiary. Pretty high stakes for a drink, if you ask me.

One of the first jobs I landed inside the camp was as an apprentice electrician. It was my job to repair the lights on the perimeter that inmates smashed with rocks so they could slip away from the camp undetected. Thick wire covers for the lights stopped most of the breakage. The liquor still continued to flow inside the prison, though.

One guard named Sam gave liquor to the inmates on his work crew. I felt sorry for him, because it was obvious to me that he needed help and was going to really screw up his life. I observed him several times both driving and working under the influence of alcohol, even when he was inside the prison. I just didn't know how to approach him. As an inmate, it is difficult to get involved in anyone's life, so I painfully watched Sam self-destruct. He was eventually fired from his job, and of course I never saw him again.

Alcohol had a fatal grip on this man, and it destroyed his life just as it had so many other men I had known. It was sad, because Sam came across to me as a decent human being. He was just sick, like any other alcoholic.

Teaching Again . . . Behind Bars

Carl was an inmate doing a seven-year stretch. He was an innocent young black man. Actually, naive is a better word than innocent. Apparently, he had needed some money, so he agreed to take a bag to someone. He didn't know what the contents were, and he certainly didn't know he was being set up. The people he delivered it to were federal agents. He was arrested and found guilty of dealing drugs. It was his first offense. But Carl had had a tough life long before that. I was drawn to him because of his sincere faith in God, and his determination to make a better life for himself. He was going to school while in prison, taking advantage of the Pell Grant system.

I know it is not a very exciting part of my story, but it was very important for me to do service work and help others while I was in prison. There were several inmates in there whom I helped with their studies. Unfortunately, inmates lost their ability to go to school on Pell Grants when people outside the prison system filed complaints.

I really enjoyed meeting with Carl in the evenings and helping him with his study skills. It was very beneficial for me to feel useful in this way, and I got a great deal of satisfaction watching him grow as a person and as a student. He is out of prison now, and I pray he is okay and doing well. Having to face the world as a convicted felon is a very difficult proposition, even for someone like me who had a tremendous support group and a loving family unit.

The Drunken Guitarist

One afternoon, when I was walking around the yard in the camp, I heard what sounded like an electric guitar being played live. I followed the sound and, to my amazement, found a small room with some instruments in it. There was a drum set, occupied by a beginner drummer who was having a hard time keeping a beat. The guitarist, on the other hand, was pretty good. He was playing some great blues guitar while barking orders to the other musicians. It took me a few seconds before I figured out he was trying to teach the others the chords of the song they were trying to play. This was a thrilling sight for me: a drum set that I might get to play! I took a seat and watched as the guitarist, "Jim," played and sang as the other members of the makeshift prison band struggled to keep up. Jim was in his own world when he played the guitar, and he was good at it.

Over the course of the next few weeks I watched the prison band practice whenever I could. Different musicians played at different times. It was pretty much first-come, first-served. None of the inmates knew I could play drums. One day, when no one was playing the drums, I asked if I could give it a try.

"You play the drums?" asked Jim, in complete surprise.

"A little bit," I answered, sitting down behind the kit and picking up the sticks. Within a few seconds I was jamming with the band. For the first time in a long time, these musicians heard a steady, interesting beat. A big smile spread across Jim's face. "You can play with us any time you want."

After that, all the musicians made me their drummer of choice. I played rock and blues with the white dudes, jazz and funk with the black dudes, and Latin rhythms with the Hispanic dudes. It was the best possible escape for me, and the musicians became some of my closest friends in prison.

One day, one of my musician buddies told me that Jim really liked to drink, and from time to time got very, very drunk. Jim lived in a part of the building distant from me, so I never had the chance to observe this behavior or talk to him about it first hand. One night, however, I spotted Jim walking through the dorms shouting at someone or something. He was staggering as he walked. Concerned for his safety, I tried to help him, but he wouldn't listen to reason.

However, the guards couldn't help but hear him, so they were forced to arrest him. They took him behind the wall of the penitentiary and tested his blood-alcohol level. Jim was positive—way positive. That put an end to his guitar-playing days in the prison camp.

They put him in "The Hole" for punishment, and we learned he got the hell beat out of him by the other inmates there. I heard that his injuries were so extensive that he was hospitalized under guard at a hospital in Atlanta. Several months later Jim returned to the camp. His eye socket had been smashed and was full of post-surgical scars. His eyeball actually drooped about one-half inch below where it should have been.

Jim was never the same after that. I remember him sitting with his wife and seven children in the visitation room the first time after he returned to camp. The look on their faces was heartbreaking. His hideous injuries frightened the kids, who were mostly too young to fully understand what had taken place. Of course, he didn't tell them what had really happened, opting instead for a story about falling out of bed and cutting his eye. All I know is, the doctors who sewed him back together were not too concerned with his appearance, because when they were finished he looked like a monster. I can still see the three large red scars around his eye and cheek where his face had been split open during the violent attack.

Jim did have a sharp tongue, and maybe that's what had gotten him into trouble. I just felt bad for him. I tried to show Jim how important recovery and sobriety were to me and tried to share my literature with him, but he simply refused to acknowledge that he was sick or had any problem at all. I never could get him to go to one of our jailhouse twelve-step meetings. All I could do was pray for him.

Come On, Just One Drink

One night, a friend of mine named Ralph offered me a drink. I watched him as he poured the liquor—out of an empty bleach bottle he stored in the janitorial supply closet with all the other bleach bottles—into a cup and handed it to me.

I stared at my cup for a few seconds. "I'm an alcoholic. I can't drink like other people, Ralph."

I was bound and determined not to have another drink, ever again. My last drink had cost me at least a million dollars in lost wages and other financial opportunities I would have had if I were still flying. I handed the cup back to Ralph.

Our conversation turned to my story of recovery from alcoholism. Ralph told me he was in prison for stealing a large crate of hand grenades off an Army base where he had worked. He was discovered when the local sheriff caught his little brother helping himself to the grenades to use in a pond for fishing. The pond was in a populated neighborhood. Ralph's little brother was not too bright.

A few months after the drink offer, Ralph was busted for getting obnoxiously drunk. Like Jim before him, he was sent to "The Hole" "behind the wall." I never saw him again.

Love Makes the World Go Around

My salvation in prison was when my friends and family came to see me on Saturday visitation days. We were not allowed to touch, hug, or kiss anyone except for a last minute goodbye peck. Of course, some of the inmates violated this in some huge ways, and they lost their visitation privileges for a long time.

Deborah came to see me every week. She made the four-hour drive down from Nashville by herself. Saying goodbye was always the hardest part for her. I would stand between two buildings and wave to her in the parking lot as she stopped to look at me one more time. I don't think she could tell that I had tears in my eyes. I just hated the fact that she had to go home without me.

Sometimes when we got together she showed obvious disappointment in me. Usually it was because I didn't have much to say. But what does a man tell his wife about life in prison? The last thing I wanted was for her to sit at home and worry more about my plight, so usually we passed the time talking about family and friends. But no matter the topic, the minutes flew by too fast in the visitation room.

Mac, a visiting friend who was a retired Delta Captain, was sympathetic to the fact that the prison guards had taken my property away in Montgomery. He knew that all I had were some very uncomfortable prison shoes that really hurt my feet. One day he walked into visitation with a brand-new pair of comfortable tennis shoes on his feet. When the visitation ended, he walked out of that prison—wearing my old prison shoes. Nobody spotted the difference. Those were the most comfortable shoes I have ever worn in my life.

A Crafty Smuggler in Our Midst

If you knew her, you'd never guess my mother to be a notorious smuggler. But my mom sewed a false pocket into her purse so she could smuggle in some Easter candy for me. She went overboard, though, stuffing in an excessive amount of candy. The guards have seen it all, and she was busted at the entry door to the visitation room. Everyone who worked at the prison got a kick out of her efforts, and, lucky for her, the right people were working in the visitation room that day. The wrong people would have tried to make her life (and mine) miserable.

I cannot say enough wonderful things about all of the people who came to visit me. They touched a special place in my heart and sustained me in the most difficult of situations. I love them all and will never stop being grateful for what they did for me.

Angels in the Midst of Hell

Modern prisons, at least the one in Atlanta, offer the opportunity for willing individuals to grow spiritually. Campus Crusade For Christ came in once a week. The Salvation Army also came in once a week, and on select Sundays brought in a choir and band members. Of these visitors my personal favorites were an 83-year-old man and his wife: Dr. and Mrs. Grimm. Dr. Grimm had been a Christian missionary in India for forty years. His messages to the inmates were always inspirational, really quite moving and beautiful. He said things in such a gentle yet powerful way.

Some of the inmates argued with him about what this meant or what that meant in the Bible. He told the guys who wanted to beat him up with their "interpretations" of the Bible, "The older I get, the less I understand about the Bible, yet the more I understand about the living God, and the Good News of Jesus Christ." The inmates were so wrapped up in telling him what they thought they usually missed his message entirely.

One of these people in particular, Conrad, had a short temper. One day, he got very angry and almost assaulted me over something I enjoyed in Dr. Grimm's Bible study. Conrad was a generally good fellow, but his temper got him into a lot of trouble. If you didn't agree with him, sometimes you found yourself on the ground wondering how you got there. His friend Billy barely managed to keep Conrad from attacking me one night. Conrad told me the next morning that he was sorry about his behavior—a rare event in a prison environment.

One thing Dr. Grimm said I will never forget: "Some people confound the vehicle with the reality. They think that they have to do something to get to heaven, to go 'up' to God. But the wonderful thing is that God comes down and works through us, and we have the awesome privilege of being a part of God's new creation each and every day."

Dr. Grimm was my angel in the midst of hell. I can still see in my mind the image of him and his elderly wife walking hand in hand down the long sidewalk to the prison camp from the parking lot. They walked slowly and with purpose, and my heart rejoiced with the reassurance that God had put them in my life as a real blessing. Their inspiration helped keep me alive. As a result, I looked forward to opportunities to be a part of God's new creation each and every day in the Atlanta Federal prison.

Speaking of Gratitude

I sang in the choir in the prison camp. I found it enjoyable to get together a few nights a week and give some praise to God. One afternoon Neil Walker, my electrical boss, told me that an appreciation banquet was going to be given by the prison camp for all the volunteers who came in off the street to give Bible studies and the like. "We need an inmate to give an appreciation talk about the Salvation Army," he explained. "Would you be interested in doing that?"

I fondly remembered my gifts on Christmas Eve. "I'd be happy to."

My dad had played in the Salvation Army band as a young man, and he always gave us children money to put in the Salvation Army's red kettles at Christmas. I remember a time when my dad wrote an angry letter to the editor of the *Fort Lauderdale News.* Some of the chain stores had announced they were not going to allow the Salvation Army to ring the bell in front of their stores; that didn't sit too well with my dad. And so I shared my story about the Salvation Army in front of a large crowd that night. I had nothing but admiration and gratitude for the Salvation Army, and I made that very clear in my speech.

The warden was one of the guests, and he was visibly moved by what I had to say. An upshot to all this was I discovered I had a talent to touch and inspire a large crowd with the spoken word. This was my introduction to public speaking. Standing there that night, I knew that speaking would be a part of my future; I just wasn't sure how yet.

Chapter 28

Oh No, Not "The Hole!"

I shared my "cell" or cubicle with a guy named Barton. He was doing a long sentence for repeated offenses of drug dealing and possession of illegal firearms. Barton was a tall man, over six-feet, six-inches. He rarely spoke to me, and I was never comfortable around him. He found it difficult to get along with people at his job, so the bosses let him walk around by himself for most of the day; that kept him away from other inmates.

In the evening, however, Barton was *my* problem. Lots of things bugged him. Even my mail bothered him. He seemed annoyed by the quantity I received from family and friends. One afternoon, just before mail call, Barton was standing next to my locker peeling an apple over my locker, on the top of which was a framed picture of my wife. Every time he peeled the fruit, apple juice dripped on the glass, making a real mess.

"Barton, would you please peel your apples over the garbage can?" I asked.

Obviously annoyed by my completely reasonable request, he shot me a dirty look and grumbled something under his breath. He continued, the juice dripping down on my wife's picture. Barton didn't like anyone telling, or even asking, him to do anything. He lived in his own little world. The tension in the air was already thick and heavy.

"Please go peel that apple over the garbage can," I said again, this time with a little more force.

I would not have believed what happened next if I hadn't witnessed it myself. I turned around, and without warning he struck me on the head with something hard. The blow dropped me to my knees and had me seeing stars for several seconds. I knelt there, my head resting on the floor. I surrounded my head with my arms and tried to take stock of my situation. When my senses returned, I heard someone yelling "Hey! Hey!" and felt the air move as a man jumped over me and grabbed my assaulter, shoving him away from me.

As I later learned, Barton had been rearing back to kick me in the head with one of his steel-toed shoes. Coming from a man as big as he was, the blow would have crushed my skull and caused serious damage. I would have become another prison casualty, with no reasonable explanation for my injury. Barton was an extremely volatile man, and I never really understood what he was doing in a minimum-security prison camp. Sadly, he was not an isolated case; there were many like him in the camp.

The guy who saved my life, Johnny T., was a big man fully capable of holding his own against a tough like Barton. Johnny held Barton at bay with one hand while he picked me off the floor like some downed prizefighter in the 12th round. Prisoners normally do not intervene on behalf of other prisoners being assaulted, unless it is a riot situation. Fortunately for me, Johnny T. was a different kind of person: he had real integrity. Maybe he looked after me because I had shared some of my art supplies with him. It took several months to get these supplies in prison, so they were especially valuable to me, but I didn't mind sharing and that must have made an impression on him, because he really stuck his neck out by intervening as he did. This was a rare blessing for me.

Barton now told the other inmates that he had attacked me because I read too much. For some reason this "atrocity" made perfect sense to those inmates who were Barton's friends. Soon we all left our cubicles for mail call, which took place in the common area within eyeshot of the guards. Johnny T. walked slowly with me, steadying me so I could make it to mail call. My head was throbbing away, and the pain from whatever Barton had hit me with was excruciating.

"You got a hell of a bump up there," said Johnny T.

I raised my hand up and felt the top of my head. The blow had raised a large, six-inch-long bump on the top and back of my head. The size of the swollen area scared me. Realizing it could be something serious, I asked for medical attention.

That proved to be a serious mistake. I wasn't going to get any medical attention, and the guards knew it.

"The only way you can get an injury like that is by being in a fight," replied one of the guards. "I think you need some time in the 'The Hole.'"

I could not believe what was happening. They handcuffed me and marched me under armed guard to the penitentiary across the way. I can tell you that the man who made that long walk back to the penitentiary was a very dizzy and disheartened individual. He was also very scared. I knew "The Hole" was a horrible place, and surely the last place you wanted to go if you needed any kind of medical attention. Besides, I just didn't want to come anywhere near that thirty-foot-high wall again, and all that was inside it. Now and then while I was in the visitation room in the camp I would look at that place, and thank God I was not in there any more. Now I was going back, and physically I was not in any shape to defend myself; I would have to defend myself with my wits alone, and with God's help and protection.

"The Hole" is where they put troublemakers from inside the penitentiary to segregate them as a form of punishment. They processed me back into the penitentiary, and I was taken into a large room filled with "Captains" of the guard and supervisors from inside the pen. They were all joking about a poor, stupid "inmate" just sent to "The Hole" for fighting.

One of them looked at me. He must have recognized me, because he said, "Didn't you like the food and the accommodations in the camp?" All the men laughed loudly, as if on cue.

I knew enough to bite my tongue and keep my mouth shut; but by this time I was nauseous and so dizzy I could barely stand, so I had to say something. "Please . . . get me a doctor and have him look at my head," I finally asked. My skull was pounding like a bass drum and getting worse by the minute. One of the guards snickered at the request, and the others turned away and continued their conversation; they couldn't have cared less about me.

They escorted me down the hall and outside into an enclosed corridor that was familiar to me from my first visit to the Atlanta Federal Penitentiary. This time, however, we went inside a building within the walls of the prison that I used to pass when we were being paraded to the chow hall during the day. Now it was nighttime, and the sound of our footsteps echoed off the cold, granite walls of the prison.

Back at the prison camp, meanwhile, the guards and inmates were rifling through my stuff. Everything I had—my clothing, personal property, etc.—was up for grabs. It takes lots of time to get a decent wardrobe in prison, but only seconds to lose it all. Many were special items, gifted by a friend who promised you the item when he left the prison. Things of value were stolen from me, never to be seen again. A guard stole a special Cross pen that my father had given me as a graduation gift; he simply put it in his pocket, and even forgot where he had acquired it. He also threw away some very beautiful drawings of a rainbow trout I had drawn. I had poured my heart and soul into the effort, and that fish had come alive on the paper. Now it was on its way to a prison dumpster.

As the looting of my property was taking place, I was being paraded under guard to "The Hole" deep in the bowels of the maximum-security prison.

Into "The Hole"

The building they shoved me into had a long, underground corridor with cells lining both sides. We stopped at an internal guard post, where two very obnoxious guards ordered me take off my good sweatpants, sweatshirt, and tennis shoes, and leave them behind.

Then they joked at my expense about who they were going to stick me in with. "Let's put him with Mr. P.," joked one of the guards. "He's doing seventeen back-to-back life sentences for murder. Let's see how much this 'camper' likes being in with Mr. P." With that, they led me down the hall and locked me in a cell with four other men. One of them was Mr. P.

As the guards were walking away, I blurted out, "I know my rights, and I'm not going to let you get away with stealing my personal property!" Anger washed over me. I was tired of being abused and kicked around like an animal. "I worked for those tennis shoes for months!" I shouted. "I saved my eleven cents an hour from my job! It took three months for me to save that money, and I'm not about to let abusive guards steal my shoes and keep them!" My yelling actually worked. The guard who had my shoes turned around, walked back, and handed them to me. From the looks on their faces and the chuckles they uttered, I think the inmates in "The Hole" enjoyed the show.

The four other inmates in "The Hole" were, for the most part, down and out in just about every way. They had been in there for a long time, and the lack of color in their skin showed it. All four were as white as ghosts, except for the youngest inmate, whose entire body was covered with tattoos. Mr. P. had two bunks to himself; he used the top bunk to stack his books and other personal items. I gravitated to an empty bunk and sat down.

At first, the inmates didn't say anything to me. It was as if they were waiting for Mr. P. to begin the questioning. I don't know why, but the guards in the camp had let me bring some of my food with me that I had purchased that morning at the prison commissary. I generously offered some to my new cell mates. One of them took an apple and thanked me for it; it had been a long time since he had eaten any fresh fruit. The smile on his face showed how much he really enjoyed it. He was still eating it when the interrogation began.

"That's one hell of a bump you've got on your head." The soft voice came from the bunk of Mr. P. I nodded my reply. "What are you doing in prison?" he demanded sharply.

"I'm in here for flying a commercial airliner under the influence of alcohol."

"That is bullshit!" Mr. P. snarled. "You made that up. Nobody ever gets put in this place for doing something like that. Fess up. You're a child molester, aren't you? You're just making that airplane shit up so we don't kill you down here. But we might kill you anyway, just because you're a camper!"

A "camper" is what inmates in the maximum-security prison call inmates in the minimum-security prison camp. Inmates "behind the wall" harbor a serious resentment toward "campers" because our living conditions are so much better than in the penitentiary behind the wall.

The other inmates watched closely, enjoying the drama as it unfolded before them. I knew I had to think of something fast or I was going to take another beating, possibly a fatal one. Out of the corner of my eye I noticed the stub of a pencil on the floor. It gave me an idea . . . and possibly my only hope.

"I am an airline pilot," I declared, "and I can prove it!" I stood, picked up the nubby pencil, and began drawing on the wall of the cell. After a few minutes I stopped, stepped back, and gestured toward my rendering.

"What's that?" the guy who had just finished the apple asked.

"It's the flight engineer panel of a Boeing 727," I proudly announced.

I had put everything right where it was supposed to be. I stepped up and added the battery switch, and explained how the engine-driven generators worked. Next came the fuel system. I explained about the fuel tanks and the different fuel pumps and how the engineer could dump jet fuel overboard in an emergency to make the airplane lighter for an emergency landing. I stopped a moment and looked at them. Each man was staring at me. No one said a word. I continued, telling them about the air-conditioning and pressurization systems, and why it was so important to have a pressurized cabin for high-altitude flight. I knew I was winning the battle, but my head was pounding, I felt like vomiting, and at times I believed I might pass out. Summoning my strength, I launched into a discussion of the hydraulic system, and explained to them how the landing gear, flaps, and other flight controls operate. An inmate asked a question. I answered it. Another question. Another answer. And so it continued.

As strange as it sounds, my "lecture" in this most unusual of classrooms lasted about one hour. Finally, an inmate named Frank, who happened to be the biggest person in the room, exclaimed, "This guy's for real! He really is a pilot!"

The discussion had transformed these murderers into semi-reasonable people. One minute they wanted to kill me, and the next they looked at me with absolute awe and respect, as I demonstrated the mechanics of an airliner. And I could tell that these men were different because of the experience. Even though they would be spending the rest of their lives in prison, they now "knew" how to fly!

After the lecture I lay down on my bunk to rest. My head still ached, and I was still dizzy. A couple hours later, an inmate turned to me and asked, "Pilot, you wanna play some cards with us?"

I knew I needed to have my head wound looked at, but my requests for medical attention had been ignored. I sat up and leaned back against the wall. Frankly, I was totally overwhelmed with fear and exhaustion. As much as I craved some camaraderie, I knew I was in no shape to participate. "Thanks, I'd like to," I replied, "but I need to lie down and see if I can get this head of mine to stop pounding."

Big Frank nodded his understanding. "Here," he said, lifting one of his pillows off his bunk and handing it to me. "You might need this."

The kind gesture hit me hard. It was one of the few examples of humanity anyone would find in "The Hole."

A Prayer for Help

With my head feeling as if it had been jack-hammered, I placed the pillow on the bunk. I gently eased the non-hematoma side of my head onto the filthy pillow and began to pray. I prayed that God's will would be done in my life. I prayed that God would keep me safe from harm, that these men would not want to hurt me, and that I could go to sleep and wake again to see another day. An unexplainable feeling of peace slowly took over my being. The calm feeling of serenity was overwhelming and wonderful. Somehow, everything was going to be all right. I fell into a deep and restful sleep.

The next morning something extraordinary happened. Frank shook me gently and said, "Someone's here to see you."

It took me several seconds to fully wake up and take in my surroundings. Once the long, dark cell came into full focus, I recognized my former boss, Neil Walker, standing at the doorway of the cell. Walker was a guard and the chief electrician for the prison. I had worked for him as an electrician's apprentice—my first job in prison. I slowly stood up and walked to him. He was the best person to work for in the entire prison system. Walker motioned for me to put my head close to the bars so the other inmates could not hear what he was going to tell me.

"Joe, I heard about the way you were attacked and that giant bump on your head," Walker whispered. "I spoke to the warden to see if he can get you out of here early." The words nearly floored me. This never happens in prison. Normally, an inmate sent to "The Hole" spends several months here. The guards considered it an "attitude adjustment" period.

"Thank you, Mr. Walker," I managed. "I don't see how that will happen."

"The warden remembers you from your speech on missionary appreciation night," continued Walker. A few months earlier I had given a speech about the Salvation Army volunteers who came into the prison. I explained how much I appreciated all of the volunteers who gave their time to us. The warden was deeply moved by my talk, and even recognized my name when Mr. Walker mentioned it.

According to Walker, the warden told him he would consider letting me out of "The Hole" early. But there was a catch, and it sent a chill down my spine.

"The deal is that they have to let Barton, the guy who assaulted you, out too." "The Hole" had several cells, and Barton was just a few yards away down a short hallway. Walker could see that the news was not sitting well with me. "Joe, if the warden only lets you out, Barton's friends will retaliate against you." He paused. "Well, what do you think?"

"Anything would be better than being here," I answered. "I'm willing to take my chances."

Walker nodded his understanding. "It might take a couple of days to get the details worked out, so be patient."

A few days later the guards arrived to escort me back to the prison camp. Getting out of "The Hole"—and especially out from behind that thirty-foot-high wall—was one of the best feelings in the world. Once again I said farewell to the machine gun towers and glistening, razor-sharp, wire fencing.

My friends in the camp were glad to see me. But many of Barton's friends turned on me; it was immediately clear they were looking for a reason to start a fight with me. Some of them were men I had sung with in the prison choir for the last six months—now they wanted to eat my lunch.

And I never did get any medical attention for my head injury, so exactly how serious it was remains a mystery.

Chapter 29

Watch Your Six O'clock

From the moment I got out of "The Hole" my head was on a swivel. My stress level shot through the roof, and my body began to break out with sores. Too many crazy things can happen when you start accumulating enemies (and you often can't tell your enemies from your friends). My mind raced with possibilities.

I had seen several people be severely beaten, and I was determined to do everything in my power to avoid trouble. I was careful not to be caught anywhere that I could be jumped by a group. I figured I could fend for myself one-on-one with anyone, as long as he didn't have a weapon. My hyper-vigilant survival state made doing time even more of a chore than usual. Many inmates are attacked at night, which made it difficult for me to close my eyes and sleep soundly. I spent every one of those restless nights counting the days I had left in prison.

I was not the only one on the lookout for trouble. Someone dumped a bucket full of urine onto the bed of the guy across the hall from me. He knew enough not to complain to the authorities. Instead, he cleaned up the mess himself and stressed out over it. I don't know why someone had it in for him, but he was always being intimidated with some disgusting form of inhumane treatment.

Prior to being assaulted, my prison counselor had informed me that I was being considered for placement in a halfway house for the last five months of my prison term. I certainly looked forward to that possibility, which would allow me to get a job, then go back to the halfway house for the night. When I was returned to the camp, however, several of the inmates told me to forget about getting out early: "Man, if you are in a fight or sent to 'The Hole,' they will never let you go to a halfway house."

They were right. One of the camp counselors informed me that my trip to "The Hole" made me ineligible for a halfway house. Instead, I was going to have to spend the rest of my sentence in the Atlanta camp. The news crushed me. I knew that one of the worst things that could happen to me was being stuck in the Atlanta Federal Penitentiary system for another six months. The odds of being attacked again and seriously injured—or worse—were very high.

Letters and Love

As I noted, I was in the prison system for several weeks before my mail finally caught up to me. But many people reached out to me in the form of letters while I was in prison. To my pleasant surprise, a backlog of more than fifty letters was delivered to me in one day; several days later, I received another batch of thirty letters. Everyone was uplifting and supportive, which sustained me and gave me hope. I did my best to answer every letter unless, as happened on a few occasions, one was stolen. Sadly, some of the inmates never received so much as a single letter at mail call, so they appropriated someone else's.

For one of my last jobs in prison I ran the motor pool and did payroll for a guard who could not read. He was one of the most decent guards I met in prison. He appreciated all I did for him, and as my reward he allowed me to use the electric typewriter in his office to answer all the letters I got from family and friends. I even got letters of support from complete strangers. Unfortunately, some of their addresses were destroyed and I was unable to answer them. I still regret this because I was committed to answering every one of them to express my gratitude.

The guards who check for contraband and drugs tear open the mail before it enters the prison. In addition to destroying the return address, cards you get from friends and family are usually a torn mess. It hurt to see a beautiful card that someone had taken time to pick out ripped to pieces. I soon learned to put the pieces of the puzzle together and find joy and gratitude in what was left.

Lightening Things Up

Given my normally cheerful nature, I tried to joke around and entertain inmates who were friends. A lighter side to things makes life in prison a tad less miserable. One guard named Jones was particularly cantankerous. I always called him "Mr. Jones." He often developed a grin on his face when I spoke to him; he seemed to enjoy the fact that I was an inmate.

One afternoon Jones was in charge of a group of us. We were being paraded single file in a line of thirty inmates on our way to a recovery meeting. I was at the front of the line, and started whistling the famous theme from the movie *Bridge on the River Kwai*. When Jones finally caught on to what I was doing, he got a big kick out of it.

True Dedication

As I noted earlier, my wife Deborah tried for several months to get my personal property back from the Bureau of Prisons. (This was the property guards had taken from me at Maxwell Prison when they let all the other inmates go inside with their personal items.) It took two months just for it to show up at the house in Tennessee.

Then the new challenge was to send the box of property to the prison in Atlanta and get it past the female, administrative guard in the R&D section. This particular guard was a real piece of work. She absolutely *hated* inmates. She was also on a huge power trip, so when my property finally reached her, she sent it back to my wife—four or five different times! But she didn't know who she was dealing with; my wife was not about to take "no" for an answer.

A buddy of mine from the dorm named Pete, a strong, 250-pound guy, worked in the R&D department. He feared this woman guard as if she was a wild lion. Each time my property came in, she gave him the box and told him to return it to my wife. Pete didn't even tell me this was going on because he was afraid the woman would retaliate against him.

After this happened several times, my wife had had enough. One day she walked into the visitation room carrying my property and all of the return postage receipts. She promptly sought out and found Mr. Craig, the head guard of the prison camp. It soon became clear to him that my package had reached the prison many times, only to be returned to Deborah, for no apparent reason, by this vindictive guard in the receiving department. Mr.

Craig told my wife to make sure the package came directly to him the next time, and he would take care of it. In the end I got my property back, but it took six months.

Looking back, the property war turned out to be a good battle for my wife to fight and win. It went a long way toward alleviating the feeling of helplessness she had been experiencing since that first day of my induction, when she was verbally assaulted by the female guard and forced to leave without telling me goodbye. The day I walked into visitation and announced to my wife that my property was now in my possession was one of her happiest days there.

Big Raise

During my last few months in the prison camp, I earned forty cents an hour as the motor pool clerk working for a guard named Blake. He was a decent man and we became friends. Blake even stood up to his boss when the boss tried to get me to take down some family pictures from my office, because Blake liked the fact that I worked so hard for him. I even managed to get the other inmates on the work detail a twenty-cent an hour raise, which really made them happy.

The Phone Racket

The easiest way to get into a fight in prison is to argue with another inmate. It could be about the television, your phone privileges and usage times, drugs, alcohol—you name it. I stayed away from the latter two and rarely watched television. The telephone, however, was so important to my sanity that I was willing to go to great lengths, including bodily harm, to defend my time slots on the sign-in sheets.

Before I showed up at the camp, one of the inmates had taken it upon himself to try to control the phone usage. Some of the inmates were intimidated by him and, as a result, never used the phones to call their families. But I figured out his system and came up with a way to beat it: by having my own friends who worked back in the dorm during the day—when the big guy and many others were away—reserve slots for me. When the intimidating inmate figured it out, he was pissed, but there was nothing he could do other than threaten me or eventually beat the hell out of me. Very stressful, but I figured it was worth the risk.

The best part about having access to a phone was all of the people who wrote and told me to call them "collect" as often as I wanted. It was a wonderful gift to give an inmate. Phone calls to the outside world always kept me going for another day, and helped me overlook the evil that surrounded me in prison.

My friends Skip, Mary, and Sam sent me beginner piano books, and I went to the chapel every day to practice and play. One fellow inmate—who was always accompanied by another inmate doubling as a bodyguard—would come in and listen to me every time I played. I found out later that he was the "Godfather" of a large Hispanic drug ring in the outside world; in prison, he was respected and protected by his men.

At a certain time of day, the Islamic inmates entered the chapel to pray. I always stopped playing when they did and told them to let me know when they were finished praying. We had a mutual respect for one another, and they smiled at me and said hello when I encountered them in other areas of the camp.

Almost Time to Go

Several prison officials told me I would not be allowed to leave for a halfway house because I had been involved in a fight. When an inmate receives disciplinary action in prison, they reminded me, he loses that opportunity. It didn't matter that I never threw a punch, or even tried to defend myself. According to their logic, I was *present* at the time I was assaulted, and that was all that mattered. Indeed, they added, I was just flat lucky to be out of "The Hole."

So you can imagine my surprise and elation when, in July 1991, I received word from the warden that I was going to be transferred immediately to a halfway house near my home in Nashville, Tennessee.

Goodbye to My Property

News of an inmate being "short" (a few days from release) travels quickly in prison. As soon as the other inmates got word I was going home the next day, they walked up to me to ask for some personal effects. Some of these guys were complete strangers.

I gave careful thought to which inmates should get my property. I gave away all of the jackets and prison pants I had, especially the "dress" clothes that I wore in the visitation room. Mine were in especially good condition, and my close buddies enjoyed receiving them. Finally, I gave my new tennis shoes to a fellow I barely knew, but who I felt really needed them. He didn't have much of anything, and the look on his face when I walked up and handed them to him gave me great satisfaction.

Goodbye to My Friends

Neil Walker, my former electrician boss, drove up to the camp exit with a pickup truck full of the guys I had worked with on the electrician crew. One of these guys, Gene, had been a mechanic on a boat that was being used for smuggling cocaine when he was arrested. The new RICO conspiracy laws made it easy for the government to arrest ancillary people such as Gene. He was doing a long, nine-year sentence, and was trying to make the best of his circumstances.

"I had no business getting on the airplane in Fargo as a Northwest Airlines pilot," I told Gene before I left. For some reason, my saying this made him very happy. I was beginning to see the past with more clarity as I continued on my journey as a recovering person.

It is impossible to find the words to express how happy I was to be leaving prison. As I lay in bed the night before my release, I reflected on my prison experience. The indignities I had had to endure to survive were incomprehensible to me. From the outset, when I turned myself in to a minimum-security camp only to be chained at the wrist, waist and ankles and hauled away elsewhere, to being thrown into "The Hole" for absolutely nothing, exemplified the unpredictability and insanity of it all. This uncertainty led me to an even greater dependence on God.

I focused on simple forms of gratitude in my attempt to look to the future with some hope. I reflected on the pile of letters from family, friends, and perfect strangers who had reached out to support me in this heinous environment. Even though I tried to keep the ugliness of prison away from those closest to me, their letters helped me survive the physical pain and dangerous consequences of being a target and being assaulted in prison.

I thought of all the corruption, gangs, violence, addiction, and anger that bulge from the bars and walls of prison. Looking back today, I realize that, inside the walls, I shut down emotionally in order to survive. There were some ways in which I had reached deep within myself, down to where I had hidden, as in my music and art. But people in prison are violated in many ways, and almost everything that happened to me was humiliating. I knew it would take a great deal of time for me to get over it, if I ever did. Somehow I had made it to the finish line, but I certainly was the worse for wear.

Now I was about to head into the scary world of the unknown again. God had made a path where He placed feathers on the ground; but some had great distances between them, and I had to look hard for them. As I think back today to that time, my soul continued to carry the heavy burden and deep wounds of the indignities I had suffered in prison. It was a breath of fresh air to get it behind me in a physical way, but my search for a safe place would be long and hard. Only slowly was I able to place these feathers on the wings of my soul until, one day, I was free again.

I woke the next morning, said my goodbyes, and was led out of the camp. Someone drove me from the prison to the bus station in Atlanta. My "shoe smuggling" friend Mac the Delta Captain met me at the bus station. His original plan had been to fly me to Nashville in his airplane—but the prison officials didn't like that idea! Mac sent me off on the bus with a hot pizza and a big smile.

Chapter 30

"Halfway" Home

The ride home to middle Tennessee was incredibly beautiful. So many months had passed since I had seen the woods and green hills of the Volunteer State.

The air conditioning inside the bus was very cold. A woman with a baby was sitting in front of me. The baby had nothing on but a diaper, and was obviously very cold and hungry. For some reason the mother and child seized my attention; everything about them bothered me. The mother didn't seem to care about her baby at all, but she was not about to accept help from anyone, either. I saw the similarity to me as I had been before, unable and unwilling to let people into my life to help me in any way. I wondered how that child was going to turn out and what would become of him.

Three teenage girls giggling in the back of the bus noticed the frozen smile on my face. One of them caught my eye. "Why are you so happy?" she asked.

"I was just released from prison," I replied, with an even wider smile.

All three girls gasped and answered in unison, "OH!" Fearful looks crossed their faces when they realized they were on a bus with a convicted felon.

But I offered some of my pizza, and one of them accepted a slice. I offered the lady with the baby a piece, but she refused. She was probably not used to getting any help from anyone. She appeared locked into a sad place.

Homecoming Fool

My next move was that of a real bonehead. A few days earlier Deborah had told me on the phone that she would not be able to meet me at the bus station, so I didn't expect to see her there when the bus pulled in. What I did not know was that she had been able to rearrange her schedule at the last minute, so she and several good friends were waiting for me at the bus station to welcome me home. Deborah wanted it all to be a big, happy surprise, and we did exchange delightful hugs, kisses, and warm greetings.

And then I climbed into my friend Skip's pickup truck. Skip had been afraid to come see me in prison, so this was the first time I had seen him in months. What I didn't realize at the time was that getting into his truck instead of riding with my wife really hurt Deborah's feelings. Later, after we talked about it, she began to understand that I was extremely disoriented after my prison experience, and my decision-making process was somewhere between rattled and confused; I had shut down. Making the transition from prisoner to free man was a slow and difficult struggle. I tried to relate this to my wife, but found it very difficult to do so.

A caravan of cars and a pickup truck meandered its way to a hamburger stand so we could all have lunch together before I turned myself in to the halfway house. Everyone kept saying how happy he or she was that I was not in prison any more. They were mostly people who had supported me and had come to prison to visit with me on Saturdays. They had all gone well out of their way to welcome me home.

But as they all noticed quickly enough, the man who climbed off the bus was not the man they had known before he went to prison. As my friend Skip later told me, "The look in your eyes was next to impossible to describe." Skip had a good friend who was shot down in a war zone and before being rescued eluded the enemy longer than anyone else in the entire war. They found him buried in mud, with his nose sticking up out of the ground. "You had the same look in your eyes as he did," Skip continued. "I have never seen that look on another human being since."

Prison is supposed to be a controlled, orderly system, but it is actually upside down because the prisoners have more power than anyone. While I was in the penitentiary I was figuratively in the same prison as any child who has an alcoholic parent. I survived because I had had a lifetime of taking the world as it is and maneuvering, running, and hiding. Now I was stepping into the next phase of my life, but I was still very damaged from tremendous turmoil, discomfort, and suffering.

I had run on adrenaline for nearly all of my time in prison. To this day, I still cannot remember much of what it was like to reunite with my wife. I was still in pure, hyper-vigilant, survival mode, and I would not be able to really relax and feel any peace for a very long time. My wife needed someone soft, caring, and gentle, but my prison demeanor was tough, defensive, and abrasive. I was always on guard, always at the ready, always prepared to fight for my life. I had shut down emotionally and was not available to her; sometimes it was like I wasn't even there. This is not where you want to be emotionally for someone who really needs you, which was very hurtful to my wife.

Healing from the damage done to me was going to take a long time.

New Roommates

On a warm and sunny July day in 1991, I said good-bye to my wife and friends and turned myself in to the halfway house. It looked like an apartment building from the outside, but I knew better: on the inside it was a jail, just without the bars.

My two new roommates (or inmates) in the halfway house could not have been more different from each other. They were both named Jim. Jim O. was in for embezzling, and his sentence was a short one. Luckily for him, all of it was to be served at this halfway house. His family was in Nashville. Despite his good fortune, he whined constantly about the way he was being treated and the living conditions he had to endure. But compared to what I had been through, this place was the Ritz, so I gave Jim O. a few words of wisdom, telling him about some of my "minimum-security" experiences inside a maximum-security setting. He looked shocked as I explained what I had undergone, and for a brief moment seemed relieved that he was in this halfway house instead of a prison in the federal system. I also sensed some embarrassment for subjecting me to all of his whining about how bad this place was, and how poorly he thought he was being treated.

The other Jim, Jim "X.," had just completed a stretch of seventeen years of hard time in a maximum-security prison. According to Jim, when he was nineteen years old he went drinking with friends, then passed out in the back of a car. His buddies decided to rob a bank, and shot and killed a man during the holdup. Jim woke up in jail with no knowledge of what had happened.

Jim X. was a calm guy who appeared grateful to be out of that horrendous environment. He told his story without any bitterness or resentment. His numerous tattoos made him scary to look at, but I soon discovered that the guy had a heart of gold. His laugh was similar to that of the original Bozo the Clown, and he laughed frequently at little things. He proved to be a blessing, and I was happy for him to be out of maximum security.

It was obvious that Jim X. was a man ready to get on with his life. His attitude reinforced what I had learned from Buddy, my first sponsor and counselor: "We do not have to dwell in the past; instead, we learn from it and continue to move forward."

I was proud to call Jim X. my friend.

Slowly Back Into the World

The idea of the halfway house system is to transition people out of prison and back into society. But as I noted, a halfway house is really another type of jail. Inmates are required to have a job on the outside in the "real" world, or they have to go back into prison to serve the remainder of their sentence. So inmates are allowed to go out and work in approved jobs, but must be back in the evening for lockdown. I had to find a job quickly.

A Safe Place for Slumber

Skip made bamboo fishing rods. He graciously shares his craft with anyone willing to learn about hand-planed, bamboo fly rods. On my second day out of the Atlanta prison system he took me to his small shop in a barn out in the country. I sat down in his lounge chair and immediately fell into a deep sleep. It was the first time in eight months I had been able to do so without feeling my life was in danger while I slept. When I woke up, it took me a while to realize I was not dreaming: I really was out of prison.

Skip was sitting at his work desk making a rod. "Welcome home, boy!" he said, when he realized I was awake. "We need to go find you a job!" So Skip commenced to drive me around in his old pickup truck while I looked for work.

It is very difficult for an inmate to find meaningful work. I wanted to try to get a teaching job, so Skip drove me down to the flight school at the Murfreesboro airport. I met with the director of the school and, luckily for me, he needed someone to teach advanced aircraft systems. My experience and passion for teaching was a perfect match. Hugh, the director, was a retired Air Force Colonel who was willing to give me a chance. He agreed to pay me $6.00 an hour to work with the foreign flight students.

Most of the students were from Norway and Sweden, and we hit it off quite well. This was a perfect environment for me, and a real blessing. I taught advanced Boeing 727 turbojet aircraft systems ground school. I must say, it was more relaxing than "teaching" in "The Hole" in an effort to save my life!

I also taught a class called Cockpit Resource Management. This instructs students how to work together with other pilots as a team member for the common good of the flight. I was teaching them to be conscientious leaders, open and willing to listen to the other pilots as the leader or Captain of a crew. The course also taught them how to work with a difficult Captain, and how to be assertive in certain situations. The students liked me, and I keep in touch with many of them to this day.

Probation

A few days after my arrival at the halfway house, I had to go to downtown Nashville and meet my new probation officer. This Federal Building was a pretty cold place, as most of them are. I found my way up to his floor and introduced myself to his secretary. "My name is Joe Balzer, and I am here to see Jim Ray."

The secretary pointed to an open door off the lobby and told me to go on in. I had heard from other inmates that probation officers could make your life tough. I didn't know what to expect.

"Hi, Joe. Close the door," he instructed as he shook my hand. The next words out of his mouth shocked me. "Joe, I think you got fucked!"

I didn't know what to say, so I stood there with my mouth hanging open.

"This whole deal got way out of hand," Jim continued, "so I am going to make this as easy on you as I possibly can."

By this time I was smiling from ear to ear. A great sense of relief came over me as I felt true freedom edging closer in my direction.

Jim Ray was a fine fellow, and he treated me with respect and kindness. He was a fair man from the start. "Here are the basic rules," he told me. "You are on supervised prison release for three years. You will need written permission to leave town."

I nodded my understanding. "Ok."

"I will come out to your job and visit you unannounced a few times a month," he continued. "I will also be stopping by your house to visit you after you leave the halfway house in a few months."

As strange as it sounds, I enjoyed the time I spent with Jim Ray. I had long hoped that the U.S. Probation Office personnel would treat me fairly, and they turned out to be a group of really good people.

One afternoon during my lunch break from work, Skip picked me up and drove me out to the little house my wife and I owned. I will never forget the feeling, sitting on the couch for the first time. "Skip, this place is a palace. Before long, I'll have my own private toilet and shower, and a nice, quiet place to sleep." My mind raced with images from prison. One was the blood of HIV-positive inmates running into the drains of the showers. (They shaved in the shower and cut themselves without any regard to the implications for other inmates.) There was also a tuberculosis outbreak in the prison when I was in there. Several inmates in my immediate vicinity were being aggressively treated for TB. Yes, indeed: my little house, nestled down a country road in Murfreesboro, Tennessee, was a palace fit for a king.

A New Look

Shortly after beginning my new job, my wife took me clothes shopping. She bought me four new pairs of pants and several colorful shirts and ties. I looked like a million dollars when I showed up for work at the school. One of the French students jokingly commented on how nicely I was dressed: "You look so good that I have lost my advantage."

Chapter 31

Home Sweet Home

Iwas officially released from the halfway house and moved back home in December 1991. I will never forget how safe it felt. "This place is absolute paradise, Deborah," I told her. "I have my own bed and my own bathroom, and can have some peace and quiet for the first time in more than a year."

Family members came to visit for the holidays. One particular incident remains vividly in my mind. It was around midnight on Christmas Eve, and everyone else in the family was in bed. I was standing alone in the kitchen in the dark. The only light in the room was from a miniature, ceramic Christmas tree my mother had made. These trees had been one of my favorite things when I was a little boy. My mom made this one while I was in prison, and had given it to me earlier that day as a Christmas gift.

The thought of finally being at home and surrounded by family after all I had been through, coupled with the thought of all the good people I had met in prison who were alone, afraid, and unable to reunite with their loved ones, overwhelmed me. I began to cry, softly. Within a few seconds my tears gave way to heavy sobbing. There had been times in prison I had walked in the prison yard as far away as possible from other inmates to try to have a good cry, but the tears never came. I was emotionally locked up, and had shut down inside. Now, on Christmas Eve, whatever it was that had my emotions locked down finally released them. I was once again in a place safe to cry. The security of my family made that possible.

I cried so loudly I woke up my sister and my mom. When they came into the kitchen to find out what was wrong, I told them what I was so upset about. To my everlasting thanks, they understood and embraced me. It was at that moment I realized it was time to move forward with my life and put the past behind me as best I could. I was so grateful to be home with my family.

Powerlessness

The situation with my job changed rapidly. The owner of the company was desperate to sell and get out of town: another operation he owned had experienced several plane crashes, and the FAA pulled the company's operating certificate. The company flew checks and banknotes in the middle of the night from Nashville to several small cities in Tennessee. The pilots were mostly young men trying to earn their hours and piloting experience, but in a hazardous environment full of mountains and rough terrain. They also flew the airplanes without the added safety of weather radar, and certainly didn't have any of the terrain-avoidance equipment with which modern airliners are equipped. It made matters worse that most of the flying was done late at night, "behind the clock." The flying involved single-pilot operations in mostly single-engine airplanes. The pilots didn't have anyone else in the cockpit with them to question their judgment or correct them if they were making a mistake. When these airplanes go down and crash it rarely makes national news, but sometimes people in the piloting community hear about them.

I was working for the International Flight Center when its sister company, TAC Air, had an ugly crash. I had flown with the young pilot, named Jimmy, as an observer just a few weeks earlier. He did some reckless flying when I was riding alone with him. Afterwards I spoke to him about it, and then the director of the company, but neither man took my warning seriously. Jimmy acted as if he were bulletproof.

One afternoon I was in the office and overheard Jimmy complaining to the Director of Operations about a check ride that he had failed with the FAA. In a check ride an FAA safety inspector rides along with a pilot and "checks" his competency level; there are certain criteria that must be met for a successful outcome. In most cases, a command pilot needs a check ride every six months. The day before his check ride, Jimmy was out flying all night, yet decided to go ahead and take the check ride first thing in the morning, while he was fatigued. That was not a good decision, and he failed the test.

A few weeks later he piloted his airplane into known icing conditions. Not only is that against FAA regulations, it is "reckless" (an FAA term) because the airplane, a single-engine Piper Lance, didn't have any anti-icing equipment on board to keep the props and wings free of ice in flight. Jimmy encountered ice somewhere between Knoxville and Nashville late at night. According to air traffic controllers, his flight rapidly disappeared from radar. It took the search party a while to find the wreckage; the airplane was buried so deeply into the ground that the only thing anyone could see was a small, six-inch section of the tail sticking up out of the hole. There was little left to identify as human remains. So much for being "bulletproof."

As the weeks passed, the employees of our company realized that the owner of the company was going to sell. In the meantime, I continued working hard and doing a good job. As my confidence rose, I began dreaming about the possibility of flying an airplane again. The conditions of my supervised release with the government forbade me from flying as the pilot in command for at least another two years, so I was trying to be productive while making plans for the future.

The road ahead was difficult. The FAA had revoked all of my pilot's licenses and certificates. It was going to take a monumental effort on my part to get certified all over again, beginning with the basic private pilot's certificate. Would it be worth the effort? Would anyone give me a chance to fly for them with such a big, black mark on my permanent record as a pilot? Was I chasing a "pipe dream," thinking that someone would eventually give me a shot?

In my recovery groups, I learned a very valuable lesson: do all of the footwork, then leave the rest to God. The odds were against me, but I decided to put my nose to the grindstone and, as my friend Skip would say, "move into the friction of life."

I didn't have a clue about the immense struggles awaiting me.

More Uncertainty

With the flight school being sold, the operation scaled down drastically. Since no new students were coming in requiring ground school, I was no longer needed, and was laid off in February. I begged the young college student who ran the desk to give me the job as the grass cutter and gardener for the airport. He looked at me as if I were crazy, but I made it clear I was serious. He was aware I was being rejected every place I went looking for a job. Plus, I enjoyed being out at the airport, and wanted to continue to have a presence there. Even though he didn't think I'd last the week, he hired me to cut the grass at the Murfreesboro Airport.

Believe me, I did it with a relish. I rode a big farm tractor with a huge power takeoff to drive the cutting blades on the bush hog. It took an entire week to get all the grass around the runway and taxiways cut, and then it was time to start all over again. I also put in a petunia garden in the spring, and frequently people who came out to the airport told me happily that it was the best the property had ever looked.

Unexpected News

One afternoon a student from the school approached me with a newspaper clipping. According to the article, the Captain of our fateful flight had been offered his job back at Northwest Airlines. I stood there with my mouth open, stunned beyond belief. "Aren't you going to get your job back, too?" asked the student.

News like this travels fast: my wife called me a few minutes later. A friend had called to tell her the same news. "Joe," she asked, "what are you going to do about getting your job back?"

The Captain had gotten his job back, and with Northwest?! It just didn't seem real to me. And it would get more bizarre as time went on. I had to be really careful how I reacted, because, as my sponsor Buddy put it, if I dwelt on this fact, I could easily end up "naked and penniless."

All I can say is that the event challenged every part of my being, and actually sent me into an emotional tailspin. I was pretty weak, anyway, from living in "survival mode" in prison, and my body and soul were far from healed after my incarceration. Now I had to endure the fact that Northwest Airlines had given the Captain his job back, without so much as even calling me up to ask how I was doing! This deal really messed me up. I spent way too much time thinking about it. Deborah offered me encouragement to try to get my job back at Northwest, but I pressured myself even harder, which didn't help matters. Honestly, I just didn't know what to do.

It is difficult to write or think about this even today, so, for the purpose of this book I simply will write the following: it is a shame the airline didn't consider bringing Bob and me back at the same time. The pilots I spoke to at Northwest felt the same way. But the airline didn't. So, for my sanity, I had to find a way to accept it and move on with my life. In some strange way, what Northwest did made me really mad, which motivated me to succeed in the impossible quest of becoming a pilot for another major airline someday; so, I guess I should thank them for the twisted inspiration.

At the time, however, the news sent me into a huge, downward spiral into a dark pit of emotional challenges that would change me forever. My struggle for the future became that much more difficult.

Depression Regression

After surviving the ordeal of federal prison, I was glad to be out of the system of incarceration. Something was wrong with me mentally, though, and I really didn't understand what was happening.

As the days turned into weeks, I slowly sank into a deeper, darker, depressive state. As discussed earlier, I had been living on adrenaline for so long that my brain could not take it any more. My hyper-vigilant state of mind from being in prison already had taken a toll, and was still doing a number on me.

This was one of the darkest places I had ever been. It is hard to explain to someone who has not experienced it before, but it felt as though my mind was shutting down. There was nothing, absolutely nothing, that I wanted to do with anyone, or wanted to say to anyone. I went to my twelve-step meetings and listened, but shared little. I can't remember much of what was said today, and couldn't then, either. My memory, especially my short-term memory, had left me. That part of my brain was no longer working or connected to the place it used to be connected to. In fact, my brain was shutting down in general: it got to the point where I was so depressed that I could not even read the written word. My life was totally void of any joy. I hadn't had any real sleep for months. Sleep deprivation, post traumatic stress disorder and depression can be very ugly things.

Today, I have a much better understanding of what depression is: a severe chemical imbalance in the brain that can be brought on over time by many factors. But at the time it was gut-wrenching for other members of my family to try to talk to me on the telephone; the old happy Joe had gone away somewhere, and nobody knew how to get him back. They quietly worried about me and wrung their hands trying to figure out what to do to help me.

One morning, I had been wearing the same clothes for some seven days, including the same flannel shirt. It was my favorite shirt, and I never wanted to take it off. That night, while at a friend's daughter's wedding reception, my good friend Skip encouraged me to go see my doctor and get on some antidepressants. He believed that I really needed to do something about my depression, and that medication would help me a great deal. Deborah was sitting across the table from me. She looked at me, nodded, and said, "I just want Joe back, the old Joe." Who could blame her, after all I had put her through?

I was too far gone to see it myself, but Skip, Deborah, and other people were right: it was time for me to get some medical attention. Therapy, meetings and even my faith in God were not doing the trick. Finally I figured it this way: God had helped man make the medicine, and the medicine was what I really needed. I took the plunge and set up an appointment.

Doctor R. explained to me that the antidepressants would "take the bumps out of the road for me." That is, *if* they were effective: he told me that they do not work for some people. I also knew of a few people who were supposed to be taking the medicine but, for whatever reason, just would not take it. That never really made any sense to me, until I realized that some people, including myself at times, have a hard time helping themselves. Certain people, for some unknown reason, choose to stay stuck in their problems for their entire lifetimes.

I wasn't sure what to expect when I started taking the antidepressants. I learned that in some cases it takes days or even a week or more for the positive effects to become evident. Luckily for me, it was the next day! It was an astronomical awakening. I was able to read again. I noticed the sun shining outside. I felt as if I could leap tall buildings with a single bound. The best part of all was being able to lie down and actually fall into a deep sleep and wake up refreshed, not burned out as if I'd just ran a marathon; I could not remember the last time I'd had a restful night's sleep. The medication did so much for me, way beyond my hope of just "leveling out the bumps in the road;" it was helping to save my life. I thanked God for the people who had developed this wonderful medication.

As my brain came back to life, I felt there was hope again. I was coming out of a very, very dark place, a place where I had been living on adrenaline in a hyper-alert state for too long. To this day, I hope and pray that I never have to go back there again. It is so sad to think that millions of people suffer from depression today and believe there is nothing they can do to help themselves. What a tragic shame. I was so blessed to have this ray of sunshine in my life.

Those Beautiful Rolling Hills and Streams

Several of the flight students in the area offered to take me up for airplane rides. There is nothing like a ride in a light airplane over the beautiful state of Tennessee. These rides brought back wonderful memories of learning to fly for the first time, and rekindled my interest and desire to earn back my pilot certificates. The feelings of pure joy inspired me to move forward with my life as a pilot. Each night before falling asleep I relived every detail of each flight in my mind. The feeling of being above the earth, with the freedom to explore the sights below, shook something deep in my soul, something once shattered, but whose parts I had subconsciously stored deep within me to protect them from complete destruction. Those parts were beginning to reassemble.

I decided to gamble my future and everything I had to pursue my dream of flying again—a complete leap of faith. I bought the books and began to study for my private pilot written exam. My flight plan was straight ahead into unknown territory, and there was no turning back. My survival kit was my prayers, and learning to depend on God.

Unsolved Mystery

One afternoon during a lunch break in the office I overheard some of the flight instructors talking about their shenanigans the night before. Some of their stories were about how much they had had to drink. Curious as to the quantity they had consumed, I asked them. Not a single one of them could tell me. They all knew at least some of my story. One of them quipped, "We consume alcohol in a responsible manner."

"How did you guys get home last night?"

They looked at one another with puzzled frowns plastered on their faces. They couldn't even remember whose car they had ridden in. In fact, after lightly arguing about it, they reached the same conclusion: they didn't know for sure. So much for the slogan "Drink Responsibly." I saw in them myself at age twenty, and it was painful to realize.

A Pattern of Christmas Sorrow

The next few years were packed with struggle and rejection. An unfortunate pattern developed in which every year I would lose my job just before Christmas. It was a painful state of existence for me. Looking for work was difficult because I had to put up with so much rejection. A well-known electronics chain store, whose name I won't mention, "lost" my application several times. After the third time I finally got the message, and stopped applying for a job there. All my effort made me realize how incredibly difficult it is for a convicted felon to get meaningful work.

Just Let Me Contribute

Being unemployed was very difficult for me to handle. I was falling behind in where I should be in life. Thank God for the 12-step program and meetings, which saved me by teaching me to accept life on life's terms. I discovered little things that made my painful life worthwhile, such as gardening, and watching the stars at night. I learned to talk and to share my feelings with other people. What I was really doing was trying desperately to piece my life back together.

I bounced around through several different odd jobs. At one point my quest for work brought me to downtown Nashville's Printers Alley. One night I was jumped after work and pistol-whipped by a desperate prison escapee. I came out of the assault with some broken ribs, broken glasses, and a deep cut on my skull where he bashed me a few times with the butt of the gun. My heart nearly stopped when he placed the gun inside my mouth and threatened to blow my head off. He demanded I give him my wallet, but the fact that he was sitting on top of me made it impossible for me to bend around and pull my wallet from my pocket. I was pinned to the ground and semiconscious, and every time I tried to get my wallet he whacked me in the head with his gun.

I had nearly blacked out when a fellow musician, to whom just minutes before I had given parking instructions, sped back down the alley with his car toward the assailant and my almost-limp body. The crazed robber jumped up off me and ran up the alley, leaving me lying in a pool of blood.

I will never forget that robber's face. I went downtown the next morning and identified him easily from a group of pictures. The police caught him that afternoon attempting another armed robbery on another private citizen. The police told me that this time the guy he was trying to rob also had a gun, and it ruined the criminal's whole day.

Chapter 32

Angels and Wings

Rock Merryweather was a local Nashville aviation legend. He had more than 30,000 hours of flight time and seemed to have worked for everyone and flown everything. At some point in his career he became an FAA-designated check airman, which meant that he could give pilots the flight and oral examinations required for them to become licensed pilots.

The flight school I had worked at kept Rock very busy giving check rides to the students. Rock was admired and respected by all of the young pilots. He had the ability to share his knowledge and wisdom of flying with the young people in the area who had aspirations of becoming pilots. Rock always had a smile on his face, and I got to know him casually by just being around him and hearing him interact with the flight students at the school. His level of experience and expertise, coupled with his love for teaching and sharing information, gave him a knack for showing even the most experienced pilots something they didn't know without hurting their feelings. If you have ever spent any time being around pilots, you know that this is a real art, and Rock was one of those rare people who possessed this extraordinary gift.

I knew the FAA was giving him a hard time because while doing his check rides he also did a great deal of teaching. One observer from the FAA told Rock that he could not tell when the check ride had begun, because Rock was teaching instead of asking questions. (In our aviation system we seem to have a punitive way of doing things, unlike what I have observed of the Canadian check ride system.) You just knew that if you had a check ride with

Rock that you were going to learn something, and he made sure that you did. This man deserved some sort of award rather than harassment.

Rock decided to make a large, triangular, wooden sign like one of those fancy executive desktop nameplates. On one side it said, in large capital letters, "THE CHECK RIDE HAS BEGUN;" on the flip side it said, "THE CHECK RIDE IS OVER." If an FAA observer was going to watch him give a check ride, he had his sign with him, and he would flip it to the appropriate side at the appropriate time so the observer would know what he was doing. Rock had a great sense of humor, was a joy to be around, and an even bigger joy to fly with. I had more than 7,000 lifetime hours of flight time when I took my check rides with Rock; but in spite of my extensive experience, Rock found interesting things to teach me, and we had fun while he was doing it.

I also received some flight instruction from a fellow named Roger Reed. Like Rock, Roger was one of the most competent flight instructors I have ever flown with. He was also a man of compassion, and he had a strong desire to help me. Great flight instructors always have packed schedules because they are in high demand. Roger gave up his precious time for me, and would not allow me to pay him for his time. He even worked for the flight school that competed with IFC for students; but he saw past the obstacles and reached out to help me in many ways. I cannot thank him enough.

Before I could take any check rides, I had to re-learn all of the maneuvers that are required of a pilot to obtain a private pilot, instrument pilot, and commercial pilot rating; I also had to re-train on twin-engine aircraft. In addition, I went for my flight instructor ratings, both multi-engine and instrument. All of this took a great deal of effort and concentration; but for the first time in several years, I felt I was accomplishing something worthwhile.

I remember flying with Rock as if it were yesterday. On my instrument check ride, we started at 7:00 a.m. in a small classroom attached to the terminal building in Murfreesboro. Rock walked into the room with his trademark joyous greeting, "Howdy, partner!"

"Good morning, Rock," I answered.

I'm not much of a morning person, and a pilot is always nervous on check ride day—we pilots call this "checkitis." So much is on the line any time a pilot is taking a check ride; any mistake easily can cause a pilot to fail. Pilots encounter this kind of stress every time they get into the cockpit with someone from the FAA who is scrutinizing everything they do. But Rock had a gentle way of setting pilots at ease.

On that particular morning, Rock brought in a briefcase, opened it up with a glimmer in his eye, and pulled out a sheaf of "old" aviation instrument charts from the 1930s era. These charts were fascinating to me, and Rock knew I would appreciate them. They were nothing like the charts of today, because the older navigational aids were constructed very differently. It was amazing to see how the Nashville airport approaches had changed, and how the old DC-3 pilots in the 1940s would fly the approaches in the clouds. Almost everything was based on time and bearings, and the pilots really had to be on top of things or they could easily run into something. Of course, this is true today as well, although advances in electronics have made flying airplanes a bit more efficient insofar as visualizing where the airplane is in space.

Rock and I spent several hours on the check ride before finishing up about 9:00 that night. He wanted to be very thorough with me, and to make sure that no one watching us go through all this could in any way think we had taken any shortcuts in the process.

The Murfreesboro airport didn't have a control tower with an air-traffic controller, which made it an uncontrolled field. Pilots had to be vigilant monitoring a specific radio frequency, and hope that other pilots in the pattern used this frequency to call in their positions and intentions. All was quiet at the airport as we came in for our night landing. I was confident: I knew that I had just passed my instrument check ride with an old master of the game. My sense of accomplishment was substantial as we slowly taxied into the terminal.

During the course of the next several days, I flew and passed my commercial pilot check ride, my multi-engine check ride in a twin-engine airplane, and my flight instructor check ride. Then we flew an instrument flight instructor check ride, and also performed this in the twin so I could get my multi-engine instrument flight instructor rating.

All of these check rides were expensive—especially for a fellow struggling to get a job paying more than minimum wage. Pilots often pay examiners between $250 and $350 dollars per rating and/or check ride, and I had just flown eight check rides in ten days or so; I owed Rock a great deal of money. I asked my brother to loan me the money to pay for these check rides, and he did. Rock and I were sitting together in the little back room of the Murfreesboro airport, and the time of reckoning had arrived: it was time to pay up. He was finishing the paperwork for my final license when I reached down into my flight bag and pulled out my checkbook.

Rock shot a glance in my direction. "No, no, no, Joe!" he exclaimed. "These are all on me. It was an honor and a pleasure to fly with you, and I'm really happy that you're back into the cockpit and flying again." He had a look of pure joy on his face. Before Rock could finish what he was saying, my eyes welled up with tears.

Rock was a man of compassion. He, too had suffered incredible pain in his life when his daughter was murdered while attending college. Yes, this man knew about pain and loss, but he also knew about redemption and grace, a priceless gift for any man, especially when he knows it well enough to give it away.

That day was one of the best of my life. There was no audience. The celebration was between two fellow aviators sitting in the quiet back room of a Tennessee country airport. One was a master, a mentor, a healer, and a kind teacher who offered hope and encouragement to the other, a man struggling for acceptance and a way to bring meaning back into his life. After giving Rock a big hug and thanking him for what he had done for me, I made the drive home along the winding country road to my little house. My heart was singing. It was as if the wheels of my car never touched the ground.

A "New" World

After I earned my medical certificate back from the FAA, under special issuance for alcoholism, I decided it was time to actively pursue a flying job. I pulled out all the stops. I contacted anyone and everyone I had ever known in the airplane business and sent them my resume. I made hundreds of phone calls and interviewed with at least a hundred different companies.

I was always honest with people and told them up front of my past mistakes, and, if they were interested, what I had learned from them. I was used to being rejected in the free market as a felon, so being rejected as a pilot applicant came as no big surprise to me. My huge blunder at NWA in 1990 continued to keep me from getting any job offers.

A Blessing

After I was allowed to fly with passengers on board I wanted to start an Aviation Explorer Post in Murfreesboro. However, I was concerned that the

Boy Scouts might reject me as a leader because of my criminal record. I had a meeting with a regional Boy Scout director and told him my background. "We would love to have more people with the kind of enthusiasm you have for helping children involved in the Boy Scouts," was his welcome reply.

With that encouragement, we were off and running. My good friend John Wallace, whom I had met a few months earlier at the airport, was an Army helicopter pilot and officer. He helped me form the post, organize the parents, and raise a great deal of money. We shared in the teaching of flight lessons and ground school of several young students, and took four airplanes up to the largest air show in the world, the EAA fly-in in Oshkosh, Wisconsin. I was grateful for all the help from the parents of the explorers. This was a very positive experience for me, and kept my passion for aviation burning deep inside me. I continued to hope that someone would give me a chance to fly for pay.

Never Quit

What should be obvious if you have read this far is that I am not a quitter; giving up easily is not a trait I possess. As one of my former drum teachers from the Cavaliers, Jim Rousell, liked to say, "Quitters never win, and winners never quit." I also inherited the natural perseverance gene from my parents, both of whom are tremendous survivors.

In the middle of all this, in October 1994, Deborah told me she was pregnant with our first child. I remember how excited we were, but I also remember wondering how I was going to support a family with a trail of minimum wage jobs behind me and no real prospects for gainful employment in the future.

As luck would have it, an East Tennessee man named Daryl Huskey introduced me to his friend John Finch, who gave me a chance with his construction company as an assistant project manager. He also had me fly him in his private airplane to different job sites. This air time, albeit limited, continued to stir the fire deep inside me.

One winter afternoon I was stranded in Dallas during a rare Texas snowstorm. A company there called Kitty Hawk Air Cargo was flying Boeing 727s and Convairs. I had experience on both of these aircraft types. I decided to drive over and "walk in" my application. Although they advertised that they did not accept "walk-in" applications, what did I have to lose?

Mustering up as much confidence as I could manage, I marched in, met a secretary, and handed her my pilot application. She immediately noted my experience on 727's and Convairs, and told me she might call in a day or two to check on my availability. "I'll stay in town for an interview," I answered with a smile.

When the call came, I got all dressed up and went in for the interview. I met with a chief pilot who acted as if he wanted to hire me, in spite of what had happened at NWA. I was very encouraged—until I interviewed with the Director of Flight Operations. His name was Tej, and he told me that Kitty Hawk's POI (Principal Operations Inspector with the FAA) would not like it if Kitty Hawk offered me a job.

Something about Tej told me that was a line of bull. I looked on his desk and saw a letter with the POI's name and phone number on it, which I quickly memorized. "How about if I call your POI and ask him what he thinks about you offering me a job?" I asked.

"Oh, no," Tej answered, snapping up the letter. "That won't do any good."

I realized at this point that the interview was over. I politely thanked Tej, but told him I would be calling the FAA to see what they thought about me working for Kitty Hawk.

That afternoon I was ready to take another chance. I called Bud Ehman, Kitty Hawk's POI. Unbeknownst to me, Mr. Ehman had been a Chief Pilot for American Airlines before he went to work for the FAA. I told Mr. Ehman my complete story, and to my surprise he listened with interest. "I have rebuilt my life and have been sober for several years," I added. "I only want someone to give me another chance."

Imagine my surprise when Ehman replied that he was already upset with Tej for lying to him. He said that the previous week Tej had fired the Chief Pilot at Kitty Hawk—but Tej had then lied, telling Ehman the Chief Pilot had resigned. "I know the Chief Pilot Tej fired was a good man," explained Ehman, "and that Tej is hiding something from me. Joe, I am going to call the DO and tell him that he needs to offer you the job at Kitty Hawk."

It was a fine and welcomed gesture, but I wasn't sure he would follow through, or whether Tej would be receptive to his request. But Mr. Ehman is a fine fellow and he did exactly as he said he would. The question was what would become of it.

Chapter 33

Yonder the Wild Blue

Aweek later I stopped by a friend's fly shop in the Smoky Mountains. Skip and some other guys there were talking about a fishing trip to the Caribbean. What I didn't know was that just that morning, while I was driving to the mountains, someone from Kitty Hawk had called the house to offer me a job. The rep told my wife that the company wanted me to come and start a pilot training class in a week. Mr. Ehman had indeed followed through.

An ecstatic Deborah called Skip to tell him about it; he greeted the news with equal excitement. But now, in front of all these guys who were in on it, he decided to have a little fun at my expense.

"Joe!" exclaimed an animated Skip. "We're going fishing, and were thinking about hiring you to be our pilot." Then he sighed. "Oh, but you really can't go on the trip, can you?" He paused for effect, before adding, "Because . . .you have to go to work and fly . . . Convairs!"

"What?" I asked, completely stunned by his words. "Are you kidding?"

As I began to realize what they were talking about, everyone in the fly shop shouted their congratulations to me. We stood there in that fly shop and celebrated the moment. They had watched me struggle for so long, and were eager to show me their support with hugs, smiles, and encouraging words.

I accepted the job and became a professional pilot for the first time in more years than I cared to remember. The long road back to the cockpit had been difficult, with obstacles along the entire way. I just felt grateful that someone was finally going to give me a chance to fly!

A Shock in El Paso

One of my first assignments as a Convair First Officer was in El Paso, Texas. We had two Convairs down there, so there were always at least four pilots staying in an apartment the company had near the airport. We would fly the Convair down to Chihuahua, Mexico, in the morning and fly back in the evening. Our cargo consisted largely of engines and related components for General Motors that were manufactured at their Mexican plant. I really enjoyed meeting the people down there, and I was even learning to speak Spanish.

The pilots were mostly young men using Kitty Hawk to build time so they could apply to a major airline. They were not used to having someone fly with them who had been with a major airline. They also were not used to having someone tell them what they could or could not do; they were quite happy in their little world, flying in El Paso and partying every night into the early hours of the morning. I found out that many of the Captains drank like fish the night before they had to fly. Guess who would end up flying with them? You're right: me, the new guy. So, trouble and controversy right out of the box: here I wanted to keep a low profile and rebuild my credibility and my resume. Instead, my first flying was about to be broadsided by the pilots flying as Captains in El Paso. The first Captain I was assigned to fly with was not drinking before he flew, but I knew that eventually I would be scheduled to fly with one of the Captains who was drinking to excess.

I had to do something. Pat, my new friend, classmate, and experienced pilot, was disturbed by the amount of "drinking and flying" going on in El Paso. He empathized with my feelings because he knew of my story and hardships. We decided to confront the Captains one evening at the apartment when everyone was back from flying to Mexico. We explained to them that we had observed them driving drunk back to the apartment from the local bar several times. Their speech was slurred and, on more than one occasion, they could barely walk. We knew that they had had a large quantity to drink, that the alcohol would still be in their systems in the morning, and that it was dangerous to fly in that condition.

"Climbing in a cockpit within four hours of your last drink," I explained, "guarantees that you are flying under the influence. This behavior needs to change." When I realized they were listening and not giving me a hard time, I opened up and shared some of my story with them. I told them how I had drunk the night before the Fargo flight—and that it was nothing close to what these fellows were drinking. "I was convicted and ended up going to prison. I lost my airline career."

The looks on their faces turned from initial interest to hostile frowns, but I continued anyway. "You guys need to understand that I am not going to be able to fly with you any time after you are out drinking into the early morning hours. I am just not going to put myself in that position, and you don't need to put yourself into that position, either."

Bill, the youngest (and wildest) of the Captains, unfroze his frown and yelled, "Who in the hell do you think you are, being the newest First Officer with this company, and coming down here and telling me what to do? You're lucky to even have a flying job, so shut up and stop giving us trouble!"

I couldn't believe my ears. Then I remembered that this type of denial is typical when you confront someone about his or her drinking behavior. But I had to make it crystal clear to all of them what I would do if I observed them showing up smashed or hung over before a flight. I glanced from one to the next as I replied, "Guys, you have a good thing going down here for yourselves, but you must know that I am serious, and the flight will have to be cancelled if you show up hung over."

"Up yours, buddy!" Bill barked back. "I am going to ruin *your* career!"

I smiled and said, "Too late, Bill, my career has already been ruined. But if you're not more careful, you're next. You're going to ruin both your career and your life."

I couldn't sit around and worry about what other people were going to think about me. Word of the dangerous El Paso situation had spread throughout the company, but my warnings fell on deaf ears. As a result, I was shunned by many of the pilots at Kitty Hawk.

I was sent to fly an assignment in Cleveland. Tom, the Captain there, was good friends with Bill, and had already been briefed about my attitude as a "party pooper." He would not even talk to me the first few days we were in the apartment together. Without any provocation on my part, Tom said, "I hate you, and really didn't want to fly with you, but I have no choice." It was a very uncomfortable situation.

I think the company moved me out of El Paso because it didn't want me to stir things up any more down there. My friend Pat, who remained in El Paso to fly, had to threaten to kick some butts if they didn't modify their drinking behavior while they were flying as his Captain. Of course, they resented him as well. Pat was a good friend to have, and was one of the few pilots who supported me throughout my short-lived "career" at Kitty Hawk.

Pat eventually left Kitty Hawk to become an FAA Federal Safety Inspector. He loves what he does, and we still talk about the drinking boys at Kitty Hawk. The administration at the company was just not going to do anything to help the pilots change their behavior.

Captain Tom in Cleveland never did warm up to me much. But one time in the midst of several other Kitty Hawk pilots, he actually paid me a huge compliment. "I may not like that Joe Balzer guy," he said, "but he is one of the best pilots I have ever flown with." Coming from someone who said he hated me, that was an outstanding compliment.

Chapter 34

Just Call Me "Captain"

I really looked forward to the chance to fly as a Captain and set the operational "tone" for my own crew. I took my Captain check ride during the deep winter months in Ypsilanti, Michigan. John, the FAA check airman, was also a Chief Pilot with our company, and he was known to be very thorough with his questioning. John held our pilots to very high, demanding standards—just as he should. I studied long and hard for three months prior to my check ride, and my efforts paid off. The Convair has a particularly complex propeller system, and I had it down cold. It must have impressed John, because he told my system Chief Pilot, "That guy gave me the best oral exam I've ever heard. He really wanted it!" Knowing he said that made me proud.

The flying portion of the exam was just as tough. To complicate matters, the Convairs we flew didn't have an autopilot system, so all of the flying had to be done manually. I had such a death grip on the yoke, while trying to maintain perfect altitudes, that my forearm was sore for two weeks after the flight!

It was obvious to John how badly I wanted to fly as a Captain. He also knew of my past struggles, and told me he was impressed with my perseverance. Then he sat down and filled out my temporary airman's certificate. "You'll get your permanent copy from the FAA within ninety days," he told me. The certificate read: "Airline Transport Pilot, Type Rating, Convair 600, Convair 640." I was elated when he handed me my certificate and shook my hand. "Congratulations, Joe, and best of luck to you!"

Now I could call my family and friends and tell them the good news. I was a new FAR 121 airline Captain! My wife had tears in her eyes when I got home. Part of me was still in shock just thinking about what I had gone through to get there. Skip honored me with a box with the words "Captain Balzer" written on the side. Inside the box was a beautiful, antique reel for fly-fishing.

Man Overboard

I chose to fly my Captain assignments in El Paso because the flying was during the daylight hours as opposed to all the night flying and behind-the-clock flying that the rest of the Convair fleet did. After returning from Mexico one afternoon, my First Officer, a very experienced and competent pilot, slipped on the airplane ladder and fell almost ten feet down out of the plane. He cut his leg open on the way down, cut his back on a latching mechanism attached to the door, and sprained his ankle when he landed on the ramp. I called the paramedics, but he didn't want to go to the hospital in El Paso because it was a Friday night and it would be jammed; besides, we were finished with our flying for the week, and he wanted to get home to his family. He told me he wanted to leave for the passenger terminal and catch a flight home to Detroit. He promised me that he would see his own family doctor the next morning. I wished him well and asked him to please give me a follow-up phone call the next day and tell me how he was doing.

In the meantime, we had another airplane break down in Chihuahua with a load of freight. One of the engines was not developing enough power for a safe takeoff in the high-altitude environment of Chihuahua. This left the cargo for one of our customers stranded on the ramp in Mexico. The company wanted me to fly my airplane back down to Mexico, pick up the stranded freight, and fly it back to El Paso. All of that would have been fine, I explained, except my First Officer was not able to fly due to his injuries. They wanted me to fly with the injured copilot. I told them I couldn't, because he had already left for Detroit—but that was a moot point anyway, because I would not let him fly in that condition.

My decision really made some people mad. I added gas to the fire the following week when I refused to fly the airplane that had broken down in Chihuahua. This airplane had a history of problems with its engines and its water injection system, which allows the engine to develop more takeoff power. The system was a must for the Mexico operation: without it the aircraft could not fly with any cargo on board.

The mechanics working on the airplane had tried everything to fix the problem, to no avail. The company decided to send the maintenance director to El Paso to perform a "shady" mission. He installed a clever system in the airplane, accompanied by his own four-page, typewritten instruction booklet on how to operate the system. If the pilots followed the instructions, the system was supposed to work. It had one major drawback, however: the system was jury-rigged and was not approved by the FAA, which made the whole thing illegal. With this in mind, I told Tej, the Director of Operations, that I would not fly the airplane in that condition. My refusal to fly drove Tej nuts. He set into motion the paperwork to fire me from the company.

The younger Captains were intimidated into flying this rigged airplane for fear of losing their jobs. But if the makeshift system failed during a takeoff from the high, hot, mountainous terrain in Chihuahua, there was a good chance the pilots would be killed. That airplane was a ticking time bomb, and I had no interest in getting killed trying to help this company maintain its image. As the Captain and pilot in command, I was responsible for the safe operation of the airplane and the safety of my crew. The FAA is well aware of this fact, and its officials would take swift action to revoke any Captain's pilot certificates if he or she operated an aircraft with such an illegal system installed. As difficult as it would be, I was willing to take my chances on finding another job.

One-Upmanship

I was hopeful the company would get its act together. However, a few weeks later the dreaded phone call arrived. Tej asked me to come to headquarters for a meeting. When I arrived, the first thing he said was that I was not a "team player." I thought that was interesting, because a few weeks before the company had given me a bonus for doing such a good job. My bonus was as large as any Convair Captain flying the line!

I came to the meeting armed for bear, and knew what I wanted: to make sure I received all of my back and vacation pay when I "resigned." I also knew why Tej wanted to fire me, and I was willing to let him—with one catch. Kitty Hawk was notorious for letting pilots go and then trashing their reputations. But a few weeks earlier, I had had the presence of mind to slip into the illegally-rigged airplane and take photographs and copy other pieces of evidence. During the meeting at headquarters, I happened to have with me a copy of the illegal manual and several pictures of the illegal system they had installed on the Convair.

"See, Joe, you are not a team player. Not the sort of pilot Kitty Hawk needs to . . ." Tej stopped in mid-sentence, with his mouth agape, when I dropped the manual and photos on the desk in front of him. If he wanted to play hardball, I was ready to hit one out of the park. I left his office with an agreement that the company would pay me one month of severance pay—which was unheard of then.

When I was done with Tej, I walked into the office of the President of the company and showed him what I had just gotten through showing his Director of Operations. He understood my position, and knew I could go to the FAA and have the entire fleet grounded. Kitty Hawk could have lost its operating certificate as a result of the pictures and evidence I had, coupled with my willingness to do something about it. But I also realized that if the FAA grounded the Convair fleet, the few friends I had there would be out of a job. So I was happy to leave it alone.

However, at the same time, I was devastated about losing my job again. I anticipated that it would be very difficult to find another one.

My Only Opportunity

My severance pay was running out, along with my options. My wife and I had a new baby at home, born on the fourteenth of June, 1995, and we needed my income to make ends meet. Job opportunities for me were more than hard to come by: they were virtually nonexistent. Finally, I found a small company in El Paso desperate enough for a First Officer on a Lear Jet to offer me a job. The catch was I had to study and get current on the systems of a Lear Jet again, and also take a check ride with the FAA. Interestingly, everyone else to whom they had offered the job had turned it down; I didn't know why, but surely the reason would reveal itself over time. In the meantime, I had a family to feed. I studied, passed my check flight, and took the position.

We flew that jet around for seven weeks with a disabled autopilot. Several mechanics made attempts to repair the autopilot without success. It is challenging to "hand fly" a Lear Jet at high altitude because the aircraft is not very stable up there, and the concentration required lends itself to additional mental fatigue. Imagine hand-flying a high performance jet at

FL410 (41,000 feet above the surface of the earth) in the middle of the night into the wee hours of morning. You are already tired from flying "behind the clock," and the intense focus necessary for hand flying takes everything you have left out of you.

Brian, the Captain I flew with, was intimidated by the demanding owner of the company and thus always agreed to fly the airplane—even when both of us were way too tired to be flying.

Of course, before they hired me, I told them my story, and their only real concern was whether, unlike all the other copilots before me, I would stay around for several months and not quit. The Captain kept telling me I was lucky they'd offered me the job. The truth was, they couldn't find anyone else who really wanted it, and if they didn't hire me, they were going to have to ground the airplane for several weeks, which would have ended up costing them a great deal of money.

I knew why Brian kept using the "you're so lucky" ploy; he was trying to get me to ignore some of the safety issues with the operation. But it didn't work. You just don't go through what I had and overlook safety issues. Brian and I started butting heads after a few weeks.

Federal Aviation Regulations regulate how much a pilot can fly in one day, but there are no time provisions for a private pilot or a pilot who is flying for a wealthy individual who owns his own airplane. Those regulations are called Part 91, and there is no flight time limit. Charter operations, or pilots on call in the "for-hire" world of flying, are allowed ten hard hours of flight time a day within a fourteen-hour duty period—but I have friends whose bosses have had them fly twenty hours in a day!

Brian frequently wanted to fly beyond the legal duty period according to the FARs, but I wasn't about to do so. He wanted to combine a Part 91 unlimited flight duty period with the end of a 135, all-night charter period, so we could fly back to the base in El Paso and be "legal" or "rested" to take a flight out again the next night. Of course, he had ongoing pressure from management to do that. Still, I wasn't about to fly fifteen or sixteen hours straight without any rest, at night, behind the clock, in all kinds of weather, in an aircraft that was questionable to begin with.

One night, after flying all night and being at the legal limit of Part 135 flying, we found ourselves in Delaware. Brian wanted to fly the jet back to El Paso, even though both of us were really tired. When I refused to go, Brian threw a fit and yelled and screamed at me. I spent the night on the cold, vinyl floor of a small, fixed-base operator, which is like a gas station for small airplanes. After getting my eight hours of so-called "sleep," I told him I was ready to fly.

The job served its purpose, and I was grateful for that. I was able to get current on the Learjet, including what is known as a "135 checkout" with the FAA. This letter would allow me to fly with any Learjet operator as a First Officer, and eventually get checked out as a Captain. I had the ambition and drive to succeed.

But my past remained a handicap. All I had to do was find someone willing to hire a felon who had lost his pilot certificates, but had a real story of redemption to tell. I had seven good years of sobriety. I was always honest with prospective employers about my background and aviation history. In recovery, it becomes obvious how important honesty is in all that you attempt to do. There had been a great deal of rejection in my life, but I firmly believed that the continuous cycle of rejection would only make things sweeter when someone out there decided to give me a chance to show them what I could do as a sober, willing employee.

A Job Closer to Home

In 1997, for the first time in several years, I had a job at Christmastime. The owner of the Learjet freight operation was even gracious enough to give me holiday pay, which I used to get some nice things for my wife and growing family for Christmas. (My son was born just a bit less than one year earlier.) However, deep down I knew this job wasn't going to work for me in the long term. If I had been in my early 20s, inexperienced, naïve, and looking to build flight time, I wouldn't have known any better. However, I was too far down the aviation highway and had too much experience to tolerate a slip-shod operation any more. I used my down-time wisely, setting out to find another job. One turned up only ten miles from my house!

Arlington Jet was a small company based in Arlington, Texas. The company was owned by a fellow who had won millions in the Texas lottery. Unfortunately for him, he demonstrated the characteristics of a stage-three alcoholic. He wasn't around very much, but when he was, he was drunk. After being around the office and observing his behavior, I realized that he had a very serious issue with alcohol. I just couldn't seem to get away from people who had drinking problems or were suffering from the effects of alcoholism. He struck me as the kind of guy who would fire you from your job if you even mentioned that he might consider getting some help.

Arlington Jet needed a First Officer and hired me right away, at $30,000 per year. The Director of Operations and owner both told me I would get a raise to $35,000 per year when I checked out as a Captain. After the DO had a chance to fly with me and check my performance, the company was interested in promoting me to Captain quickly. After a few weeks, I began studying for my ATP Captain check ride in the Learjet.

Since the company was small, we used the company's airplane to fly the check ride with an FAA-designated examiner. Larger companies can afford to send their pilots to a first-rate training organization such as Simuflite in Dallas. At Simuflite the training is done on state-of-the-art flight simulators; but Arlington Jet didn't want to spend the money for that, so I ended up taking my check ride with the FAA and studying the books on my own. I had only been with the company for a few months when I completed my training and passed my Lear Jet Captain check ride with the FAA.

My first trip as a Captain came a few days later. We had a charter to Hot Springs, Arkansas, for some wealthy horse owners from Dallas. While laying over for the night in Hot Springs, I brought up the subject of my raise with the DO as we sat in the bar of a restaurant.

"When am I getting the raise you promised me?" I asked.

"You'll have to wait another six months."

That wasn't what I expected to hear. "That isn't the deal we made when you hired me," I protested.

He wouldn't budge. But I didn't want to really get into it with him: he was beginning to drink heavily—I learned enough later to believe he was an alcoholic, too—plus I knew he was just the mouthpiece of the owner, anyway. So I just said, "Look, I am not going to play this game. I'll give you twelve hours to change your mind and pay me what I was promised, or you can start looking for another Learjet Captain."

"There's no way you can quit! We just spent $10,000 getting you trained!"

"Then all you have to do is give me what you promised, and that will save you the money and the trouble of having to find someone else. If you lied to me and you can't change that, then I'll be leaving this job tomorrow afternoon."

I wasn't sure what the company would do, but it called my bluff. They lost. I quit.

Arlington Jet's Lear ended up grounded for weeks. The decision to let me quit rather than pay me what we had agreed upon cost them thousands of dollars in revenue. Finding a Captain to fly their jet for $30,000 a year was harder than they thought. I am certain the DO was an alcoholic and I really felt compassion for him, but he didn't want any help from me or from anyone else. The owner entered into alcoholism's final stage and eventually drank himself to death. The company went out of business.

I was really tired of dealing with alcoholism in the workplace. This time my approach had been very different than in the past. It was a risky move to quit Arlington Jet, knowing how tough it was to find a job in the Dallas area to begin with; but there was no way I would fly with an alcoholic again, at least knowingly. I knew it was time to move forward again with faith and courage, hoping that God would provide a challenging and rewarding job for me, one that would allow me to provide for my growing little family: my wife, baby daughter, and newborn son.

Incredibly, I found another job the next day, making more money, in a wonderful and exciting environment.

Yet Another New Beginning

It was as simple as this: the next day after our layover in Hot Springs, I walked into Simuflite in Dallas and told the President of the company my story. I also told him how much I enjoyed teaching. He hired me on the spot.

The job at Simuflite was a perfect fit for me. I trained the pilots of corporate America, and enjoyed working with the professional clients. I did miss being a pilot, however, and I still dreamed of flying with a major airline.

Chapter 35

Dreaming the Impossible

W ith the encouragement of other pilots in recovery, I began telling my story to college students, church groups, and pilots attending FAA safety seminars know as "wings weekends." One of my first speaking engagements was the National H.I.M.S. Conference. H.I.M.S. stands for Human Intervention Motivational Study. It began in 1972 as an experimental program to help recovering alcoholic pilots so they could return to work as healthy individuals and regain their careers in recovery.

Prior to 1972, any pilot diagnosed as an alcoholic ended up losing his pilot's license for life. (Remember my friend Herb?) H.I.M.S. includes special doctors with the FAA and other health-care professionals who specialize in addiction treatment. It also includes a group of pilot union officials who volunteer their time to help pilots in recovery, and work in unison with company doctors and aftercare workers to aid in a pilot's recovery efforts, to help insure a successful and lasting rehabilitation. The conferences are dedicated to educating interested people and pilots about the disease of alcoholism. The national conference meets once a year and is attended by personnel from most of the major airlines, and some regional carriers who either have or are attempting to have a state-of-the-art employee assistance program (EAP) within their companies.

When I attended my first conference I was shocked that so many people were dedicated to helping pilots. I have to admit I was very nervous the night before my presentation. There were so many people there—hundreds of them! I prayed that God would give me the right words to say, and thanked Him for the opportunity to share my story.

When I walked up onto the stage, I was stunned at the size of the audience. The room was jammed to the rafters! I said a quick prayer, cleared my throat, and began to speak.

"I know all you see up here on this stage is me, but there are so many people who are standing behind me you cannot see. But I can assure you that they are there, for they have sustained me, supported me, talked to me, cried with me, laughed with me, and prayed for me throughout my entire ordeal."

As part of my presentation, I publicly made amends to Northwest Airlines for embarrassing and humiliating the company by my actions in March of 1990. (Shortly before the conference, I had written a letter of apology to the pilots of Northwest Airlines and mailed it to their union newsletter. To my great disappointment, it was never published.)

The crowd was quiet, respectful, and very attentive. I simply told my story, as if I was sitting down in a living room with a friend who had never heard it before. There were times when laughter burst forth, and times when crying could be heard. The words were inspired and seemed to flow out of me. When I finished, and humbly thanked them for inviting me, the reaction from the crowd was so devastatingly wonderful that I broke down. They stood and cheered for what seemed like a very, very long time. I couldn't move. In fact, in my state of overwhelming emotions, I could hardly breathe.

When I looked up at their smiling faces through my tear-soaked eyes, something deep in my soul was renewed. They gave me *hope*. As they stood there and embraced me with their kindness, they empowered me with the strength to move further on my journey—and take the biggest risk of all. I made up my mind that day that I was going to be a pilot for a major airline again. I was not going to give up until I had exhausted every possibility.

Some of the people I met at these alcohol conferences held influential positions with several major airlines. The Chief Pilots from American Airlines, Southwest Airlines, Alaska Airlines, and American Trans Air did their best to give me encouragement. They told me to try applying to their companies, and that they would do everything in their power to help me land a flying job.

I knew that was probably impossible, but I like to believe in the impossible; I always have. However, I wasn't sure if I could bear the added pain of even one more rejection. Would a rejection at this stage in the game send me into an unrecoverable tailspin? I had been bruised and bloodied by the onslaught of continuous rejections and disappointments I had endured during the past several years. But my "courage to change the things I can" kept me moving forward into the "friction of life," as my good friend Skip liked to say. I decided to move ahead and fill up my rejection container to the very brim, and get this idea of flying for a major airline behind me. I was ready to expose yet another part of my tender heart.

Sometimes people try to help you, yet things just do not seem to work out. It is all very disappointing and disheartening, but you really do have to keep trying until you are absolutely certain that your opportunities are exhausted for good. I nearly reached that point. I applied to every major airline, and every major airline turned me down—by pretending I did not exist. I couldn't even get them to send me a postcard acknowledging that they had received my job application.

I was down to my last bit of aviation hope. All of my other contacts had fallen through, even though the people helping me had the best of intentions. To move forward I had to risk the final rejection in my pursuit of a good flying job, but I was willing to take that last chance. So in 1998 I spent several days filling out a pilot application for American Airlines. I had held up playing this last card for a whole year after they started hiring pilots. Like an obsession, the words of one particular pilot at one of the airline conferences kept going through my head: "After these Chief Pilots heard your story, they really wanted to go to bat for you to try to help you get hired by American Airlines." Captain Mike Smith and Captain J. C. Doerr explained to me that I might have a chance to fly for American. Their willingness to tell me that made me that much more willing to fail, that much more willing to get kicked in the teeth again, that much more willing to be rejected one last time. With so many people going to bat on my behalf, inside my heart I applauded their courage to at least take a chance on a man who was down on his luck. It was American or nothing.

However, filling out that application was difficult because even while one part of me kept urging that I not give up on my dream of flying for a major carrier again, another part of me screamed that I was wasting my time.

Chapter 36

Go Ahead, Make My Day

One Monday morning in December of 1998, I was dressed in a flight jacket and tie at Simuflite waiting for the FAA to show up and give me a check ride. For some reason they didn't come, so I had the rest of the day off with nothing to do. I was feeling particularly courageous that day, so I drove home to pick up my copy of the American Airlines application. As I drove back across town, the events of the past several years raced through my mind. It was an emotional time, and I was taking my final chance. When the American Airlines headquarters building came into view, I was overwhelmed with the thought of how a job with American would change the lives of everyone in my family.

It was time to move forward again, through the fear of rejection, into the realm of possibilities and dreams. I have learned in recovery that courage is putting fear into forward motion. Was each step that morning bringing me closer to my dream of flying again for a great company?

Remember my friend Kurt, the airline pilot? (He was the one who had said I would never go to jail.) We had talked the night before, and he told me I should introduce myself to Captain Cecil Ewell, the Chief of all Chief Pilots at American. Kurt's encouragement made me realize that I had waited long enough. But was Kurt right this time, or wrong again?

I parked my car and stepped out. As I walked toward the headquarters of American Airlines, I realized I was going for broke, that this would be my last opportunity. Things were stirring deep inside of me as I walked up the sidewalk with my application and resume in hand.

A locked security door swung open, and a man wearing a coat and tie stepped out. He stopped to look at me. He was obviously an employee of

American Airlines in the Flight Department, but I couldn't tell from his ID card what his position with the company was. He looked at me cautiously, because I was eyeing the door, and his eyes had searched my jacket for a company ID card and come up empty.

"Hello, sir, my name is Joe Balzer. I would like to apply to American Airlines for a piloting job, but there is no way that my application is ever going to get through the personnel department. You see, sir, I was one of the Northwest Airlines pilots, back in 1990, who went to prison for flying under the influence of alcohol. I went through total revocation of all of my flight certificates and have completely rebuilt my life. I'm here to try to meet Captain Ewell and tell him my story."

The man looked at me in amazement, then nodded, smiled, and pointed toward an elevator across the room. "Joe, you need to go to that elevator right there and press the button for the third floor. Get off the elevator and turn right. Go down to the end of the hallway, and there will be a really nice woman named Linda sitting there at her desk. Tell her you are here to see Captain Ewell, and don't tell anybody how you got in the building." He winked at me and held the door open for me. When he knew I was safely inside the elevator, he walked away. I never saw him again.

I rode up that elevator and made the long walk down that hallway. Linda was right where he had said she would be. As I stepped closer to her, I could hear someone in the room behind her speaking in a loud, deep voice on the telephone. She looked up as I approached. "Hello, Linda," I said. "My name is Joe Balzer, and I was hoping that I might be able to have a very short meeting with Captain Ewell?"

"It's three-oh-five," she replied, "and he's already late for a three o'clock meeting with the Board of Directors all the way across the complex. I don't know if he can see you, but if you would like to wait you may have a seat over there until he gets off the phone."

"Thank you," I replied, trying to hide the tension I was feeling. "I would love to wait and see him." I walked over and sat down on the couch.

As I waited, an American Captain in full uniform walked up to Linda just as Captain Ewell got off the phone. He walked right into the office and sat down and spoke with him for about five minutes. My heart raced. As the Captain walked out of his office I heard Captain Ewell bellow out, "Send in Joe Balzer!" Linda motioned for me to go in.

As I walked through his door into his office, he was looking down and signing individual congratulatory letters to the new pilots he was hiring to fly for American Airlines.

I stood in front of his desk and said, "Hello, Captain Ewell, my name is Joe Balzer." I swallowed, took a deep breath, and continued. "I have to attach my heart to this application, or it is never going to get through your personnel department. You see, I'm a convicted felon, I have been fired from a major airline, and I went through the total revocation of all of my flight certificates to pilot an airplane."

Captain Ewell stopped what he was doing and looked at me. I could tell he was in deep thought. "I am a recovering alcoholic with more than eight years of sobriety," I continued. "I was the flight engineer on the Northwest flight back in 1990, and I spent a year in Federal Prison."

"Have a seat, Joe," offered the Captain. Then he said one of the most profound things I have ever heard in my life: "Joe, sometimes something bad can happen to you when you are a young man, and it seems to ruin your whole life. But sometimes in life, things have a way of coming full circle, and you finally run into somebody who's willing to give you a second chance."

I sat there in stunned silence. *Did he really just say that? Did he say that he might be the person who gives me a second chance? Was that what he was implying?*

Captain Ewell continued to praise me and make me feel really good about all the hard work I had put in. He told me that my efforts were nothing short of heroic—defying the odds and never giving up. He asked me several important questions about my recent flight experience: "How many hours have you flown this past year?"

"About five hundred hours as a simulator instructor, and I am very confident I am current; and I have obtained more than a thousand hours of new flight experience since earning my licenses back, most of it in jets."

My answer seemed to please him. "How much total time do you have?"

"More than 7,500 hours," I replied.

He leaned back a little and smiled. "Now, that ought to be plenty of flight time." Captain Ewell rolled his chair backward and pulled the telephone off the bookshelf. My mouth, literally, fell open. I quickly learned, to my surprise and delight, that he was phoning the personnel office. "Renee," he said calmly, "I have this fellow in my office named Joe Balzer. He is going to be down there in twenty minutes to see you about scheduling a pilot interview with us."

My heart swelled with joy. I am sure he could tell that I was totally overwhelmed, because when he got off the phone he said, "Joe, you need to go get yourself a cup of coffee and take your time getting over there." Then he went on. "It was great meeting you today, and I wish you the best of luck in your interview. You won't be getting any special treatment, if you know what I mean. Just go in there and show them what you can do."

I shook his hand and looked into his eyes. They were the eyes of a wise man, and I was very grateful for that. I realize today that Captain Cecil Ewell is a man who understands something about grace and redemption in his own life, and that is why he is able to offer it to others.

The applications for pilot jobs at all of the airlines go through tremendous scrutiny. I'm sure the ladies in the personnel office were not used to looking at the application of a convict, with its pages and pages of menial jobs. Yet after reviewing my application, the young lady asked, "So, when would you like to interview, this Thursday or next Tuesday?" I was not expecting such an early interview date, so I went for Tuesday.

An hour later I walked into the door of our house feeling as if I was in a dream. My eleven-month-old son was lying on the floor playing. My two-year-old daughter shouted, "Daddy, Daddy!" as she saw me walk into the house. Deborah walked into the living room and offered a smile.

"I have something important to tell you, honey," I began. "I just got an interview with American Airlines."

Her surprised scream scared all three of us. She has never jumped that high in her life! I enjoyed the moment to its fullest. I still had a long way to go, but I was going to get an interview with American Airlines, and I was ready for the challenge.

The Crucial Interview

I arrived on the day of the interview knowing that the odds of me getting a job with American were slim. The interview process at any major airline is always highly competitive, and I would be the only one in the group with such a colorful past. But I just wanted to go in there and do my best, and I felt confident that I could do just that, and the results were going to be up to God. I felt deep gratitude for the opportunity to interview, and also humility in realizing that someone was willing to at least give me that chance.

After taking a battery of computerized exams, we applicants were divided into pairs to take the simulator check ride. We flew a DC-10, and something was really bothering the guy who was my partner, because he ended up crashing the simulator. I tried to talk to him about what was going on. It seemed that something was happening in his life that was having a dramatic effect on his concentration, but he wouldn't share any of it with me. I tried to encourage him to talk to someone about it, and maybe American would let him come back for another interview when his troubles were over. But he was simply shut down. I felt really bad for him.

I was in quite a different place. I was very excited, and seemed to be hitting on every cylinder. I smoked my simulator check ride, and moved on to the next phase of the interview, which involved speaking to a panel of Captains.

As I awaited my turn, I sat in the room with all of the other pilots who were interviewing. What an outstanding group of individuals they were—the best of the best. I wished them all luck as they got up to go to their interviews with the Captains' panel.

And then, finally, my name was called. "Joe Balzer, time to interview with the Captains."

I picked up my things, took a deep breath, and walked into "the friction of life," into the unknown, into my ongoing journey, and into the possibility of rejection and disappointment. But rejection and disappointment were not on my mind. All I could think of was how this opportunity could change my family's life in a positive way, and for the rest of our lives.

I walked into the small room and was quickly taken by surprise. I had overheard one of the earlier interviewees saying as he left that there were two Captains in the room when he was interviewed, so I was expecting to see two officers. Now, however, there were *three* Captains sitting on the other side of the table: three on one. Now, that is what I call zone coverage. Were they ganging up on me in particular? For some reason, it didn't really bother me. I just asked for the strength to carry on and be myself. In that moment, right before they started asking me questions, my mind flashed an image before me of all the people who were praying for me that day, and I was comforted with a feeling of peace.

I didn't know it at the time of the interview, but the third Captain in the room was in the upper echelon of American Airlines pilot management. A man in his position was powerful, and he didn't usually sit in on pilot interviews.

They began by asking me a lot of technical questions. Those are easy to answer when you are working full-time as a flight or simulator instructor. Then they switched gears and got a little more personal: "What would you do if you were flying along and *this* happened or *that* happened?"

After I answered several of these scenario-type questions, the Captain leading the questioning looked at me intently and asked, "So tell us, what is the worst thing that has ever happened to you?"

I took a deep breath. I slowly began to tell them my story from the very beginning. I shared what I had learned from my mistake. I told them how much I wanted to help other people who were struggling with alcoholism. The story just poured out. And they were listening to every word! About forty minutes later, when I reached the part where I was getting out of prison, I could not talk any more. I was so overwhelmed with emotion that I broke down and cried. I put my head down and grasped it with my hands and leaned on the desk. I had no idea what they were going to think about all of that, but it was the truth, and I owned it all. What you see is what you get; there was nothing to hide. I was just spent emotionally.

The small room was suddenly quiet. You could have heard a pin drop. After what was for me an eternity, one of the Captains—his name was Burt—broke the silence. "It's all right, Joe. I know a little about what you went through. My precious daughter is in recovery, and it's the best thing that ever happened to us. What a remarkable story, Joe. My hat is off to you. You have done some extraordinary things, and you've set a fine example for us all."

I looked up. All three Captains had tears in their eyes. They were deeply moved by what I'd shared. The interview was over. "We can't tell you anything now, or give you any indication of how you did, or what we are going to do or recommend," Burt continued. I thanked them and left.

I had given it my all, and the results were up to God.

Back for a "Thank You"

The next day I decided it was important for me to try to see Captain Ewell again. I wanted to express my gratitude for the interview, in person, if possible. Captain Ewell welcomed me back into his office, and I thanked him for the opportunity to pursue my dream again. I told him how exciting it was for my family and me to think that someone might be willing to give me a chance.

He looked at me and said, "You know, Joe, you've been through so much, and I really admire your perseverance. We're going to close this office down next week for the Christmas holiday, and I'm not going to leave you hanging, wondering whether or not American Airlines is going to offer you a job to fly for us. You've suffered enough. The pilot board [a group of at least twelve pilots who interview candidates and discuss the results and recommendations] is going to meet this week on Friday. If their review of your interview is positive, I'm going to hire you."

But then he shifted in his seat, and I could detect that he wasn't totally confident. "There's only one catch," he continued, "and I have to be right up front with you about this. I'm going to have to take this to my boss, Bob Baker. Mr. Baker runs this airline, and he's going to have to make the final decision."

I nodded my understanding as I thought to myself, *Here is an honest man. He is telling me right up front what to expect.* I didn't know anything about Mr. Baker. I didn't know that he was the most respected airline executive in the industry, a man who started at the bottom throwing bags, just as I had. I didn't know that he came from an aviation heritage. I didn't know that he was a man of compassion, courage, and honor.

There was a part of me that wanted to believe that all of these people were just being nice to me, or trying to do something impossible. But the bigger part of me was full of hope and anticipation that something wonderful might happen.

Chapter 37

The Day of Reckoning

Early the following week, before the flight office closed for Christmas, I received a phone call from American Airlines. Deborah answered the phone. Normally, Captain Ewell personally called the pilots he was going to hire to congratulate them; but the person on the other end of the line was not Captain Ewell. I could see the disappointment on my wife's face as she handed me the phone. "It's someone from American Airlines," she said flatly. I could hear the disappointment in her voice. I took the phone from her.

I was certain that I was being rejected one more time. I had played my last card—and lost. I would never fly for a major airline again. There was the familiar tightness coming in my chest as I braced myself for the cold and impersonal exchange. "Thanks for coming for the interview," I would hear, "but . . ." My wife had already left the room. I could tell she was not only sad but emotionally defeated.

"Hello," I said, "This is Joe Balzer."

"Hello, Joe," said a female voice on the other end. "This is Renee with American Airlines. How are you doing on your Christmas shopping?"

I was taken aback by her cheerfulness. "Well, to be honest with you, with all of the preparation for my interviews, I haven't had time to do any Christmas shopping," I answered. "And that's not good, because this year I promised my wife I would help her with it." We both laughed a little about that.

"Well, we just wanted to know if you are still interested in a flying job with American Airlines?"

Silence.

"Hello? Joe? Are you there?"

More silence. I had dropped the phone on the floor. It beat my falling body there by about a half a second.

I was totally overcome by a joy I had not felt in a very long time. My moving ahead with courage had finally catapulted me over the walls of rejection. My future changed in that instant, and I was overwhelmed by the possibilities. I tried to gather my thoughts. After all, all I needed to say was "yes," but for some reason, I couldn't get a single word out.

My wife could hear me crying from the other room, and, as I would soon learn, was certain I had been turned down one last time.

I fumbled for the receiver and shoved it in front of my mouth. "Yes, I would love to!" I said, with heartfelt gratitude. As I rose to my feet in disbelief, Renee told me my class training date would be in February of 1999. "Congratulations, Joe! Captain Ewell was very sorry he could not call you personally, but he had to rush out of town to handle an emergency."

When I hung up the phone I started yelling, "I just got hired by American Airlines! I just got hired by American Airlines!"

"What? What?" screamed Deborah, as her heartbroken tears quickly turned into tears of joy.

We were so excited we jumped up and down. I called all of our family and friends to share the good news. It was one of the happiest days of our lives. We spent the next several days calling our supporters to share the great news with them.

A Leader and a Mentor

After initial ground school training, new-hire pilots with the airlines are required to fly a period of Initial Operating Experience, or IOE, with a check Captain. My check Captain's name was Jake Jacobs. One tradition at American Airlines is that a new pilot is given his wings from his check Captain when he has completed the IOE and is ready to fly as a line pilot. A line pilot is someone who has completed all of the training requirements and is qualified to fly with passengers on board as part of the regular operations of the airline.

After flying with Captain Jacobs for a few days, I made my final landing with him at Chicago's O'Hare field. We taxied to the gate, and I anticipated passing my official "line check." As Captain Jacobs set the parking brakes, he called for the parking check. I called out "Brakes," and he said, "Set." I called out "Seat Belt Signs," and he said, "Off." And so on, until we got down to the last item. I handed him the aircraft logbook so he could sign it, and add any discrepancies for the people who keep us flying—our outstanding mechanics.

I passed him the logbook, but he did not immediately take it. I looked at him, only to see tears welling up in his eyes. With a wide smile on his face, Jake said, "You are out of uniform! You'll need to put these on." He handed me my pilot wings. That was his special way of telling me I had passed my check ride. He also wrote a heartfelt letter that found its way to the desk of Mr. Bob Baker.

Welcome to Our Family

A few days later I received a personal phone call at our house that I never would have expected. "Hello, Joe," a deep voice said. "This is Bob Baker. I just wanted you to know that I have a letter here from Captain Jacobs commending you for your skills and attitude. I also want to say that we are so pleased to have you as a member of our family, and I wanted to personally welcome you to our company."

After recovering from my shock I replied, "Thank you, Mr. Baker. I am deeply grateful to have the opportunity to be a pilot for American Airlines."

"This is Your Captain Speaking"

Life Goes On—Happily

I have been flying for American Airlines for over ten years. I have enjoyed the journey, in spite of the many challenges airline employees have faced over the last couple of decades. I remember with gratitude the people who were willing to take a chance on me and give me the opportunity to show them what I could do.

I am blessed with a wonderful family. My wife Deborah is a loving wife and dedicated mother. As of 2009 we have been married more than 21 years. She faced tremendous challenges during this time. Deborah is the ultimate good sport, and "hung in there" with a husband whose life came apart very rapidly. Deborah is an International Flight Attendant and loves her work; she still enjoys traveling and exploring new places. She has been voted by her peers as one of the "Professional Flight Attendants of the Year." Her fellow employees have supported her greatly, especially at the onset of our tragedy.

Our first child, my daughter, came at a time when our struggles were raw and very real. That little girl lit up the room, and we cherish the joy she has brought into our lives. Now 13, she loves reading, music, and dancing, and has many warm relationships outside our family.

Our second child, my son, was born eighteen months after my daughter. His laughter adds to our joy. Now 12, he is a very inquisitive, kind, and caring young man. He loves playing guitar, skateboarding, sports, and video games. I was flying Convairs when he was born, and when he learned to talk he told people with great enthusiasm that his daddy flew planes "way up in the sky." He also said, "Daddy, I want to have a job that nobody else has." I replied, "What will that be?" He answered, "I want to invent the future." I have no doubt he will do just that. Both kids are precocious readers, love school, and attack learning with great enthusiasm. Both of our children have been tremendous blessings for us and our families at large.

My parents, Bob and Rose, had a great time last July at their 60th wedding anniversary party hosted by their four children. Also present were their seven grandchildren, five great grandchildren, and several cousins, brothers and friends. Both of my parents are very giving, and spend a great deal of their time volunteering at church and raising money for people in need. My dad is President of the Korean War Veterans in Florida, and they just raised more than $45,000 for the Wounded Warriors Foundation, which helps broken soldiers coming back from the current wars. My parents' contributions to their community are numerous and outstanding. They set a great example for all of us.

My in-laws, Billy and Norita Duffey, are my friends and great supporters. They have been a pillar of strength, and we enjoy a close relationship. He is a retired professional truck driver and missionary, and she always has some little day care center going along. Their sons and their wives are great people. Among them, son Daniel is a professional pilot whom I have been proud to mentor.

My brother and sisters are all doing well. The oldest, Brenda, and her husband Dick are retired from their small business. Brenda is a retired flight attendant, a career she took on after raising her family. They have two fine children and enjoy spending time with their five grandchildren, splitting their year between Arizona in the winter and Michigan in the summer. My brother Jim is happily married to Annie, and proud papa of a little girl. Annie loves drum corps as much as I do, and we are great friends. Jim is an active pilot and continues to add ratings to his pilot's license; I am very proud of him. Jim raised three fine boys in his first marriage. My sister Barbara continues to do well, and is pursuing her goal of becoming a college professor. She is my hero, as she led our family into recovery and continues to live a happy, sober life. She volunteers with Habitat for Humanity and does a variety of other important community service for those less fortunate than ourselves.

Then there is me. I have been the beneficiary of tremendous love from my family and friends. I do not take for granted the miracle that my children have never seen their father drunk, and have never seen their Grandpa Bob drunk either. The people in my family who are in recovery continue to flourish and do well. We make the humble attempt to help other people in need who still suffer from alcoholism.

My family came to support me this year during the Cavalier Reunion Corps 60th anniversary performance. It was fantastic to see their smiling faces after our show. I enjoy my music and drumming, and love to work with young people. I coach little league, go fly fishing, and—though I haven't played much in twenty years—I think it is time to start golfing and playing tennis again.

Spreading the Word

I love to go to meetings and share my story, and welcome any opportunities to speak to and encourage others. I have found that this is one of the most rewarding things I can do: share my story with other people, especially those who suffer from alcoholism, drug addiction, or have a family member or friend who does. My life experience has shown me that almost everyone I encounter has a story to tell about someone in his or her own life who has suffered, or is still suffering, from substance abuse. I meet people on airplanes every week, and it is stunning to hear the stories they tell me after I have shared a part of mine with them. Of course, I tell them about all the things that have been beneficial to me: the books, the programs, the counselors, the sponsors, the fellowship of twelve-step meetings, and the patient struggle to learn to be a healthy and sober person.

The benefits of sobriety are wonderful. Recovery from alcoholism offers hope for those who still suffer from the disease. Think about my five-day trip to hell with the Captain and First Officer Bob, described earlier in this book. In contrast to the "synergistic dysfunctionalism" that occurred on our first trip together, today that same flight would be different, because today that same Captain is a sober man. I didn't write about the Captain to be mean; rather, it was my attempt to describe what the experience was like for me. He, like me, is now a changed man. The true miracle is that we are both sober, and have overcome tremendous obstacles to stay that way. I wish him well, and my prayer for my "old" Captain is that his story will continue to change people's lives for the better. God bless you, Captain. May all your flights be safe.

The healing journey is the best and most important journey that I have ever been on in my life. Nothing makes me feel more useful than reaching out and helping people, and seeing the look in their eyes when they "get it" and are willing to make a change for the better in their own lives.

I am a very fortunate man. So many people have died from this terrible disease. So many people live shattered lives. The thought of contemplating the numbers and the damage is overwhelming. But my choice is to focus on the greatest gift that God has given me, or as Dr. Grimm would say, "to be a part of God's new creation each and every day."

I pray that my story, my perseverance, and my very real redemption will get people's attention, and I hope it encourages them to take some kind of action in their own lives. There is hope for those who suffer, whether they are children trapped in an alcoholic environment, teenagers, spouses, family members, or close friends.

My advice to everyone is simple: "Go ahead; ask for help." Move into the "friction of life." Take a chance. Learn to trust someone, and do not give up—ever. Don't stop the first time you fail, because that is just a closed door, and you will meet plenty of closed doors. God will open up another one for you. I wish you a happy and sober life.

With the deepest of gratitude,

Your friend,

Joseph Balzer
(A happy, sober pilot, living life one day at a time.)

Appendix

Facts Established at Trial

The following established facts are taken from the opinion issued by the United States Court of Appeals, Eighth Circuit, for the case of United States of America, Appellee, v. Norman Lyle Prouse, Appellant. V. Robert John Kirchner, Appellant, v. Joseph Wesley Balzer, Appellant, Nos. 90-5585 to 90-5587. 945 F.2d 1017.

On March 7, 1990, at approximately 11:00 a.m., Northwest Airlines (NWA) Flight 650 landed in Fargo, North Dakota. The flight crew consisted of Prouse as captain, Kirchner as first officer, and Balzer as second officer. The three men checked into the Days' Inn Motel in nearby Moorhead, Minnesota. At approximately 4:00 p.m., appellants Prouse, Kirchner, and Balzer went to the Speakeasy Restaurant and Lounge (Speakeasy) located approximately one and one-half blocks from their motel.

John Stenerson, Les Stenerson, and Bill Fellows, three local residents, arrived at the Speakeasy at approximately 8:30 p.m. They noticed that the conversation at appellants' table was getting loud. Approximately one hour later, the Stenerson party began to talk with appellants. After finding out that appellants were NWA pilots, the Stenerson party asked, at least twice, "You guys aren't flying out at 6:00 a.m. tomorrow, are you?" Appellants lied and said, "No." When Kirchner and Balzer left at 10:30 p.m., they had shared approximately six and one-half pitchers of beer and were noticeably unsteady. Prouse continued to drink with the Stenerson party. During that time, Prouse admitted that he, Kirchner, and Balzer were scheduled to fly out of Fargo at 6:00 a.m. the next morning. When Prouse finally decided to leave at around 11:30 p.m., he had consumed approximately seventeen rum and diet cokes. As he stood up to leave, both he and his chair fell over backward. Prouse got up shakily, refusing help, and made an unsteady exit. About twenty minutes later, Prouse returned to the Speakeasy and asked for directions to the Days' Inn. The waitress informed him that it was a block and a half away, straight down the road.

Les Stenerson subsequently made an anonymous call to the Federal Aviation Administration (FAA) expressing his concern about appellants' ability to fly a plane early the next morning. Stenerson told the FAA that he had witnessed three NWA pilots drinking heavily late into the night at the Speakeasy in Moorhead, Minnesota, and that by the time they left, the pilots appeared quite intoxicated. Stenerson also identified one of the pilots as "Lyle Pseudo." At 1:30 a.m., the FAA Flight Standards District Office's answering service called FAA Inspector Verle Addison and informed him of the anonymous call. FAA officials subsequently directed Addison to meet with the flight crew before their 6:00 a.m. departure.

Following Addison's arrival at the airport at approximately 5:00 a.m., NWA personnel told him that the 6:00 a.m. flight crew normally arrived at approximately 5:15 a.m. Kirchner and Prouse arrived at approximately 5:45 a.m. They had waited close to ten minutes for Balzer at the motel, but when he did not show up, they decided to continue on without him. Addison noticed an odor of stale alcohol when Kirchner and Prouse spoke to him. He also noticed that Prouse's eyes were quite red. Addison told Prouse and Kirchner of the anonymous phone call and that he smelled alcohol on them. Kirchner said that they had had dinner at the Speakeasy the night before, but he did not mention drinking. Addison informed Prouse and Kirchner that he would continue his investigation. Shortly after 6:15 a.m., Balzer arrived. Addison informed him of the anonymous call and stated that he noticed an odor of stale alcohol emanating from Balzer. Balzer responded that he had not been drinking the night before and that he had returned to his motel room early and read a book. Balzer also stated that he was late because he was up most of the night with a bad case of diarrhea. Balzer then boarded the aircraft.

Addison called Doug Solseth, an FAA aviation safety inspector in Minneapolis, to discuss the situation. Shortly thereafter, the plane took off. Addison was surprised at the quick departure because he knew that Balzer was required to perform a thorough pre-flight inspection before take-off and that Balzer could not have performed such an inspection in the short time between their conversation and the take-off. Officials later learned that Kirchner had performed the inspection, even though he was not qualified or authorized to do so.

When Prouse, Kirchner and Balzer deplaned in Minneapolis, they were met by various NWA employees and FAA officials. From a distance of thirty to thirty-five feet, Solseth noticed that they had flushed faces and bloodshot eyes. NWA employees then took appellants to the NWA Service Manager's Office to avoid creating a public spectacle. Meanwhile, Solseth consulted with Minneapolis Airport Police Officer David Kuhns and requested that Kuhns perform a blood test on appellants. Soon afterwards, Kuhns spoke with appellants, noticing an odor of stale alcohol on each appellant's breath. At the time, Kuhns believed that appellants had violated a Minnesota statute that prohibited operating an aircraft while under the influence of alcohol. See Minn. Stat. Ann. § 360.075, subd. 1(2), (3) (repealed 1990) (flying while under the influence of alcohol is now addressed at Minn.Stat. § 360.0752). Kuhns, however, also believed that he did not have the authority to arrest appellants because this offense was only a misdemeanor and it was not committed in his presence. See State v. Duren, 266 Minn. 335, 123 N.W.2d 624, 632 (1963). Consequently, Kuhns advised that one of the individuals present at the landing and deplaning should conduct a citizen's arrest. During a subsequent interview with appellants, Solseth informed them that he was performing a citizen's arrest for their violation of an FAA regulation prohibiting the operation of an aircraft within eight hours of consuming alcohol or while under the influence of alcohol. See 14 C.F.R. § 91.11(a)(1), (2) (1987). At the time of their arrests, Solseth read appellants an Implied Consent Advisory requesting that they submit to a blood alcohol test. Appellants agreed to submit to a blood test.

At 9:15 a.m., personnel at the Hennepin County Medical Clinic administered blood tests. The Minnesota Bureau of Criminal Apprehension Laboratory analyzed these tests. The results showed that Prouse had a 0.13 blood alcohol concentration (B.A.C.), Kirchner had a 0.06 B.A.C., and Balzer had a 0.08 B.A.C. Following the initial blood tests, NWA security took appellants to the Airport Medical Clinic for a second blood test. These tests took place at 11:15 a.m. Medtox Laboratory, a private lab not affiliated with the United States Government, analyzed these samples. The results of these tests showed that Prouse had a 0.104 B.A.C., Kirchner had a 0.036 B.A.C., and Balzer had a 0.054 B.A.C.

Appellants were ultimately indicted for operating a common carrier while under the influence of alcohol, in violation of 18 U.S.C. § 342 (1988). The jury trial began on July 25, 1990. At trial, the government called various witnesses who had observed appellants on March 7 and 8 to testify about appellants' conditions and actions. The government also called an expert witness who testified that he could estimate the B.A.C.s of appellants when the plane took off by using the B.A.C. data from the two blood tests. He calculated that at 6:30 a.m., appellants' B.A.C.s were as follows: Prouse's B.A.C. would have been in the range of 0.15-0.21, with a likely B.A.C. of 0.18; Kirchner's B.A.C. would have been in the range of 0.08-0.14, with a likely B.A.C. of 0.11; and Balzer's B.A.C. would have been in the range of 0.10-0.16, with a likely B.A.C. of 0.13. This expert also testified that, at 9:15 a.m., Prouse had the equivalent of approximately eight mixed drinks in his body and that Balzer and Kirchner each had the equivalent of two and one-half to three bottles of beer in his body. The government also presented expert testimony that, even at the low end of the B.A.C. range, all of appellants could be considered "under the influence" when they flew from Fargo to Minneapolis.

Appellants called witnesses who testified that they did not notice anything to indicate alcohol impairment on the morning of the flight. Prouse called several expert witnesses who challenged the use of B.A.C. as an absolute indicator of being "under the influence." They testified that individuals responded differently to alcohol, and that Prouse, who admitted to being an alcoholic, would have a greater alcohol tolerance than an average person. Therefore, Prouse could have a much higher B.A.C. and still not be "under the influence." Kirchner and Balzer each called a forensic chemist as a witness, but the district court refused to recognize these witnesses as experts on low-level alcohol impairment.

On August 20, 1990, the jury convicted all three appellants of operating a common carrier while under the influence of alcohol. On October 26, 1990, the district court sentenced Kirchner and Balzer to twelve months' imprisonment, and Prouse to sixteen months' imprisonment. Appellants also received a three-year term of supervised release. As a condition of probation, the district court ordered that appellants could not fly or operate an aircraft during the first year of supervised release and were precluded from piloting an aircraft with passengers for the entire three-year term.

The entire Opinion is available online: http://bulk.resource.org/courts.gov /c/F2/945/945.F2d.1017.90-5587.90-5585.html

About the Author

Joe Balzer is a pilot for American Airlines with more than 20,000 hours of flight experience. He has a Master's Degree in Aerospace Education and is also an inspirational speaker, traveling around the country speaking to pilots and other groups on the dangers of alcohol and other addictions. He often brings his audience to laughter and tears with his powerful message of hope. Joe is a single father and lives in Tennessee. *Flying Drunk* is his first book.